J.P.Morgan

"In today's business world, the greatest challenge is that most *Homo sapiens* think linearly—but these people are playing the wrong game. *Radically Human* offers a set of tools and frameworks to remind everybody that the business world is not linear, but exponential."

—**STÉPHANE BANCEL**, CEO, Moderna

"From emotional AI to the metaverse, digital technologies are rapidly advancing. Daugherty and Wilson offer a compelling blueprint for leaders to create business value while building a more human-centered, trustworthy, and sustainable society. A must-read!"

—**ERIK BRYNJOLFSSON**, Professor and Director, Digital Economy Lab, Stanford University; author, *The Second Machine Age*

"Leading organizations recognize the strategic role of technology in the reinvention of their businesses. *Radically Human* offers an easy-to-understand primer on cloud, artificial intelligence, and other emerging technologies and provides a clear, compelling framework that challenges current thinking with a new human-centric mindset on innovation."

—**PETER ZAFFINO**, CEO, AIG

"In *Radically Human*, Paul Daugherty and James Wilson deftly illustrate how AI and other technologies will transform our future. Building on their extensive research and client experiences, the book makes a powerful case for why a human and humane approach will enable business leaders to disrupt competitors and chart a path toward a future that works for all."

—**R. "RAY" WANG**, Principal Analyst, founder, and CEO, Constellation Research; author, *Everybody Wants to Rule the World* and *Disrupting Digital Business*

"*Radically Human* offers businesses and leaders a startlingly fresh perspective on how the increasingly human face of advanced technology is transforming innovation. Paul Daugherty and Jim Wilson provide a clear road map that enables leaders to build their future in a way that maximizes talent and human potential."

—**ARIANNA HUFFINGTON**, founder and CEO, Thrive Global

"Radically Human makes an original, provocative business case for human-centered tech. Companies that harness AI and other advanced technologies while keeping trust and talent at the fore will become this century's greatest success stories. Daugherty and Wilson's research reveals valuable insights, brilliant real-world examples, and a new framework to transform the future."

—**AMY WEBB**, founder and CEO, Future Today Institute;
Senior Fellow, Atlantic Council

"Daugherty and Wilson take on the very important work of distilling today's complex and rapidly changing business landscape. Their previous book examined the early rise of artificial intelligence, and now the authors consider how far the technology has come in transforming the traditional definitions of invention and innovation."

—**PETER CHEN**, cofounder and CEO, Covariant

"In *Radically Human*, Paul Daugherty and James Wilson offer an exhilarating perspective on the next stage of our technology development, one that puts the human at the center of a more sustainable future—a future that we will ultimately decide."

—**JEAN-PASCAL TRICOIRE**, Chairman and CEO, Schneider Electric

"Radically Human turns upside down many of the assumptions about artificial intelligence and emerging technologies. Daugherty and Wilson make a strong case for a new, human-centered approach to technology leadership and provide a road map to a better future for all."

—**DR. KAI-FU LEE**, Chairman and CEO, Sinovation Ventures; author, *AI 2041* and *AI Superpowers*

RADICALLY HUMAN

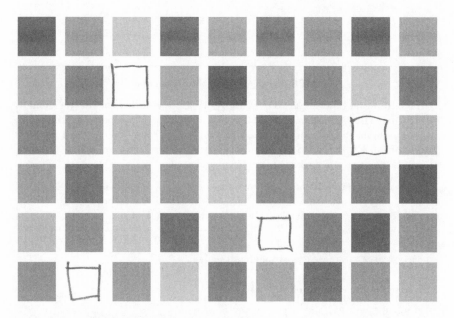

RADICALLY HUMAN

How New Technology Is Transforming
Business and Shaping Our Future

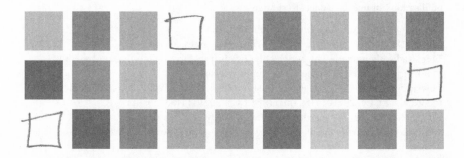

PAUL R. DAUGHERTY   H. JAMES WILSON

HARVARD BUSINESS REVIEW PRESS

BOSTON, MASSACHUSETTS

Library of Congress Cataloging-in-Publication Data
Names: Daugherty, Paul R., author. | Wilson, H. James, author.
Title: Radically human : how new technology is transforming business and shaping our future / Paul R. Daugherty, H. James Wilson.
Description: Boston, MA : Harvard Business Review Press, 2022. | Includes index. |
Identifiers: LCCN 2021044182 (print) | LCCN 2021044183 (ebook) |
  ISBN 9781647821081 (hardcover) | ISBN 9781647821098 (epub)
Subjects: LCSH: Artificial intelligence. | Technological innovations. | Business—Data processing.
Classification: LCC TA347.A78 D38 2022 (print) | LCC TA347.A78 (ebook) |
  DDC 006.3—dc23/eng/20211012
LC record available at https://lccn.loc.gov/2021044182
LC ebook record available at https://lccn.loc.gov/2021044183

ISBN: 978-1-64782-108-1
eISBN: 978-1-64782-109-8

Science and technology multiply around us. To an increasing extent they dictate the languages in which we speak and think. Either we use those languages, or we remain mute.

— J. G. Ballard

CONTENTS

Contents

RADICALLY HUMAN

Technology Takes a Radically Human Turn

When we began writing this book there was no global pandemic. No disruption of virtually every aspect of life and commerce. No desperate search for a vaccine. And certainly no expectation, against all odds and experience, that a vaccine, much less several, would be developed within a matter of months.

In our previous book, *Human + Machine: Reimaging Work in the Age of AI*, we detailed how leading companies are using artificial intelligence (AI) to augment human capabilities, not replace them. Here, we intended to extend that story with some trends that were just beginning to come into view—trends that, like human-machine collaboration, overturn longstanding assumptions about AI and innovation.

Then the virus intervened.

The successful search for vaccines validated much of what we were seeing. So did the work of pioneering researchers and companies large and small across industries, as organizations of all kinds found themselves trying to compress what would have been ten-year technology transformations into one or two years. Rather than a temporary disruption to be overcome before a return to normal, the pandemic fast-forwarded all of us—every company and every individual—into a future that had previously appeared only as a faint glimmer on the far horizon, a future beyond what we imagined in *Human + Machine*.

The Great Acceleration

Two studies tell the story. Prior to the pandemic, we undertook one of the largest studies ever of enterprise systems and technology adoption. Encompassing C-level executives at more than 8,300 companies across twenty industries in twenty-two countries—half in information technology (IT) and half not—it included data on their IT systems strategies, their use of twenty-eight technologies, their approaches to talent and culture, and specific performance indicators between 2015 and 2023 (expected).[1] During the pandemic, we undertook a second study covering the same range of issues and encompassing 4,000 companies; twenty industries across twenty countries; and, again, C-level executives, half in IT and half not.[2]

To say that the pandemic accelerated the pace of tech adoption is to put it mildly. Compared to just before the pandemic, the pace picked up by 70 percent. First-time adoption of digital, AI, cloud, and related technologies averaged 63 percent. Put another way, for any given technology a firm had not adopted before Covid struck, there was a 63 percent chance they adopted it during the pandemic. And they often did it in a hurry. As the chief digital officer of a major European food manufacturer reported to us, "IT changes we planned to undertake over 12 to 18 months occurred in a matter of days."

Yet, a large majority of companies used these technologies as a lifeline, not as engines of innovation. Before the pandemic, laggards and mediocre performers were already falling behind at an alarming rate: pre-Covid, the top 10 percent of leaders in technology adoption and innovation grew revenue at more than twice the rate of laggards—the bottom 25 percent. Why? Laggards adopt technologies unsystematically, isolate them in unconnected silos, and fail to harness their inno-

2

vative potential. By contrast, leaders adopt a wide range of cutting-edge information technologies and weave them into "living systems" that blur boundaries, afford agile adaptability, and create seamless human-machine integration.

When Covid compelled companies to fast-forward, the gap between leaders and laggards widened. Leaders invested in these digital technologies at historic rates to respond to new operational challenges and rapidly shifting customer demands. They scaled their investments in key technologies such as cloud and AI. This helped them not only absorb impacts quickly, but also refocus on growth. They not only survived; they thrived—and pulled ahead of laggards at an even more astounding rate. In 2019, our landmark research on enterprise technology strategies and their impact on performance showed that tech leaders were growing revenues at twice the speed of tech laggards. In our second study, the top 10 percent of companies rocketed even further ahead, growing revenues at *five times* the speed of laggards. Now, following the pandemic, laggards could find themselves falling even further behind—dangerously so—despite their embrace of new technologies.

The bottom line: every business is now a technology business. At the same time, a radically human approach to technology innovation, often diametrically opposed to existing approaches, has now burst forth—and brought companies to a new moment of truth.

Innovation Loses Its Innocence

The breakthroughs we examine here arrived at a time of gathering pessimism about the technological road we had been traveling for the past decade. The 2010s dawned with an unprecedented burst of technology-driven innovation. AI promised driverless vehicles, error-free surgery, great leaps in productivity, and much else. The savvy use of social media helped elect America's first Black president. Homes, buildings, energy grids, and even cities got "smart" and were getting smarter. Opportunities for disruption seemed boundless—every upstart company aspired to be the Uber or Airbnb of its industry.

But as the decade wore on, innovation lost its innocence. Autonomous vehicles sometimes turned deadly. A massive federal study of facial recognition systems widely used by law enforcement found that Asians and African Americans were up to 100 times more likely to be misidentified than white men. Malign actors appeared to hijack social media to influence US politics and subvert democracy across Europe. Cambridge Analytica harvested the personal data of 87 million people. By the end of the decade, countries and municipalities across the globe were using advances in facial recognition and datamining to create pervasive surveillance systems trained on billions of their citizens. In 2020 and 2021, key agencies throughout the US government were hacked. Ransomware attacks caused transportation problems, created gas shortages, hampered meat processing, and led to worries about food shortages.

Those were just the stories playing out in public. Other challenges emerging from the trajectory of innovation took place largely out of sight. Though seemingly more mundane than the headline-grabbing events, these developments were just as consequential for citizens, companies, and societies.

In many businesses and organizations, algorithms produced biased or unexplainable results that directly affected individuals applying for loans, seeking jobs, or confronting the criminal justice system. Among companies and institutions, "big" IT widened the gap between the haves and the have-nots, as innovations in IT architecture brought ten-fold growth each year in computing power. That's more than 300,000-fold growth since 2012. Yet, startups, many companies, and academic labs don't have the resources to pay for the exponentially increasing costs of training data-hungry AI systems to capture the potential of this growing computing power.

As lumbering legacy IT systems struggled to keep up with new technology, leaders found that making wise tech investments had become more difficult than ever. "Yes," we often heard from CEOs in the course of our work, "we know we have to become a technology company, but *what* technology?"

The time was ripe for a new departure. But it would not be in the direction of more imposing technology and ever diminishing human involvement. Instead, the trajectory of innovation is taking a dramatic turn that is changing the terms of competition and charting a path toward a more workable future.

Radically Human—Innovation Turned Upside Down

The way in which humans interact with intelligent technologies is entering a third stage. In the first stage, AI was used to automate repetitive tasks. Humans were subservient to machines and often replaced by them, leading to dire predictions of a dystopian future of joblessness for many workers. Happily, the second stage proved the pessimists wrong. As we detailed in *Human + Machine*, a number of leading companies used AI to augment human capabilities, not replace them. These leaders defied the conventional expectation that technology would render people obsolete. They used the power of human-machine collaboration to transform mechanistic processes into highly adaptive and human-centered activities, transforming their businesses and their bottom lines. This collaborative stage, leveling the playing field between humans and machines, is now giving way to a third stage in which humans and the human are in the ascendant. Leading organizations are not only out-innovating their competitors but taking an even more decisive turn toward human-centered technology—a radically human turn, as we see it, that is upending the very nature of innovation as it was practiced over the previous decade.

This turn is radical in both senses of the word—*revolutionary* and *rooted*. Revolutionary in that it is rewriting the terms of competition. Rooted in that it engages with the deepest attributes of humans—how we understand, feel, and think. Intelligent technologies have long endowed us with superhuman abilities, but now they are beginning to encompass the inherently human. That includes not only our abilities but our fallibilities. Just as behavioral economists have incorporated human fallibility into the formerly "dismal science," tech innovators are taking into account the biases and other human faults that have crept into previous generations of AI and related technologies.

This radically human approach is turning assumptions about the basic building blocks of innovation—intelligence, data, expertise, architecture, and strategy—upside down. Taken together, this upending of reigning assumptions in **I**ntelligence, **D**ata, **E**xpertise, **A**rchitecture, **S**trategy—**IDEAS**—offers a new innovation framework for companies large and small that they can use to chart a new course to the future, turbocharge revenue growth, and prepare to compete in a world where the human—and the humane—will be the means by which companies will succeed and the measure by which they will be judged.

- **Intelligence.** Technologies based only on deep learning have little sense of causality, space, time, or other fundamental concepts that human beings effortlessly call on to move through the world. Now a number of pioneering researchers and companies are creating applications and machines whose reasoning ability is adaptable and savvy—more like the way humans approach problems and tasks. For example, a new generation of robots can generalize in real-world settings like warehouses, manipulating items without being told what to do. Or consider "emotional AI," which grew out of work with autistic children to help them understand and express their emotions. It is now evolving into onboard automobile AI that could be as effective in saving motorists' lives as seatbelts. By leveraging the most powerful cognitive characteristics of humans—awareness and adaptability—these developments promise potentially more intelligent solutions to pressing commercial and social challenges.

- **Data.** The voracious data appetite of deep learning and the need for massive infrastructure to support it has increasingly put AI out of reach for many organizations. In the future, however, we will have top-down systems that don't require as much data and are faster, more flexible, and more affordable. Companies, like e-commerce retailer Wayfair, are effectively training AI in contexts where big and noisy data, like an enormous number of products, would previously drown out the small subset of relevant data. As AI continues to evolve, researchers and organizations are developing techniques ranging from data echoing, where a system reuses data; to active learning, where the system indicates what training data it needs; to synthetic data, where usable data is created where none exists. The size, shape, sources, and implementation of data are changing and, in the process, giving companies even more powerful insights and adding agility to their operations.

- **Expertise.** The human turn in intelligent systems is upending many of the assumptions about the role of people and their expertise in the emerging technological ecosystem. This is one of the most consequential human turns of all: from machines "learning" by processing mountains of data to humans teaching machines based on human experience, perception, and intuition. Rather than training systems with bottom-up machine intelligence, people are guiding them with top-down human knowledge, imparting natural intelligence to what was previously artificial. At Royal Dutch Shell, for example, an engineer or other in-house expert puts a layer of high-level machine teaching on top of an AI drilling system to dramatically shorten the time it takes the system to figure out how to operate when conditions change. Tesla uses its hundreds of thousands of car owners to teach its Autopilot feature how humans drive in virtually any situation. Etsy, the online marketplace for vintage and handmade goods, has developed a product recommendation system based on aesthetics, a notoriously difficult challenge for AI, by having the company's experts school the system in subjective notions of style. For almost any company, machine teaching unleashes the often-untapped expertise throughout the organization, allowing more people to use AI in new and sophisticated ways.

- **Architecture.** Because all businesses are now, in effect, technology businesses, architecture matters more than ever. The conventional IT "stack" spans software applications, hardware, telecommunications, facilities, and data centers. But this conventional stack simply can't handle today's hyper-digital world of mobile computing, AI applications, the internet of things (IoT), and billions of devices. And it wasn't designed to adapt to the human turn in intelligence, data, and expertise that is setting the new terms of innovation. In place of the rigid conventional stack, innovative companies are creating "living systems"—boundaryless, adaptable, and radically human architectures that bring an elegant simplicity to human-machine interaction. Epic Games, creator of the software framework called the "Unreal Engine," is a great example. This architecture is fast and adaptable, allowing more than 8 million simultaneous users to engage in graphics-intensive game play in addition to collecting a large and steady stream of data for AI-enabled analytics. Harnessing the power and elasticity of the cloud and combining it with AI and edge computing, the human turn in architecture has ignited a new era of business where competition, no matter the industry, has become a battle between systems.

- **Strategy.** Leading companies are pioneering a fundamentally
  new approach to strategy and, in the process, creating powerful
  engines of value creation. Enabled by intelligent technologies,
  these business models are built on an unprecedented integration of strategy and execution that advances both nearly simultaneously. Given the great acceleration in digital transformation
  and the speed with which new intelligent technologies are
  arriving, these companies know they can no longer afford to
  sequentially devise a strategy, experiment, and then execute.
  Their new approach is ushering in some novel business strategies.
  Among these strategies, three stand out: Forever Beta, Minimum
  Viable IDEA (MVI), and Co-lab. Forever Beta strategies are seen
  in products like the Tesla, digitally updateable through the cloud,
  allowing customers to see the value and utility of their purchase
  grow over time rather than fade. MVI strategies use one or more
  elements of the IDEAS framework to precisely target weak links
  in a traditional industry, provide a superior customer experience,
  and make immediate inroads in the market. Lemonade, an
  upstart online insurer, combined AI chatbots, machine learning,
  the cloud, and an approach that made the customer the linchpin
  of a unique human-in-the-loop process to eliminate the mutual
  distrust between insurance companies and customers. Co-lab
  strategies produce superior results in the sciences or other
  knowledge-intensive environments through human-guided,
  machine-driven discovery. Nowhere can the power of IDEAS and
  the marriage of strategy and execution be seen more clearly than
  in the remarkable part played by Moderna and Pfizer/BioNtech in
  the development of Covid-19 vaccines in record time.

With the IDEAS framework at hand, both technical and nontechnical executives can better understand each of the distinct elements of
the emerging technology landscape and innovate in all areas of the
business. Possibilities span everything from R&D and operations to

talent management and business models. Executives with deep knowledge of tech may be inspired to further push the boundaries of their disciplines to capture even more value from digital transformation using the framework.

Most importantly, for specialists and nonspecialists alike, the IDEAS framework provides a common point of reference to guide business and technological initiatives—the radically human dimension that will increasingly drive competition.

Who Will Win in the New World of Radically Human Innovation?

To gauge how companies are faring in this emerging environment, we have drawn on both of our studies—pre-pandemic and post-pandemic—of enterprise systems and technology adoption. We have drawn also on targeted case studies of leading companies, our hands-on client experience, and extensive conversations with business leaders and innovators around the world that have grown out of *Human + Machine.*

In part one, "Transforming Innovation—The Power of IDEAS," we explore the new approaches to intelligence, data, expertise, architecture, and strategy that are redefining innovation. In part two, "Competing for the Radically Human Future," we explore how companies will use IDEAS to differentiate themselves along four key dimensions: talent, trust, experiences, and sustainability.

All four of the areas outlined in part two have been of concern to a greater or lesser degree for many companies throughout this century. Now they loom larger than ever. Tech-literate talent is in short supply; trust has been thrust to the fore by the pandemic; unique experiences, enhanced by technology, offer nearly limitless possibilities for customers, employees, and citizens alike; and sustainability grows more urgent daily.

What's different now is the outsized role AI and related technologies play in how companies perform along these four dimensions of competitive difference. Companies of all kinds—traditionally tech oriented or not—will need to come to terms with the ways radically human technology and innovation are redefining these more-important-than-ever sources of differentiation. Talent, trust, experiences, and sustainability will be major components of every company's value proposition, brand promise, and financial performance.

Who will come out ahead? The answer is far from obvious. The fact that leaders in our second survey were growing revenue five times faster than laggards might imply that we are moving into an era of winner-take-all competition. But in this second survey, conducted during the pandemic, we found a number of organizations that have been able to break previous performance barriers.

These "leapfroggers," representing about 18 percent of our sample, have adopted advanced and emerging human-centered technologies and scaled them across their enterprises while fostering the right kind of organizational change needed to take advantage of these investments. And they have shifted their IT budgets from operations-related activity to innovation-related activity. Between 2018 and 2020, leapfroggers grew at four times the rate of laggards. During the pandemic, their growth rate was even higher than that of the average leader. By pursuing *compressed transformation*, these breakout companies demonstrate the possibility that even the least technologically advanced organizations can make enormous and profitable leaps forward.

A More Human—and Humane—Future

What could radically human technology mean for individuals and society? What role do companies play in helping society move toward a more general social prosperity? How can companies actively foster

11

well-being for customers and communities? And do it all while aiming for financial success?

Just as we shape our tools, our tools shape us.[3] This adage offers an excellent philosophical foundation to begin to think through these questions. From the hammer to the wheel to television to AI, each tool created for making or doing in turn forces us to rethink our environments and ourselves, to reconsider who we are and what's possible for the future, for better or for worse.

In *Human + Machine*, we reported that leading companies aren't pitting humans against machines in a fight for jobs. Instead, they are putting people and machines in symbiotic relationships, each pushing the other to achieve what neither could do on their own. The symbiosis between people and our tools is what undergirds the radically human IDEAS framework and what shines a light through the differentiators of talent, trust, experience, and sustainability.

While not all solutions should be tech solutions, modern technology is, without doubt, one of the most potent and scalable tools for accelerating positive change in our world, especially when coupled with strong policy and healthy guardrails for human safety and dignity. That today's technology holds this kind of power is all the more reason to understand how to better shape it so as to better shape ourselves. This sentiment includes acting quickly to fix our tools as well as our own understanding of them, when they, or we, falter.

What follows are the stories of innovators, researchers, companies, and organizations that are putting new, radically human technologies to work for and with human beings and, in doing so, shaping our future tools, the world we live in, and ourselves. In some ways these stories are as old as civilization, and in some ways they're brand new. All aim to inspire future trajectories of innovation through the very old story of doing well by doing good. What will it take to get us there together? This book will be your guide.

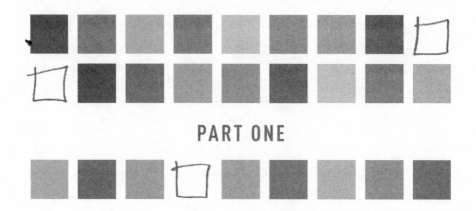

PART ONE

TRANSFORMING
INNOVATION

The Power of IDEAS

1

INTELLIGENCE

More Human, Less Artificial

"Can machines think?"

That's how Alan Turing began his celebrated paper entitled "Computing Machinery and Intelligence," published in 1950.[1] Ever since, there has been much argument about what came to be known as the "Turing Test"—turning on the question of whether a computer could fool us into believing it was human. Though Turing himself never claimed that machines could actually think, that hasn't stopped fantasists and casual observers from imagining—usually with horror—machines endowed with human consciousness.

That is not us.

The radically human turn in AI that we are seeing is not about recreating consciousness. It's about solving problems by leveraging the most powerful cognitive characteristics of humans and supplementing them with the most powerful abilities of computers. It promises not domination by machines, but a more comprehensive, more effective, more affordable, and more innovative means of solving pressing commercial and social challenges. It is fully under way at the furthest frontiers of research and in enterprises of all kinds, with profound implications for us all.

And a Little Child Shall Lead Them

No machine powered by AI can yet match the ease and efficiency with which even the youngest humans learn, comprehend, and contextualize. Accidentally drop an object and a one-year-old child who sees you reaching for it will retrieve it for you. Throw it down on purpose and the child will ignore it.[2] In other words, even very small children understand that other people have intentions—an extraordinary cognitive ability that seems to come almost prewired in the human brain.

That's not all. Beginning at a very young age, they develop an intuitive sense of physics: they begin expecting objects to move along smooth paths, remain in existence, fall when unsupported, and not act at a distance. Before they've acquired language, they distinguish animate agents from inanimate objects. As they learn language, they exhibit their remarkable ability to generalize from very few examples, needing to experience only an instance or two of a new word to grasp its meaning.[3] They also learn to walk on their own, through trial and error.

Yet AI can do many things that people, despite being endowed with natural intelligence, find impossible or difficult to do well: recognize patterns in vast amounts of data; defeat the greatest champions at chess, Go, and Jeopardy; run complex manufacturing processes; efficiently aid callers to customer service centers; analyze weather, soil conditions, and satellite imagery to help farmers maximize crop yields; scan millions of internet images in the fight against child exploitation; detect financial fraud; predict consumer preferences; personalize advertising; and much else. Automating such tasks lies beyond not only the capabilities of humans, but also of traditional procedural logic and programming. Most important, AI has enabled humans and machines to complement each other, transforming mechanistic processes into highly adaptive, organic, and human-centered activities. And, contrary to automation doomsayers, such collaboration is opening up an array of new, high-value jobs.[4]

No wonder, then, that adoption of AI is rapidly accelerating through-out industries around the globe. According to a 2019 survey, compa-nies planned to double AI projects in 2020 and, by 2022, to have an average of thirty-five AI or machine-learning projects in place.[5]

What's driving this acceleration in adoption? More AI models are being put in production. Specialized hardware is increasing AI's capac-ity to provide quicker results based on larger datasets. Simplified and smaller tools are enabling AI to work on nearly any device. The cloud is allowing access to AI resources from anywhere and the ability to scale up and scale down as business needs evolve. Rapid adoption is also being driven by the need to integrate data from many sources, by complex business and computer logic challenges, and by competitive incentives to make data more useful. And, of course, there was the great acceleration driven by the pandemic.

Our firm's recent research shows that more than three-fourths of major companies currently have deep learning initiatives under way.[6] Deep learning is a powerful subset of machine learning. It works through neural networks consisting of simple neuron-like processing units that collectively perform complex computations. AI based on deep learning must be trained from the bottom up on massive amounts of data and, often, fine-tuned with additional data. But this data-hungry approach is beginning to run into significant challenges—of capacity, affordability, and sustainability, as we will see in the next chapter.

Meanwhile, on the frontiers of research, the nature of machine intel-ligence is taking a radically human turn: becoming less artificial and more intelligent, less like the autonomous vehicle that has to be labori-ously taught everything and more like the human infant who comes equipped with a remarkably efficient capacity to learn.

These developments should give pause to senior leaders contemplat-ing how to allocate their technology spending over the coming three to five years. On the one hand, the challenges facing deep learning are formidable and, for many organizations, insuperable. On the other hand, deep learning has provided so many insights and valuable outcomes, it won't vanish anytime soon. As the plans of companies in our survey attest, these technologies are no longer optional; they're required. At the same time, however, the quest for more human-like AI, after lying dormant for decades, has taken on new life, impelled by the limits that current approaches to intelligence are now running up against. For senior leaders, navigating this dilemma begins with an understanding of those limits.

The Trouble with Intelligence

MIT Technology Review analyzed twenty-five years of AI research, encompassing 6,625 scholarly papers, and concluded that deep learning could be nearing the end of its explosive ten-year dominance.[7] Deep learning won't disappear. It will remain a powerful tool for certain narrowly defined problems. And it will be an important element in some of the wide range of complicated techniques that will tip the balance in machine intelligence in favor of the human over the artificial. But the notion that deep learning, if only given enough time and fed enough data, will get us to general AI looks increasingly unlikely.

Many AI Systems Aren't All That Smart

For starters, deep learning systems are often stumped in ways that can't be explained. Consider AI image-recognition. It was one of the great AI success stories of recent years. But, since 2017, it has seen little progress. ImageNet, maintained at Stanford University, is an open-source collection of more than 14 million hand-labeled images in more than 20,000 categories. It has been used to train many familiar AI image-identification applications such as Microsoft's Bing. But researchers have collected some 7,500 real-world photos that confuse state-of-the-art computer vision systems. (For instance, a picture of a young man running was absurdly identified as a unicycle.) When fed these images, the systems' accuracy drops from over 95 percent to as low as 2 percent.[8] That means that some of the most powerful computer vision systems in the world will correctly identify these images in only 2 of 100 attempts. And when what's at stake is not simply correctly classifying an image but genuinely recognizing an object, as with self-driving cars or delivery drones, failures could have fatal consequences.

Complex Systems Suffer from the "Black Box" Problem

AI systems are often used to help make highly consequential decisions: who gets approved for a loan, who gets hired, who wins parole, how long a prison sentence someone gets, why a driverless vehicle makes a critical maneuver, where and how a company's ads are distributed on social media, and more. But many of these systems, especially those that employ deep learning, are opaque. It's impossible to explain how their algorithms, working with enormous numbers of parameters and many intricately interconnected layers of abstraction, reach their conclusions. And those conclusions can sometimes be disastrous—resulting in racial discrimination in loans and criminal justice, vehicles that tragically crash, or respected brands whose ads on social media show up next to neo-Nazi content or conspiracy theories.

The drive to make AI "explainable"—enshrined in law in the European Union's General Data Protection Regulation—demands the question be asked: Explainable to whom? Different stakeholders seek different kinds of explanations. The problem arises even with a relatively simple loan risk assessment system.[9] Software developers and system administrators want an explanation in terms of architecture and processing parameters. A seasoned loan officer, who makes the final decision, might want to know how various factors have been weighted in the system's recommendation. An applicant who has been denied a loan wants to know precisely why—*is it my age, my race, my zip code, an inaccurate credit history?* A regulator wants to be assured that the system doesn't compromise data privacy, violate anti-discrimination laws, or leave it itself open to financial fraud. A layperson, contemplating the black box problem generally, might want to know why anyone would build a machine they don't understand.

Deep Learning Systems Can't Read

We can compile all the books in the world in a massive searchable database (as in Google Books) and devise machine reading programs that can extract all kinds of correlations. But no existing AI can read with even the rudimentary comprehension of a young child. Researchers Gary Marcus and Ernest Davis asked Google's Talk to Books tool this simple question: "Where did Harry Potter meet Hermione Granger?" None of the twenty answers the tool returned came from *Harry Potter and the Sorcerer's Stone,* and none addressed the question of where the meeting took place.[10]

Smartphones may be relatively good at correcting writing mistakes or predicting the next word in a sentence. Translation programs render serviceable translations among many languages. But none of those applications—or any others—brings the background knowledge, sense of context, and countless assumptions about reality required to read with genuine comprehension.

They Lack Fundamental Knowledge Frameworks

Those frameworks include concepts like space, time, and causation that humans, like the pencil-retrieving infant, acquire without apparent effort.[11] Take causation—an essential component of common sense. Much of the success of deep learning has been driven by a powerful ability to find correlations, such as that between a constellation of symptoms and a particular disease. But, as we should all know by now, correlation is not causation. If machines understood that one thing causes another, then they wouldn't need to be retrained for each new task.[12] Instead, they could apply what they know in one domain to a different domain.

The Future of Radically Human Intelligence

Despite advances in cognitive psychology and neuroscience, we don't really know exactly how the human brain does the amazing things it does with its very limited computational resources. But, at a high level, we do know what some of the basic building blocks of human intelligence are, and pioneers are beginning to create machine versions of them. The authors of "Building Machines That Learn and Think Like Humans," a seminal piece on this new direction in machine intelligence, put it: "As long as natural intelligence remains the best example of intelligence, we believe that the project of reverse engineering the human solutions to difficult computational problems will continue to inform and advance AI."[13]

The question for senior leaders is which more human-like cognitive abilities, detailed next, might be most relevant to capturing value for their businesses and delivering value to their customers.

Generalizing in Real-World Settings

While theoretical arguments rage over deep learning versus some ideal version of artificial general intelligence as *the* means of getting to more human-like intelligence, practitioners aren't waiting. They're drawing on all the disciplines of AI to open up new possibilities for machine capabilities and performance.

Consider the coming generation of logistics and warehouse robots—a technology that can have an enormous impact on the operations and bottom lines of companies in many industries. For instance, in highly automated product fulfillment centers with miles of warehouse shelves, robots do a lot of the heavy lifting and initial steps in product picking. But faced with hundreds of thousands of SKUs that change often, automated picking systems must be designed either to pick a specified category of items, or they must be trained on every item they might need to pick. That means that when new items are added to inventory, they must be hand-coded into the system, which is highly impractical at an industrial scale.

That's why humans are, in many ways, superior to the current generation of "dumb" robot pickers. Humans don't need to be constantly retrained on each new SKU. They can generalize from their experience, easily distinguish one object from another, and quickly figure out the best way to handle something without damaging it. But fulfillment centers, aiming for same-day or even same-hour delivery, suffer from high employee turnover and limits on the volume and velocity of work that is humanly possible.

At Obeta, a German electronics wholesaler whose warehouse is run by Austrian warehouse logistics company KNAPP AG, a new generation of smarter robot pickers is changing the game. Equipped with AI from Covariant, a startup founded by robotics researchers from the University of California at Berkeley and research lab Open AI, the robots are taught general abilities. Those abilities include 3D perception, physical affordances of objects, real-time motion planning, and few-shot learning (mastering a task after only a few training examples). These general abilities enable them to quickly learn to manipulate objects without being told what to do.[14] Their job is to pick items from bulk storage bins and add them to individual orders to be shipped.

A visitor to Covariant's headquarters described the technology in action: "I watched three different robots masterfully pick up all manner of store-bought items. In seconds, the algorithm analyzes their positions, calculates the attack angle and correct sequence of motions, and extends the arm to grab on with a suction cup. It moves with certainty and precision, and changes its speed depending on the delicateness of the item."[15]

The robots employ an off-the-shelf industrial arm, a suction gripper, and a vision system. The vision system is coupled to the gripper by Covariant Brain, a hardware-agnostic software platform. It is intended to be a universal AI for robots in any customer environment—a single neural network that can adapt to many different environments.

"Our system generalizes to items it's never seen before. Being able to look at a scene and understand how to interact with individual items in a tote, including items it's never seen before—humans can do this, and that's essentially generalized intelligence," says Pieter Abbeel, one of the company's founders. "This generalized understanding of what's in a bin is really key to success. That's the difference between a traditional system where you would catalog everything ahead of time and try to recognize everything in the catalog, versus fast-moving warehouses where you have many SKUs and they're always changing."[16]

To say the system is a hybrid hardly does justice to all of the techniques that have been brought to bear to endow it with the ability to generalize. Covariant uses a wide range of such techniques, including imitation learning and reinforcement learning. For instance, to train the robot on a new set of items, they put new objects in front of it and see if can successfully adapt to them. When it fails, it can update its understanding of what it's seeing and try some different approaches. And when it succeeds, it can get a reward signal to reinforce learning. When a set of SKUs differs totally from other sets, then Covariant has to revert to supervised learning—collecting and labeling a lot of new training data, as happens with deep learning systems.

To succeed in a commercial environment, the robots must perform to a very high standard. Previously, KNAPP's robot pickers reliably handled only about 15 percent of objects; the Covariant-powered robots now reliably handle about 95 percent of objects.[17] And they're faster than humans, picking about 600 objects an hour versus 450 for humans. Nevertheless, no staff have been laid off at the Obeta facility. Instead, says Peter Puchwein, vice president of innovation at KNAPP, they have been retrained to understand more about robotics and computers.[18] Meanwhile, Covariant is looking to build out its Brain to power robots in manufacturing, agriculture, hospitality, commercial kitchens, and, eventually, people's homes.

Survival of the Fittest Algorithm

For e-commerce sellers like Zappos, irrelevant search results are a perennial headache. Because queries can have multiple different meanings to a website's search engine, getting accurate search results among the enormous inventory can be difficult. Potential customers who enter search terms for a particular style of dress shoe, but are shown dresses instead, will soon get fed up and move on to competitors. To solve the problem, Zappos is pitting algorithms against each other in a digital game of *Survivor*.

These so-called genetic algorithms are essentially randomized search algorithms that imitate the mechanics of natural selection—a process of stumbling upon useful results and then moving toward optimization of delivery routes, for example, or designing lightweight yet sturdy structures. First introduced in 1960 by John Holland, a polymath in psychology, electrical engineering, and computer science, genetic algorithms have only recently become useful because of their computing power requirements. Zappos began experimenting with genetic algorithms in 2017. At the time, the company's website encountered about a million unique search terms each month. The search engine had to match those terms with the more than 100,000 items in the company's product catalogue.[19] Borrowing a page from Darwin, genetic algorithms simulate the process of natural selection. The Zappos system, for example, produces algorithms that work out the intent of a search phrase. One algorithm might see the word "dress" as a strong signal for retrieving dresses. A competing algorithm pays more attention to other words in the phrase. A "relevance test," which simulates how users behave, rewards the winning algorithm by passing on its traits to the next generation of algorithms. The best-performing algorithm goes live on the website until it is superseded by a "fitter" one, continually improving the performance of the search engine.

After less than a year of using the genetic algorithm technology, the company found that customers were shopping faster, were applying fewer filters, and didn't need multiple searches to find what they were looking for. And, says Ameen Kazerouni, lead data scientist at Zappos, "At the end of the day it's not a recurring expense—once it's working, it's working."[20]

Making Better Bets

Humans routinely, and often effortlessly, sort through probabilities and act on the likeliest, even with relatively little prior experience. Machines are now being taught to mimic such reasoning through the application of Gaussian processes—probabilistic models that can deal with extensive uncertainty, act on sparse data, and learn from experience.

Almost a decade ago, Alphabet, Google's parent company, launched Project Loon, designed to provide internet service to underserved regions of the world through a system of giant balloons hovering in the stratosphere.[21] Their navigational systems employed Gaussian processes to predict where in the stratified and highly variable winds aloft the balloons needed to go. Each balloon then moved into a layer of wind blowing in the right direction, arranging themselves to form one large communication network. The balloons could not only make reasonably accurate predictions by analyzing past flight data, but also analyze data during a flight and adjust their predictions accordingly.

Although Alphabet ended the experiment in early 2021, such Gaussian processes hold great promise. Using AI-startup Secondmind's Decision Engine, powered by Gaussian process-based probabilistic modeling, Japanese carmaker Mazda was able to improve engine calibration while using 1000 times less data compared with current tools.[22]

Some experts believe the small data powers of Gaussian processes could hasten autonomous AI. "To build a truly autonomous agent, it has to be able to adapt to its environment very quickly," says Vishal Chatrath, CEO of AI startup Secondmind. "That means being able to learn in a data-efficient way."[23]

Gaussian processes don't require massive amounts of data in order to recognize patterns; the computations required for inference and learning are relatively easy, and if something goes wrong, its cause can be traced, unlike the black boxes of neural networks.

Closing In on Causation

AI is good at spotting correlations and making valuable predictions based on them. For instance, GNS Healthcare, a Cambridge, Massachusetts, precision medicine company, uses causal algorithms to help some of the world's largest pharmaceutical companies understand not only which patients respond to what drugs, but why. Using Bayesian techniques, their software platform translates data into causal models. These techniques identify which variables in a dataset appear to have the most influence on other variables, with the aim of better targeting research, designing more incisive drug trials, speeding up regulatory approval, and better predicting patient risk.

In one study, GNS, along with the Alliance for Clinical Trials in Oncology, set out to identify the clinical predictors for a subpopulation of patients with metastatic colorectal cancer (mCRC).[24] It is one of the most common cancers in the United States, with an estimated 140,000 new cases diagnosed each year. The study used the company's causal AI platform to analyze clinical data from more than 2,000 patients with mCRC. The researchers wanted to uncover predictive biomarkers for patient response to different drug treatments for the disease and predictors of overall survival among some patient subpopulations.

"We have never been in a better position to unravel drivers of disease and patient response to specific drugs," says Colin Hill, GNS chairman, CEO, and co-founder. "We built an *in-silico* patient model of colorectal cancer and were able to uncover biomarkers that tell us which patients will respond to which treatment, and most importantly, why. This is what will get us to the point of delivering personalized medicine and eradicating disease."[25]

Taking on Time/Space

Some 720,000 hours[26] of video are uploaded to YouTube each day, video that must be processed for ad rankings and recommendations. In hospitals, terabytes of sensitive videos must be used on local devices to protect privacy. In smart cities, closed-circuit cameras generate reams of video that must sometimes be quickly analyzed to avert imminent danger from potentially violent or criminal activity. All of these tasks require accurate and efficient understanding of what is taking place in any given video. But video recognition, unlike simple image recognition, requires temporal modeling—the ability to understand and predict sequences of actions. Like other AI based on deep learning, video applications have typically required vast and expensive computing power, and they're unavailable in settings that lack sufficient resources and technology.

Recently, however, researchers at the MIT-IBM Watson AI Lab have developed a new technique for training video recognition systems that is both highly accurate and saves on computation costs.[27] The researchers were able to train video recognition models three times faster than existing state-of-the-art techniques. Instead of breaking up videos into individual frames and then running recognition algorithms on each frame, the technique extracts sketches of objects in each frame and overlays the sketches to see how the objects shift in space. The increased speed could be critical for the ability of autonomous vehicles to recognize and react to visual information and to predict what is likely to take place around them.

Further, the model can run on low-power devices like phones. For instance, with a small computer and camera running only on enough energy to power a bicycle light, the model was able to quickly classify hand gestures.[28] This technique could help reduce the computation cost of video recognition and shrink its carbon footprint. Because of its hardware efficiency, it could also help put compact diagnostic devices in the hands of physicians and nurses at primary sites of care.

Calling on Common Sense

A variety of organizations are working to teach machines to navigate the world using common sense—to understand everyday objects and actions, communicate naturally, handle unforeseen situations, and learn from experiences. But what comes naturally to humans, without explicit training or data, is fiendishly difficult for machines. Says Oren Etzioni, the CEO of the Allen Institute for Artificial Intelligence (AI2), "No AI system currently deployed can reliably answer a broad range of simple questions, such as, 'If I put my socks in a drawer, will they still be in there tomorrow?' or 'How can you tell if a milk carton is full?'"[29]

To help define what it means for machines to have common sense, AI2 is developing a portfolio of tasks against which progress can be measured. The Defense Advanced Research Projects Agency (DARPA) is investing $2 billion in AI research. In its Machine Common Sense (MCS) program, researchers will create models that mimic core domains of human cognition, including "the domains of *objects* (intuitive physics), *places* (spatial navigation), and *agents* (intentional actors)." Researchers at Microsoft and McGill University have jointly developed a system that has shown great promise for untangling ambiguities in natural language, a problem that requires diverse forms of inference and knowledge.[30]

The millions upon millions of unstated assumptions and rules about how reality works that constitute common sense could almost be said to *be* human intelligence. In the early days of AI, researchers attempted to codify all those rules in the manner of symbolic logic, creating a knowledge base from which a system could draw inferences. These "symbolist" efforts foundered on the near impossibility of cataloging the untold number of such rules—and their many exceptions, qualifications, and contexts—and devising algorithms that could navigate them.

Proponents of deep learning took a different tack. They designed neural networks with interconnected layers that could discern patterns without having them embedded in advance by programmers. As we've seen, their record has been mixed—impressively guiding autonomous vehicles and hilariously failing basic tests of commonsense reasoning. But there are signs that symbolist approaches may be converging with neural network approaches in hybrid systems that produce results that more closely resemble the outputs of human common sense. With such systems, the goal is to produce both the right answer and the rationale for that answer.

Consider chatbots and voice digital assistants, which often leave users frustrated. The applications can be easily stumped, and most importantly, even when they do come up with an answer, they can't provide a commonsense explanation for it. Cloud services and CRM power-house Salesforce is working to change that with its Einstein Voice Assistant. The company's research is moving toward imbuing neural networks with the capacity to give not only correct answers, but to provide plausible explanations for those answers as well. Enterprise voice assistants are rare in general; thus Einstein gives the company a great advantage in customer experience and engagement.

In addition to conferring advantages on organizations whose voice assistant can explain its answers, advances in AI common sense have obvious relevance in sectors where explainability is critical—healthcare, finance, security, and government. Commonsense reasoning could also help overcome some of the limitations of visual recognition systems, supplying, for example, the common knowledge that hitting a traffic cone is far less consequential than hitting a pedestrian. "Common sense is a critical component to building AIs that can understand what they read; that can control robots that can operate usefully and safely in the human environment; that can interact with human users in reasonable ways," says Gary Marcus, a leading AI expert and founder of Robust. AI. "Common sense is not just the hardest problem for AI; in the long run, it's also the most important problem."[31]

Tracking Emotions

In 2018 alone, distracted driving claimed 2,841 lives in the United States. The dead included 1,730 drivers, 605 passengers, 400 pedestrians, and 77 bicyclists.[32] Any activity that diverts attention from driving counts as a distraction—texting, talking on a phone, eating and drinking, conversing with passengers, and fiddling with the sound or navigation system. Texting is particularly dangerous. At 55 mph, taking your eyes off the road for five seconds to read a text is like driving the length of an entire football field with your eyes closed. Falling asleep at the wheel is even deadlier—up to 6,000 fatal crashes each year may be caused by drowsy drivers.[33] Road rage is another major cause of accidents. Some 94 percent of all traffic accidents are caused by driver error, and one-third of those accidents could be linked to behavior characterized as road rage.[34]

Those figures could drop dramatically if an AI system designed to read the emotions of drivers becomes as ubiquitous in automobiles as seatbelts. Such a system is currently being created by Affectiva, a Boston startup founded in 2009 by researchers from MIT's famed Media Lab (and acquired in mid-2021 by Swedish company Smart Eye). Affectiva's algorithms read people's faces to detect their emotional and other cognitive states. It could help keep drivers calm, attentive, and awake by automatically providing appropriate interventions, alerts, or suggested actions. But it's an enormously complex challenge. Cognitive states like drowsiness come on gradually; facial manifestations of emotions can differ by age, gender, ethnicity, and culture.

The company has also developed an emotion tracking system that enables media and advertisers to test responses to their programming and video ads with target audiences. The system is based on the analysis of more than 7.6 million faces in eighty-seven countries. About one-fourth of the *Fortune* Global 500 have used the technology to test their ads around the world and help them predict purchase intent, sales lift, or the likelihood of content to go viral.[35]

"Affective computing" or "emotional AI," as it is known, was used early on in work with autistic children to help them understand and express their emotions. Its originators, says Gabi Zijderveld, formerly with Affectiva and now with Smart Eye, were driven by "the idea that technology could have the ability to understand and respond to human emotions, to basically improve human interactions with technology to make them more relevant, more appropriate, but also maybe to help humans get a better grasp or better control over emotions."[36]

Rana el Kaliouby, the founder of Affectiva and now deputy CEO of Smart Eye, knows a thing or two about overwhelming emotions. In 1990, when she was a child growing up in the Middle East, Iraq invaded Kuwait, her native country. "Overnight, our world changed," she writes. "My parents lost their jobs, their home, their savings. In the aftermath, I felt a flood of emotions unlike anything I'd ever experienced."[37]

The profound psychological dislocations wrought by Covid-19 set her thinking about how an emotion-enabled digital world might help. The massive moves to online learning, virtual meetings, and telehealth, and the isolation brought on by social distancing, eliminated essential elements of human connection that we take for granted in face-to-face contact. Employees suffered "Zoom fatigue." Professors and corporate presenters alike had no way of knowing how their audiences were really responding. Physicians and psychologists seeing patients virtually had difficulty assessing moods and general sense of well-being. So did people connecting with aging parents particularly vulnerable to the virus. Emotion tracking software might restore at least some of the human connection we lose in such encounters and help monitor and promote mental health.

As el Kaliouby writes, "Our reliance on technology to connect with the world will only grow stronger. Arming technology with artificial emotional intelligence might be the only way to preserve the things that make us human in the first place: empathy, emotion, and meaningful connection."[38]

Giving Machines a Theory of Mind

The child who retrieves the pencil when you drop it accidentally and ignores it when you throw it down on purpose is said to have a theory of mind. They understand that others have emotions, intentions, desires, and knowledge; and they draw on that understanding to analyze and respond to others' behavior. A theory of mind is crucial for the innumerable everyday interactions we take for granted. It is also crucial for robots working with other robots and around humans. For instance, a care-giving robot must be able to understand the emotions and desires of someone who may have limited ability to express them.

Attempts to imbue robots with a theory of mind are proceeding along several tracks, all of which are attempting to overcome the limitations of deep learning. Deep learning's bottom-up approach to intelligence is based on a thoroughgoing empiricism, the aim of which is pattern recognition. For instance, when a deep learning visual recognition system sees something, the item is processed through the neural network's vast amount of training data to find patterns of ever-increasing complexity until the system arrives at a conclusion about what the item is. As we've noted, the limitations of this approach are its voracious appetite for data and its lack of explainability.

Researchers at Google's DeepMind are trying to overcome these limitations, while still employing neural networks, with what they call a "machine theory of mind."[39] Their Theory of Mind neural network—ToMnet—uses meta-learning to build models of the external agents it encounters, from observations of their behavior alone. Through relatively few observations, ToMnet acquires a strong prior model of agents' behavior and the ability to bootstrap to richer predictions about the agents' characteristics and mental states. Like other deep learning systems, it improves with experience.

DeepMind's AI entities were simple agents in a virtual room, where they collected colored boxes for points while ToMnet "watched."[40] One of the agents was blind; one couldn't remember its recent steps; and one could both see and remember. The blind agents tended to follow along walls, the agents with faulty memories went for objects that were closest, and the agent that could see and remember strategically collected boxes in a specific order to earn more points. With some training, ToMnet was able to identify each type of agent quickly and correctly predict its future behavior.

These simple experiments are heavily dependent on a tightly bound context; they are confined to interactions with very simple agents, and ToMnet's rudimentary abilities are a far cry from the capacity of humans to fathom other minds. But the direction of such work, even though it involves neural networks, is in keeping with the turn in intelligence toward more top-down, less data-hungry approaches.

Another top-down approach assumes that the mind makes mental models of the world against which even very sparse data can be tested. Instead of learning to model other agents, the AI is equipped with simulations against which it can test hypotheses and predict what other dynamic agents in its vicinity might do.

Researchers at the University of West England have explored the potential of a mobile robot containing a simulation of itself, other dynamic agents, and its environment.[41] Operating in real time, the simulation-based internal model is able to look ahead and predict the consequences of its actions and those of other actors in its vicinity. For example, when navigating down a narrow corridor with an oncoming robot, the AI could simulate turning left, right, or continuing its path and determine which action will most likely avoid collision.[42] Robots have certainly succeeded at such maneuvers without simulations, but the advance here is to prove that such simulations provide a path toward an artificial theory of mind.

Getting Smart about Intelligence

Like objects in an auto's side mirror, these more natural cognitive and emotional abilities may be closer than they appear. As we have seen, they are being developed and refined by research organizations like AI2; specialist companies like Covariant and Affectiva/Smart Eye; and established enterprises like Zappos, Salesforce, Google, and many others. This technology is here now, gaining momentum daily, and helping lay the groundwork for future competition.

Along the key dimension of trust, more human-like intelligence will win loyal customers and further separate leaders from laggards. Radically human machine intelligence will also take us from a past in which tech was imposed on customers and employees, who struggled to learn how to use it and adapt to it, to a future in which people eagerly adopt it because it adapts to them. As that future draws closer, companies will need to ramp down older, more costly and cumbersome approaches to machine intelligence and ramp up more human-centered approaches.

While there is no precise formula for this transition, there are some steps leaders can take now to prepare, starting with leadership and moving outward from tech specialists, to encompass the entire organization and engage with the company's wider ecosystem. It starts with leadership, with the CEO, and the C-suite. They need to make sure they have AI teams that are learning and experimenting with the emerging approaches to intelligence we have been describing here, linked to the business. These teams should focus on algorithms that more closely mimic human cognitive abilities, and that produce explainable results and offer more affordable and innovative solutions to business challenges.

In the wider organization, the aim should be to propagate what we call *digital fluency*. We explore it in depth in chapter 6 on talent; but, in brief, the idea is to move from digital literacy—mere familiarity with the terms of AI and the like—to immersion in the language, techniques, and application of intelligent technologies. Digitally fluent employees, especially those closest to customers or internal challenges, are able to deliver solutions at the point of need.

Beyond the four walls of the company, you need to tap into the wider world of technology partners, researchers, and industry players, all of whom can help you move faster in assembling the elements of new approaches to intelligence that are most relevant to your business. This is also a crucial first step toward the coordinated, strategic ecosystem partnerships that increasingly characterize competition in a world where no one has a monopoly on the vast number of technological breakthroughs occurring almost daily.

In part, the radically human turn in intelligence, which will have such profound consequences for your company's processes, products, and services, will be enabled by a turn to less data-hungry AI, complementing well-established approaches to big data and potentially leveling the playing field for all competitors, the subject to which we turn in the next chapter.

2

DATA

From Maximum to Minimum,
and Back Again

The notion of leveraging something in business—capital, talent, research, technology, a process—is so frequently invoked that, like many familiar metaphors, it has lost its expressive power. "To leverage" has come to mean little more than "to use advantageously." But it's worth recalling the full power of the metaphor—what leverage really means is having a small number of resources yield a high level of return.

Nowhere is that dynamic more apt than with the use of data in AI as it travels from the "edge" of a local device to the cloud and sometimes back again to a device.

Data-hungry AI can certainly deliver some degree of leverage in an organization. As voracious and expensive as it might be, it can still yield higher return than alternatives (like manual processes). But recent developments in "small data" leverage AI at its source, processing data locally for AI uses at the "edge"—directly on the smartphones, sensors, autonomous vehicles, drones, and potentially any other device with a robust-enough microchip that generates streams of data. All this small data adds up to something big: IDC estimates that connected IoT devices such as these will collectively generate 73 zettabytes (or 73 trillion gigabytes) of data by 2025, quadrupling in size from 2019.[1]

Using small data on the edge to power big data insights can yield higher returns on AI performance itself, using far fewer resources of training time, computational power, infrastructure, people, and money. This data-leveraged AI then brings the leverage of AI generally to the organization. Mastering the art of marrying small data, big data, and AI could help make the competitive difference for many organizations, especially those finding themselves in a data arms race they're unlikely to win.

The Trouble with Maximum Data

Starsky Robotics looked to be one of the emerging success stories in autonomous vehicles. The company's proprietary AI system guided big-rig trucks over highways and on local roads and allowed a human driver, working from a remote operations center, to take over. Starsky was no pie-in-the sky venture built on a vague possibility of one day disrupting an industry. The company actually owned assets, employed former truckers as remote operators, and was pursuing a practical business model that seemed to put it commercially ahead of ambitious rivals like Waymo and Uber.

Starsky also enjoyed a string of increasingly impressive accomplishments: In 2016, its self-driving truck became the first street-legal vehicle to do real work with no one behind the wheel. In 2018, it completed a seven-mile trip on a closed Florida road without a human in the cab—the first fully unmanned truck run in history. In 2019, it became the first unmanned truck to drive on a public highway. It navigated a rest stop, merged onto the Florida Turnpike, and covered a 9.4-mile stretch of road at an average speed of 55 mph. Only the first and last segments of the trip, about two-tenths of a mile, were handled by a remote operator, sitting 200 miles away in Jacksonville.

In 2020, the company closed its doors.

What went wrong? In a wrenching farewell blog post, Starsky founder Stefan Seltz-Axmacher detailed what he called the many problems that plague the autonomous vehicle industry. The biggest problem: supervised machine learning doesn't live up to the hype—especially when dealing with unusual situations (also known as "edge cases," not to be confused with "edge AI"). "It's widely understood that the hardest part of building AI is how it deals with situations that happen uncommonly," wrote the Starsky founder. "In fact, the better your model, the harder it is to find robust datasets of novel edge cases. Additionally, the better your model, the more accurate the data you need to improve it. Rather than seeing exponential improvements in the quality of AI performance (à la Moore's Law), we're instead seeing exponential increases in the cost to improve AI systems."[2] It was a classic instance of diminishing returns. The number of training examples increased exponentially, but accuracy increased only linearly.

Unlike infants, who can learn and extrapolate from a single instance of a phenomenon, much AI runs on algorithms that must be trained on mountains of data. Driverless vehicles, like the Starsky truck, are trained on as many traffic situations as possible. (Human drivers, to receive a license, typically undergo only twenty to thirty hours of classroom instruction and a mere dozen or so hours of experience behind the wheel—and yet are able to react instantly to one-of-a-kind situations.) The first computer program to defeat a professional player in the ancient board game Go was trained on 30 million games.[3] AIs that diagnose diseases can do so because they've been fed data on how often millions of other people with the same set of symptoms have contracted a particular ailment.

These deep learning and supervised machine learning approaches to AI, requiring massive amounts of data to train and maintain, are now running up against some serious limitations, including:

Lack of Existing Big Datasets for AI

There is "Big Data" and there are "big datasets"—and it's important to distinguish between the two. Big Data refers to statistical analytic techniques brought to bear on huge volumes of data in order to extract patterns. A dataset has been organized into some type of data structure (e.g., a collection of names and contact information). Big sets of training data in machine learning—sets like ImageNet, with its more than 14 million hand-labeled images—enable the machine to teach itself. But for most AI problems, there are no existing big datasets on the order of ImageNet. That means the data must be laboriously gathered and labeled before any novel application can even be considered—an expensive and time-consuming process. And over time, as the focus of specific AI applications shifts, training sets may gradually lose relevance.

Similarly, for most business problems or opportunities that exist, there are no big datasets "cleansed" and ready for use by AI systems. In fact, in most organizations, the biggest obstacle to comprehensive AI solutions remains noisy, sparse, or incomplete data, much of it semi- or unstructured. This explosion of messy data comes from sources such as log files, call center recordings, videos, social media posts, transactions, and a wide range of devices. For example, Walmart collects 2.5 petabytes of unstructured data (2.5 million gigabytes) from 1 million customers every hour—equivalent to 167 times the number of books in the Library of Congress.[4] By 2025, each human being will create an estimated 3.4 exabytes of data per day (1 billion gigabytes), mostly through social media, video sharing, and communications.[5]

To add to the complexity of all this unstructured data, mountains of structured data are often trapped within legacy enterprise data warehouses, replicating organizational silos and thereby limiting data sharing and innovation at scale.

The Need for Ever More Massive Infrastructure

Deep learning is caught in a vicious cycle. The more data at its disposal, the better it can perform its tasks, whatever they might be, from piloting vehicles to diagnosing diseases to classifying objects in images. That requires ever larger neural networks with billions of parameters and massive hardware and computation infrastructure. In fact, says the former head of Intel's AI Products Group, "The rapid growth in the size of neural networks is outpacing the ability of hardware to keep up."[6]

Yet the volume of data—from search engines, social media, enterprise resource planning systems, and countless other sources—continues to grow exponentially. For instance, Facebook trained image recognition networks on large sets of public images with hashtags, the biggest of which included 3.5 billion images and 17,000 hashtags.[7] These vast and rapidly expanding troves of data invite the construction of larger and larger AI models that require more and more computational power. Since 2013, the amount of computational power required to train a deep learning model has increased 600,000-fold.[8]

Astronomically Rising Costs

Researchers at the University of Massachusetts, Amherst, analyzed the costs to train and develop the deep neural networks of several prominent natural language processing (NLP) AIs—the most data-hungry models of which attain the greatest accuracy.[9] They found that while training a single model is relatively inexpensive, the cost of tuning a model for a new dataset or performing the full R&D required to develop the model quickly goes through the roof. For instance, they calculated that the cloud computing costs alone for training a model called Transformer, with 213 million parameters and a "neural architecture search" feature, could run anywhere from $1 million to $3 million, which may not seem like much to a big tech company but for small companies or researchers, it's a lot. Continual fine-tuning drives costs even higher.

Increasingly Unattainable Resource Requirements

Deep learning requires resources that lie beyond the reach of many organizations. Only a limited number—Alibaba, Amazon, Apple, Google, Microsoft, and some Global 1000 companies—can keep up. Those that are digital businesses to start with can efficiently harvest training and tuning data on a massive scale. They are already fully staffed with data scientists, computer scientists, and other experts. And they, like other large companies, can afford the cost of massive deep learning systems. Many other enterprises cannot. Further, as deep learning systems grow bigger, research is becoming more concentrated in fewer hands, far beyond the means of academic labs. Professors or graduate students with a promising new idea for a computationally expensive AI simply cannot afford to test it.

Privacy Concerns

The advent of Big Data and datamining raised privacy challenges that now seem almost quaint. In our age of ubiquitous machine learning, systems can incorporate countless personal datapoints and features in complex ways that compromise privacy in ways that are difficult to understand, predict, or prevent.

These concerns aren't theoretical. Countries and municipalities across the globe are using advances in facial recognition and analytics to create pervasive surveillance systems trained on billions of citizens. Meanwhile, AI's more beneficent uses in fields like healthcare, where AI applications have helped save lives, are circumscribed by legal requirements to preserve privacy.

Government regulation, like the EU's General Data Protection Regulation (GDPR), which went into effect in mid-2018, raises particularly thorny issues for systems that depend on deep learning. For instance, the GDPR requires that individuals who are the subjects of automated decisions based on their personal data can demand an explanation of how a decision was reached—a requirement that deep learning's notorious "black box" problem is likely to run up against. The Covid-19 pandemic triggered debate about the use of smartphone GPS data to track individuals who may have been exposed to the virus, as well as the privacy implications of contact tracing apps. In the United States, congressional lawmakers have pushed legislation that would prohibit contact tracing without affirmative consent.[10]

Doing More with Less Data

For every dataset with 1 billion entries, there are 1,000 datasets with 1 million entries, and 1,000,000 datasets with only 1,000 entries.[11] By capturing the value of these small datasets, companies can unlock a thousand-fold opportunity, especially when they use them in conjunction with big datasets they can build or buy. Moreover, since 90 percent of the work in data-hungry AI involves data cleansing, normalizing, and wrangling, the use of small data allows AI workers to focus on higher-value tasks and for big datasets to be used for the most strategic use cases.

Now, a few leading organizations are learning how to leverage smaller, unstructured datasets in ways that competitors can't match. Instead of assuming that competitive advantage requires only enormous and carefully cleansed datasets, they are redefining notions of usable data, discovering where it resides, liberating it, and activating it across apps, infrastructure, and silos in their organizations as a new basis of innovation.

For example, in the fall of 2021, Apple announced that Siri will process voice instructions directly on the newest iPhones, using the built-for-AI processor Apple calls a "neural engine," rather than sending those out to the cloud for processing, something that Google has been doing on its Pixel phones since 2019 for voice transcription without an internet connection. These AI applications still need to be trained on the cloud using the latest data, but eventually scientists expect edge AI systems to learn on their own.[12] In the meantime, pioneering companies, along with cutting-edge researchers, are finding innovative ways to balance the complementary nature of big datasets and small datasets. These pioneers are addressing three distinct challenges: (1) when big and noisy data obscures the small subset of relevant, high-quality data needed to train AI; (2) when the amount of data for training AI is small; and (3) when there is no relevant data at all.

Filtering Out the Noise

The e-commerce retailer Wayfair maintains a vast catalog of more than 14 million home goods items, with product categories that range from furniture to storage to lighting to décor and more. Some of the categories include hundreds of thousands of items. That's great for range of selection but challenging if you're a customer looking for just the right option among all of those possibilities. And it's even more challenging for you and the company if you're a first-time customer with no shopping history on the site. The company doesn't know your preferences and can't personalize your experience. So, instead, Wayfair has found a way to make it easy for first-timers to find the products with the broadest appeal.

The problem is much harder than it looks. When the company's data scientists try to identify the most appealing products, they run into the conundrum of "position effects" created by the site's sorting algorithm. Products positioned at the top of the first page for a particular category tend to be ordered more frequently, regardless of their inherent appeal to a broad base of customers. In some cases, a product at the top of the page gets ordered twice as often as a more appealing product with less visibility.

To correct for position effects, you can model a product's inherent appeal as the difference between its order rate and the average of any given product in a particular position. That calculation yields each product's historical performance. With enough data, that big dataset approach would suffice. But although the site may handle as many as 9 million orders in a typical quarter, those orders are spread over millions of products, resulting in just a few orders per product. "Small integers like these can be extremely noisy, so we always have to worry that one product simply seems better than another because of random chance," write two of Wayfair's data scientists. "For example, it is hard to tell if a product that happened to attract three orders is actually any better than one that happened to attract two, or if it just got lucky."[13]

To cut down on the noise, Wayfair added information about customers' behavior at each stage of a product's potential order: clicking on the product, adding it to their shopping cart, and ordering it. Because each step depends on the one before it, they can be weighted and multiplied to arrive at a reasonable estimate of the product's likely order rate. To correct for changing appeal over time, Wayfair incorporates data from a single day's orders into the model, rather than relying on a massive amount of big data that's constantly changing. And it also shows products in a range of random positions each day, while making sure that the most appealing products are positioned prominently. Wayfair is now trying to apply these highly data-efficient techniques to other optimization and ranking challenges.

When Available Training Data Is Inherently Small

Each time a pure deep-learning AI takes on a new task, it must once again undergo training on massive amounts of data. But researchers have made great headway in recent years on techniques that can train for new tasks using far fewer examples (few-shot learning), one example (one-shot), and no examples (zero-shot). These less data-intensive techniques could help ensure that AI innovation isn't limited to large technology companies.

Few-Shot Learning

Why can children learn the difference between an apple and an orange after seeing just a few examples, while machine learning models might require orders of magnitude larger numbers of labeled pieces of data to reliably identify objects? Data scientists at companies as diverse as a Swedish pizza-snack company and the NFL are using an AI approach known as "few-shot learning" to approximate this exquisitely complex human process.

Dafgårds is a family business in Sweden that has been making popular foods like meatballs and pizza snacks for distribution around the world for more than eighty years. With its popular line of pizza snacks, it needed to make sure each item had the right amount of cheese to meet the high standards of its discerning customers. The company's IT team of twelve wanted to use a more intelligent and efficient method of quality control, but the team had limited experience in machine learning. So it partnered with Amazon Web Services (AWS) to build a machine learning system to do automated quality inspection.[14]

Using the Amazon Lookout for Vision service of AWS, customers like Dafgårds can identify defects in industrial processes with as few as thirty images to train the model: ten images with defects or anomalies and another twenty normal images. But a common complication is that modern manufacturing processes are often so finely tuned that defect rates are often 1 percent or less, and defects can often be very slight or nuanced. That yields a small dataset to use for quality control that often doesn't match the reality of what's happening on the shop floor.

To get around the relative lack of defect data, AWS built a mock factory, down to building a system of conveyor belts and objects of various types to simulate a range of manufacturing environments. It used trial and error to create synthetic defect datasets by drawing realistic anomalies on normal images of objects, such as missing components, scratches, discolorations, and other effects. This approach to few-shot learning occasionally allowed the team to work with no images of defects at all to significantly speed up quality control.

Or consider what the NFL did with computer vision to more easily and quickly search through thousands of its video and other media assets of games to find the small number of relevant images for videos like highlight reels. The people-power to tag all these assets at scale would have been time- and cost-prohibitive. Instead, the NFL's content creation teams used the Custom Labels feature of Amazon Rekognition, a service for automated image and media analysis, to apply detailed tags for players, teams, numbers, jerseys, locations, events like penalties and injuries, and other metadata to their internal media asset collection. The automated process took a fraction of the time and used a much smaller subset of examples than it previously took teams to do manually.

The system combines Rekognition's existing big-data AI training on tens to millions of images across numerous categories to identify objects and scenes with a user-provided small dataset of as few as ten images per category label. The user uploads a small dataset into the system and can start analyzing it with a few clicks. "In today's media landscape, the volume of unstructured content that organizations manage is growing exponentially," says Brad Boim, senior director of post-production and asset management at NFL Media. "Using traditional tools, users can have difficulty in searching through the thousands of media assets in order to locate a specific element they are looking for. These tools allow our production teams to leverage this data directly and provide enhanced products to our customers across all of our media platforms."[15]

More Efficient Robot Reasoning

When robots have a conceptual understanding of the world, as humans do, it is easier to teach them things, using far less data. Vicarious, a highly secretive Silicon Valley startup backed by such investors as Peter Thiel, Mark Zuckerberg, Elon Musk, and Jeff Bezos, is working to develop artificial general intelligence for robots, enabling them to generalize from few examples. The company has developed robotic arms that get better at sorting items as they do it.[16] These smarter robots have already been put to work assembling product sampler packs for makeup company Sephora, a job that previously had to be done exclusively by humans, owing to the large number of potential combinations of fast-changing SKUs, pouches, boxes, and types of sample packs. The system lowered the cost of this massive combinatorial problem by 80 percent.[17] Examples of such combinatorial complexity are common in fast-moving, limitless inventory warehouses like Amazon's, where items are often unstructured, inconsistently displayed, and constantly shifting places based on demand but still need to be found quickly and with 100 percent accuracy.[18]

Modeled on features of the neocortex in the human brain, the Vicarious models have several advantages over deep learning approaches that could only learn from big datasets: for example, they are better able to generalize, like the human brain, from a small number of examples, and they are better at handling what are called "adversarial examples," optical illusions for machines[19] that can be used to fool a neural network.[20] Dileep George, one of the co-founders, is quick to point out the limitations of deep learning models: they can't reason, understand causes, or do anything outside their experience. "Just scaling up deep learning is not going to solve those fundamental limitations," he says. "We've made a conscious decision to find and tackle those problems."[21]

Research from Vicarious shows how incorporating aspects of human learning to divide and conquer problems using "object factorization" and "sub-goaling" can enable AI systems to infer a high-level concept from an image and then apply it to a diverse array of circumstances. Researchers say such cognitive techniques are beginning to approach the general-learning algorithms of the human mind and can dramatically improve AI performance and explainability for complex problem-solving involving massive numbers of permutations.[22]

Consider those jumbles of letters and numerals that websites use to determine whether you're a human or a robot. Called CAPTCHAs (Completely Automated Public Turing tests to tell Computers and Humans Apart), they are easy for humans to solve and hard for computers. Drawing on computational neuroscience (the study of brain function through computer modeling and mathematical analysis), researchers at Vicarious have developed a model that can break through CAPTCHAs at a far higher rate than deep neural networks and with 300-fold more data efficiency.[23] To parse CAPTCHAs with almost 67 percent accuracy, the Vicarious model required only five training examples per character, while a state-of-the-art deep neural network required a 50,000-fold larger training set of actual CAPTCHA strings, owing to the millions of combinations of ways letters can be made to appear. Such models, with their ability to train faster and generalize more broadly than AI approaches commonly used today, are putting us on a path toward robots that have a human-like conceptual understanding of the world.

From Few Shots to One Shot

Google's DeepMind Technologies is using "matching networks," a neural network that uses recent advances in attention and memory, to address the challenge of rapidly learning new concepts from as little as one labeled piece of data. It's the equivalent of a child being shown a single image of a giraffe and being able to identify all giraffes in the future. The researchers devised a novel architecture and training strategy that augments its system with a small "memory matrix," or a support set of data filled with labeled information helpful to solving a problem. The approach significantly improved the accuracy of identifying images from the gigantic ImageNet and Omniglot datasets with only one labeled example, as compared to competing approaches.[24] (The Omniglot dataset, designed for developing more human-like learning algorithms, is an encyclopedia of writing systems and languages that contains 1,623 different handwritten characters from fifty different alphabets.)

At Samsung's AI Center in Moscow and Skolkovo Institute of Science and Technology, engineers and researchers have recently developed a face animation model that thrives on both few-shot and one-shot learning.[25] Called "Talking Heads," the model does have to be trained initially on a large dataset of face videos, which demonstrates the value of combining big and small data approaches. But after that, it can identify and extract facial landmarks from just a few examples of a new face and animate it into a realistic avatar that looks like actual video footage.

In a striking demonstration video, the narrator's face, as he talks, runs side by side with an almost indistinguishable avatar.[26] The model created the narrator's avatar after seeing just eight video frames of him. An avatar of the actor Neil Patrick Harris, trained on thirty-two frames, is virtually perfect. And the system can generate avatars from just a few selfie photos, which differ sharply from video frames as source material.

The system also boasts an impressive one-shot learning capability. From single, iconic photographic portraits of celebrated people, including Marilyn Monroe, Salvador Dali, Fyodor Dostoevsky, and Albert Einstein, the system has generated convincing avatars. The system has even had some success generating avatars from classic paintings like the Mona Lisa.

The video of Dostoevsky is particularly jarring, given that the great nineteenth-century Russian novelist died in 1881, before the advent of film. And, taken together, the animations of the famous raise the specter of "deep fakes"—videos in which people are depicted doing and saying things they never did, from sex tapes to outrageous political statements. The Talking Heads creators acknowledge the danger of deep fakes, but point out that tools are rapidly being developed to detect them. However, some applications use what are called generative adversarial networks (GANs) in which an algorithm that generates an image is pitted against an algorithm that tries to determine whether the image is genuine, with both algorithms constantly improving, making detection increasingly difficult.

Malicious uses of the technology aside, lifelike telepresence could transform the world in the not-too-distant future, especially as users gain the ability to create avatars themselves.[27] Potential benefits include reducing long-distance travel and short-distance commuting, democratizing education, and improving the quality of life for people with disabilities and health conditions. VR goggles have already allowed surgeons to step inside large-scale, accurate 3D models of a specific patient's brain. Today, at the Ottawa Hospital in Canada, this approach helps implant microelectrodes thinner than a human hair into the brain, with millimeter precision.[28]

Remote brain surgery is not a futuristic notion. In March 2019, Ling Zhipei performed China's first remote, 5G-supported surgery on the human brain on a patient 3,000 kilometers away. And medical students at Stanford University now use immersive systems to explore inside the human skull. Led by an instructor/avatar, they can see tumors and aneurysms from different angles and walk through the steps of surgical procedures.[29]

HOW TO DO MORE WITH LESS DATA

As AI continues to evolve, researchers and organizations are developing techniques that are rapidly advancing the ability to do more with less data. These techniques can work well in situations where companies have access only to smaller datasets, owing to the limited number of labeled examples available to study, as well as for edge cases involving small amounts of outlier data featuring rare defects or characteristics. Those small-data techniques include the following.

DATA ECHOING. Researchers at Google Brain have been exploring a technique that reuses (or "echoes") data to speed up the training of AI.[a] In a typical training process, an AI system first reads and decodes the input data and then shuffles the data, applying a set of transformations to augment it before gathering examples into batches and iteratively updating parameters to reduce error. Data echoing inserts a stage in the process that repeats the output data of a previous stage, thereby improving efficiency as the system reclaims idle computing power capacity.[b]

DYNAMIC FILTERING. Presto uses a distributed engine for big data analysis that parses a data query, assigns it to multiple "workers," and creates an optimal plan for answering that query. It collects data from different sources, using both big and small datasets, and determines if one data source is significantly smaller than another. It then dynamically filters the data in order to skip the scanning of irrelevant data from the larger source. This enables a significant performance improvement when joining data from different sources.[c]

SIMULTANEOUS TRAINING. Google trained a single deep-neural-network on eight different tasks simultaneously. It can simultaneously detect objects in images, provide captions, recognize speech, translate between four pairs of languages, and analyze sentences. The researchers showed that it is not only possible to achieve good performance while training jointly on multiple tasks, but also that performance actually improves on tasks with limited quantities of data.[d]

ACTIVE LEARNING. In this approach to AI, the algorithm chooses which data to learn from. New York University Shanghai has been employing active learning algorithms to develop a computational framework that personalizes the assessment of human vision change.[e] The system rapidly evaluates test results in relation to a large library of potential test results and converges on a set of optimal queries for each patient based on their previous responses. Researchers believe AI-driven improvements to the standard eye chart would help with early detection and treatment of many eye-related afflictions, such as glaucoma and cataracts.

LOCAL DATA. Just as global firms create geographically relevant products and customer channels, it's important that data collected locally be used to train the algorithms that drive a company's approach to interacting with local customers. Locally collected data embodies the culture, behaviors, and values that can be used to tailor a company's approach to sales and achieve greater customer satisfaction. Radically human AI models are those that are trained with data that's relevant to the populations that they will affect rather than ready-made models for the masses.

FEDERATED LEARNING. Combined with edge computing, federated learning is helping to make data smaller. In federated learning, each device on the edge downloads the machine learning model from the cloud, updates the model, and sends it back where it will then be averaged with other updates from other sources, thus training the model with locally stored data. This approach eliminates a centralized big-data store, contributes to algorithmic development, and is particularly useful in scenarios where wireless latency is an issue.

SYNTHETIC DATA. Unlike large tech companies, startups and researchers might not always have access to the data they need to train algorithms. But with synthetic data—artificial information generated by computers that mimics real data—engineers can teach an AI system how to react to novel situations. Synthetic data can help level the playing field for startups competing against the tech giants. Early-stage startup AiFi is using synthetic data to build a checkout-free solution for retailers along the lines of Amazon Go.[f] But this democratization of data doesn't mean that the tech giants are sleeping.[g] Waymo, Alphabet's self-driving car, traverses more than three million miles daily in a simulated environment, allowing engineers to test features before unleashing them in the real world.[h]

a. Dami Choi, Alexandre Passos, Christopher J. Shallue, and George E. Dahl, "Faster Neural Network Training with Data Echoing," arXiv, January 4 2020, https://arxiv.org /abs/1907.05550.

b. Kyle Wiggers, "Google's New 'Data Echoing' Technique Speeds Up AI Training," VentureBeat, July 15, 2019, https://venturebeat.com/2019/07/15/googles-new-data-echoing -technique-speeds-up-ai-training/.

c. Shai Greenberg, "Querying Multiple Data Sources with a Single Query using Presto's Query Federation," BigData Boutique, May 26, 2020, https://blog.bigdataboutique.com /2020/05/querying-multiple-data-sources-with-a-single-query-using-prestos-query -federation-veulwi.

d. Lukasz Kaiser, Aidan N. Gomez, Noam Shazeer, Ashish Vaswani, Niki Parmar, Llion Jones, and Jakob Uszkoreit, "One Model to Learn Them All," arXiv, June 16, 2017, https:// arxiv.org/pdf/1706.05137.pdf.

e. James Devitt, "A.I. Could Give Eye Charts a Personalized Overhaul," Futurity, August 29, 2019, https://www.futurity.org/eye-charts-artificial-intelligence-2146852/.

f. Evan Nisselson, "Deep Learning with Synthetic Data Will Democratize the Tech Industry," TechCrunch, May 11, 2018, https://techcrunch.com/2018/05/11/deep-learning-with -synthetic-data-will-democratize-the-tech-industry/.

g. Yashar Behzadi, "Why Synthetic Data Could Be the Ultimate AI Disruptor," Upside, June 28, 2019, https://tdwi.org/articles/2019/06/28/adv-all-synthetic-data-ultimate-ai -disruptor.aspx.

h. Nisselson, "Deep Learning with Synthetic Data Will Democratize the Tech Industry."

Creating a Modern Data Foundation

Mastering the use of big and small data to generate value from AI requires that organizations lay a solid foundation. In every industry, companies' current successes are happening in spite of their foundations, not because of them. Data is locked in legacy, on-premise platforms that are often siloed, making it difficult, if not impossible, for people to get different types of data to work together. That makes it even harder for business users to find and consume the right data they need to arrive at the appropriate decisions.

Creating a modern foundation requires breaking data out of legacy silos so it can be unified in the cloud across different dimensions and processed with cutting-edge analytical tools. As we will see in chapter 4, this requires the right architecture (the A in IDEAS): the right storage, the right warehouses, the right computers, the right access—all in the cloud—to enable agile data capabilities that create bottom-line results.

Companies that get this right enjoy substantial competitive advantage. As we noted in the Introduction, according to recent Accenture research, companies that lead in this regard grew five times faster than laggards.[30] And a significant number of "leapfroggers" scaled their investments in key technologies such as cloud and AI during the pandemic, not just to keep the lights on but also to create "second-mover advantage."

How have they made the leap? Three capabilities are key: modern data engineering, AI-assisted data governance, and data democratization.

Modern Data Engineering

In a modern data foundation, data comes from a variety of internal and external sources through a number of mechanisms, including batch and real-time processing and application programming interfaces (APIs). It gets stitched together into highly curated and reusable datasets that can be consumed for a variety of analytic purposes. A good foundation relies on reusable frameworks for data ingestion and ETL (extract, transform, load) that support diverse data types. These frameworks also handle rules for data quality and standardization as well as metadata capture and data classification, and they enable a configuration-driven approach to data ingestion, processing, and curation so that new data pipelines for analytic use cases and data products can be developed quickly and at scale on the cloud.

AI-Assisted Data Governance

Cloud-based AI tools offer the advanced capabilities and scale to help automatically cleanse, classify, and secure data gathered on the cloud as it is ingested, which supports better data quality, veracity, and ethical handling.

Data Democratization

A modern data foundation gets more data into more hands. It makes data accessible and easy to use in a timely manner, while enabling multiple ways to consume data, including self-service, AI, business intelligence, and data science. As we will see in chapter 6, the latest cloud-based tools democratize data and empower more people across the enterprise to easily find and leverage data that's relevant to their specific business needs—faster.

Together, these three capabilities help companies overcome some of the most common barriers to value: data accessibility, data trustworthiness, data readiness, and data timeliness. They enable companies to blend data from big and small datasets together in real time, build agile reporting, and leverage analytics and AI to create broadly accessible customer, market, and operational insights that deliver meaning-ful business outcomes.

With a solid data foundation—more data from more sources, AI-assisted data management, and more data in more of your people's hands—you are no longer dominated by data, but driving it to ever more powerful *and* more fine-grained uses. As with more human-like intelligence, this approach to data transforms mechanistic processes into activities requiring more, not less, involvement of people, position-ing you to unleash human expertise—the E in IDEAS—to which we turn in the next chapter.

3

EXPERTISE

From Machine Learning to Machine Teaching

In *Human + Machine*, we identified novel roles and jobs that grow from human-machine partnerships in what we called the *missing middle*—new ways of working that are largely missing from economic research and reporting on jobs. With increasingly sophisticated AI technologies that enable human-machine collaborations, developing the missing middle has become one of the key components of innovation.

Among the six human-machine hybrid activities we identified, three entail machines augmenting humans by (1) *amplifying* our powers, as in providing otherwise unattainable data-driven insights; (2) *interacting* with us through intelligent agents; and (3) *embodying us*, as with robots that extend our physical capabilities. In turn, humans complement machines by (1) *training* them, as in labeling data for machine learning systems; (2) *explaining* them, to bridge the gap between technologists and business leaders; and (3) *sustaining* them by ensuring that AI systems are functioning properly, ethically, and in the service of humans, rather than the other way around. To those latter three, we now add a fourth: *teaching* machines by endowing them with the experience of experts.

In the new world of humans teaching machines, the people who ultimately help your organization wring the maximum competitive advantage from AI will not be data scientists or computer engineers or AI vendors. All of those roles will remain relevant, but the real difference-makers for your business will be the domain experts in your organization. Machine teaching can unleash the expertise of people at all levels of the organization and greatly multiply its value as you reimagine business processes around the new possibilities that top-down AI opens up.

Three Dimensions of Expertise

In 2015, the experimental sound artist Holly Herndon released *Platform*, the then 25-year-old's second full-length album. It was something of a break-up record—with technology. Or at least a certain approach to technology. Known as "laptop girl" for performing on stage with her computer as her instrument, she had used software to manipulate her voice on her first album. But on *Platform*—the title refers to the internet—she extended those techniques to create, in part, a critique of technology's potential to dominate humans.

She's no Luddite. In the ensuing four years, she earned a PhD at Stanford University's Center for Computer Research in Music and Acoustics (the home of, among other things, the Stanford Laptop Orchestra, founded in 2008). With her partner Mat Dryhurst and computer artist Jules LaPlace, Herndon built a gaming PC that houses an artificial neural network. They called it their "AI baby," christened it "Spawn," and used it to help make her 2019 album *Proto*. The title alludes to the protocols of algorithms.

But instead of simply training Spawn on a vast set of vocal samples, Herndon and her human bandmates taught it through call-and-response singing sessions. Their style harked back to folk music from around the world, including Tennessee, where Herndon sang in her church's choir as a child. On *Proto*, Spawn's sounds are married with the sounds of the human ensemble. The result is something new: "a choir of women's voices, harmonizing and ricocheting in counterpoint that could be Balkan or extraterrestrial," as the chief pop music critic for the *New York Times* put it in a rapturous review.[1]

"The whole album is drawing on various folk traditions, and a lot of it has to do with the individuals who were in the ensemble and the different experiences they have," Herndon told the BBC. "I got really interested in this idea of all these different vocal traditions that happen all around the world as this almost inherent human technology inside of us."[2]

That contrasts sharply with approaches to musical AI trained on samples of a musical genre or a particular artist (even dead ones) and then switched on to automatically generate "new" music in that style. Says Herndon, "I don't want to recreate music; I want to find a new sound and a new aesthetic. The major difference is that we see Spawn as an ensemble member, rather than a composer. Even if she's improvising, as performers do, she's not writing the piece. I want to write the music!"[3]

Herndon is onto one of the most radically human turns of all: from machines "learning" by processing mountains of data to humans teaching machines based on human experience and expertise. Machine teaching represents the next logical step on the path of human-machine collaboration: humans tutoring machines rather than training them only; leveraging top-down human expertise, not just bottom-up machine empiricism; and imposing natural intelligence directly onto AI. "Machine learning is all about algorithmically finding patterns in data," says Gurdeep Pall, Microsoft's corporate vice president of business AI, "Machine teaching is about the transfer of knowledge from the human expert to the machine learning system."[4]

Machine teaching includes three distinct areas of human expertise that AI has long struggled to incorporate: professional experience, collective social experience, and personal experience (the innate and acquired individual abilities of human beings). For Herndon, these three areas are, respectively, her professional musical experience, the social context of folk traditions and ensemble singing, and her personal ability to compose. The result: genuine, highly specific innovation that competitors can't duplicate.

Machine teaching isn't confined to the far corners of experimental techno-artpop. In pathbreaking approaches to AI, companies and researchers are reimagining the role of professional, social, and personal experience in AI. These pioneers are finding new ways to build human professional experience into value-creating systems unique to their businesses. They're immersing powerful systems in heretofore elusive collective social systems like natural language, consumer perceptions of style, and intricate webs of other intelligent agents. And they are finding ways to leverage innate and acquired human abilities that give new life to the notion of "putting the human in the loop." Along with the radically human turn in intelligence and data, this new emphasis on professional, collective, and personal expertise—the E in IDEAS—opens entirely new avenues of innovation across industries.

Professional Expertise: Making AI Innovation Business Specific

Consider Microsoft's ambitious machine teaching efforts, begun more than a decade ago and now beginning to come to fruition. Their goal is to make it easier for workers of all kinds to use AI tools for their express purposes—to let them, in effect, "write the music" themselves. Developers or subject matter experts with little AI expertise, such as lawyers, accountants, engineers, nurses, or forklift operators, can impart important abstract concepts to an intelligent system, which then performs the machine learning mechanics in the background.

Someone who understands the task at hand decomposes the problem into smaller parts and sets up rules and criteria for how the autonomous device should operate. Then, using simulation software, the expert provides a limited number of examples—the equivalent of lesson plans—that help the machine-learning algorithms solve the problem. If the device consistently makes the same mistake, additional examples can be added to the digital curriculum. "It's not randomly exploring, it's exploring in a way that's guided by the teacher," says Mark Hammond, Microsoft general manager for business AI.[5] Once the curriculum is in place, the system automates the process of teaching and learning across hundreds or thousands of simulations at the same time.

The principal program manager for the Microsoft Machine Teaching Group, Alicia Edelman Pelton, offers the simple example of a company that wants to use AI to scan through all its documents to find out how many quotes that were sent out resulted in a sale.[6] First, the system has to be able to distinguish a contract from an invoice from a proposal and so on. In all likelihood, no labeled training data exists, especially if different salespeople do things differently. Under a pure machine learning regime, the company would have to outsource the job of creating training data, sending thousands of sample documents and detailed instructions to the vendor, whose army of labelers would need months to complete the task. Once the company was sure the data was free of errors, it would need a high-priced, hard-to-find machine learning expert to build a model. And if salespeople started using models the machine wasn't trained on, its performance would deteriorate.

But with machine teaching, someone inside the company—a salesperson or other experienced employee—would identify the defining features of a quote and keywords like "payment terms." The expert's language would be translated into language the machine could understand, and a preselected algorithm would perform the task. Thus, using in-house experts, companies can use machine teaching to rapidly build customized solutions.

Innovating in Industrial Settings

Scores of organizations are now trying Microsoft's machine teaching software.[7] Delta Air Lines is testing whether the technology can improve baggage handling. Schneider Electric, the venerable Paris-based multinational provider of energy management and automation solutions, wants to see how it works with heating and cooling controls for buildings. Carnegie Mellon University used it to run a mine exploration robot that won a DARPA challenge.

Microsoft is not alone. Amazon and Google are also working on machine teaching techniques that would enable engineers without AI expertise to program complicated AI models. Amazon's SageMaker Autopilot, for example, can be used by people without machine learning experience to easily produce a model. Google is teaching its AI to learn how humans talk by monitoring the way our faces move when we lip-sync a song. This is possible without any specialist motion tracking hardware—only a phone's camera.[8]

Teaching a machine what a human expert would do in the face of high uncertainty and little data can beat data-hungry approaches for designing and controlling many varieties of factory equipment. Siemens is using top-down AI to control the highly complex combustion process in gas turbines, where air and gas flow into a chamber, ignite, and burn at temperatures as high as 1,600°C.[9] The volume of emissions created and ultimately how long the turbine will continue to operate depends on the interplay of numerous factors, from the quality of the gas to air flow and internal and external temperature.

Using bottom-up machine learning methods, the gas turbine would have to run for a century before producing enough data to begin training. Instead, Siemens researchers Volar Sterzing and Steffen Udluft used methods that required little data in the teaching phase for the machines. The monitoring system that resulted makes fine adjustments that optimize how the turbines run in terms of emissions and wear, continuously seeking the best solution in real time, much like an expert knowledgeably twirling multiple knobs in concert.

Who Counts as an Expert?

Experts can be found at all levels in an organization, as a recent experiment our firm conducted with medical coders demonstrates.[10] In healthcare, medical coders (not to be confused with programmers who write computer code) analyze individual patient charts and translate complex information about diagnoses, treatments, medications, and more into alphanumeric codes that are then submitted to billing systems and health insurers for payment and reimbursement.

The medical coders in our experiment, all of them registered nurses, already had experience with AI, as it was used to scan charts and find links between medical conditions and treatments and suggest proper codes. We wanted to see if it was possible to transform these medical coders into AI teachers, enriching the system with their knowledge and improve its performance.

The coders could review the links within the knowledge graphs where there was disagreement between human coders and the AI in determining the relationships between nodes of the graph (symptom X is associated with condition Y, for instance). Based on their expertise, the coders could directly validate, delete, or add links and provide a rationale for their decisions, which would later be visible to their coding colleagues. In addition, they were encouraged to follow their inclination to use Google (often with WebMD) to research drug-disease links, going beyond what they regarded as the existing AI's slow lookup tool.

This overlay of human expertise has a significant multiplier effect. Instead of merely assessing single charts, the medical coders added medical knowledge that affects all future charts. Further, with the AI taking on the bulk of the routine work, the need for screening of entire medical charts is greatly reduced, freeing coders to focus on particularly problematical cases. Meanwhile, data scientists are freed from the tedious, low-value work of cleansing, normalizing, and wrangling data.

In the new system, coders were encouraged to focus less on volume of individual links and more on instructing the AI on how to handle a given drug-disease link in general, providing research when required. Links could now be considered for addition to the knowledge graph AI with a lesser burden of quantitative evidence. The AI would learn more regularly and dynamically, especially about rare, contested, or new drug-disease links.

In their new roles, the coders quickly came to see themselves not just as teachers of the AI, but as teachers of their fellow coders. Most importantly, they saw that their reputations with other members of the team would rest on their ability to provide solid rationales for their decisions. They spoke often of the importance of those rationales to the confidence of a subsequent medical coder encountering an unfamiliar link.

The medical coders also indicated that they felt more satisfied and productive when executing the new tasks, using more of their knowledge and acquiring new skills to help build their expertise. They also felt more positive about working with AI on a daily basis.

Making in-house subject matter experts and their experience the driving forces behind AI offers numerous advantages. By transforming people who are not data scientists into AI teachers, like our medical coders, companies can apply and scale the vast reserves of untapped expertise unique to their organizations at every level. Instead of having experienced people remain passive consumers of AI outputs, they become creators of AI. Instead of extracting knowledge from data alone, they put their specialized knowledge to full use. That knowledge includes not only their functional and domain expertise, but their fine-grained understanding of the business itself: how it makes money, how it competes, and where it could be improved.

Collective Expertise: Teaching AI Social Contexts

Humans operate, often effortlessly, in collective and social contexts of immense complexity. These contexts overlap and interpenetrate and are constantly evolving on short and long timescales. When we maneuver a car through an urban environment, we are negotiating a dense web of social systems: We're processing and anticipating the movements of other vehicles and the intentions of their drivers. We're reading the body language of pedestrians. We're following (and maybe bending) the formal rules of the road and engaging in the informal ones embedded in our culture. For instance, in some cultures, flashing your headlights on and off means you are yielding to another vehicle; in other cultures, it means you're coming through and the other vehicle damn well better give way.

With language, we negotiate the innumerable complexities and nuances, including formal rules, informal usage, slang, colloquialisms, jokes, tone, style, diction, and—sometimes most important of all—what goes unsaid. In matters of etiquette, we respond to well-established social cues. With art, we identify styles in works of the imagination. Any intelligible inference, prediction, action, or utterance by an individual is necessarily situated in social contexts. As Aristotle put it in *Politics*, society precedes the individual.

The Wisdom of Crowds + Machine

On May 4, 2019, North Korea's wildly unpredictable leader Kim Jong Un launched his country's first missile test in seven months. Except, in this instance, his action was correctly predicted by a group of ordinary civilians interacting with an AI system. These prescient human "forecasters" are part of a joint project between IARPA, a research arm of the US government intelligence community, and the University of Southern California's Viterbi Information Sciences Institute (ISI).

IARPA stands for the Intelligence Advanced Research Projects Activity. Staffed by spies and PhDs, its mission is to provide decision makers with accurate predictions of geopolitical events. Since 2017, it has been working with USC's ISI on a project called SAGE: Synergistic Anticipation of Geopolitical Events.[11] The goal is to generate forecasts from the combination of humans + AI that are more accurate than the predictions of a human expert or a machine.

Forecasting geopolitical events is notoriously difficult. Experts' predictive accuracy, tracked over time, has been shown to be comparable to a random guess.[12] One way to improve forecasts is to crowdsource them, aggregating a large number of human forecasts into a single estimate of probability. This "wisdom of crowds" approach, first detailed in James Surowiecki's 2004 book of the same name, holds that large groups of people outperform small, elite groups of experts at solving problems, making wise decisions, and predicting the future.[13] In other words, collective expertise in the broadest sense can sometimes be superior to highly specific individual expertise. At the same time, advances in machine learning have led to models that produce fairly reasonable forecasts for a number of tasks. The SAGE project combines the power of crowdsourcing with advances in AI—hence the term "synergistic" in its name—to generate more accurate predictions than either method could on its own.

More than 500 of ISI's publicly recruited forecasters have predicted more than 450 questions pertaining to geopolitics, sports, medicine, climate, and more. The forecasters select what they'd like to predict from a set of quantitative and qualitative questions. For instance, a quantitative question might read: "What will be the daily closing price of Japan's Nikkei 225 index on [this date]?" A qualitative question might be: "Will Pakistan execute or be targeted in an acknowledged national military attack before [this date]?"

For quantitative questions, time series data can be used to give the human forecaster a sense of a base rate (how often the historical value has fallen within each answer option) and to give the machine model historical data to create a time series forecast. For qualitative questions like political disruptions, where historical data is rarely available to generate a time series forecast, the system obtains a base rate by mapping the question to a framework for similar historical events.

In addition to making predictions based on information provided by the machine learning methods, users can interact with fellow forecasters on discussion boards and comment on forecast results. In this respect, it differs from traditional crowdsourcing, which captures input from group members, who do not communicate, and then statistically analyzes the aggregate results.

In a competition held to test the accuracy of forecasting systems, SAGE was tested against two competing systems throughout 2019. All three systems were given the same set of more than 400 forecasting questions. SAGE won.

The wisdom of crowds also gives Tesla a big advantage in the race to develop self-driving technology—a half million drivers teaching its Autopilot feature to get better. Each of those cars, with more being added every day, is connected to the internet. Combined, they are driving around 15 million miles a day, or more than 5.4 billion miles a year, collecting vast amounts of camera and other sensor data, even when Autopilot is not engaged. The data is uploaded to Tesla so that its neural network can learn how humans drive and directly predict the correct steering, braking, and acceleration in virtually any situation. Meanwhile, most competitors have to accumulate real-world miles the hard way—having (and paying) human safety drivers riding along in test cars.

The Hive Mind of Humans + Machine

What knowledge, then, can be received from the collective?

Bustle Digital Group, the largest publisher for millennial women, wanted to predict Christmas sales for eight women's sweaters from a major fashion retailer.[14] It turned to a platform developed by Unanimous AI called Swarm to leverage the expertise, intuition, and experiential knowledge of a group of randomly selected millennial women who self-identified as being fashion-conscious and having no sales fore-casting experience. Using their own personal computers, the partici-pants connected remotely to the Swarm platform and were quickly taught how to use it. They were then asked to predict the retailer's rela-tive unit sales of eight women's sweaters during the upcoming holiday season. The participants gave assessments first as individuals using an online survey and then by "thinking together" as an AI-optimized sys-tem using Swarm.

As the name of the platform implies, it's leveraging the concept of "swarm intelligence," a natural phenomenon in which groups of organ-isms appear to exhibit collective intelligent behavior without a central control mechanism. Birds flocking, bees swarming, fish swimming, and colonies of ants are all examples of collectives that work in unison to efficiently converge on optimal solutions to complex problems. Swarm intelligence has been known for decades, but only recently has it been joined with AI, with particular hope that in the future, robot swarms can perform dangerous or difficult tasks such as search-and-rescue, undersea mapping, cleaning up toxic spills, and more.

With the Bustle example, the swarm algorithms evaluated complex collective actions, reactions, and interactions of the fashion-conscious participants in real time. By relying on observable behaviors rather than participants' self-reported feelings, the system produced an opti-mized sales ranking of the items from one to eight, as well as a scaled ranking that showed the relative spacing between each. The top three sweaters were rated as having broad appeal, and being moderately to very trendy.

Ultimately, using Swarm, Bustle was able to predict two of the three top sellers from the group of eight. Significantly, the three items ranked highest by Swarm outsold the bottom three by a factor of 150 percent—a remarkable result, given that the only differences between the items were color and graphic treatments. In addition, the Swarm forecast was significantly more predictive of the actual unit sales volume than the traditional survey, predicting 34 percent of the variance, compared to only 4 percent for the survey when it came to ratings of trendiness, breadth of appeal, and sales forecast.

In another example of the Swarm AI platform, Stanford researchers leveraged the expertise from a group of radiologists who assessed chest radiographs for pneumonia, which, because it looks like other diseases, is particularly difficult to diagnose using image alone.[15] Every X-ray was examined in real time with the individual radiologists contributing their opinions. Throughout the session, each participant could manipulate an icon to express to the other participants how strongly they felt about their position at any time, while the algorithms inferred participants' confidence based on the relative motions of their icons. In the end, Swarm was 33 percent more accurate than individual radiologists and 22 percent more accurate than a Stanford machine-learning program that had previously bested radiologists.

In other industries, swarm technologies have been used to amplify the intelligence of networked teams to produce more accurate forecasts and better decisions. For instance, groups of financial traders were asked to forecast the weekly trends of four common market indices (SPX, GLD, GDX, and Crude Oil) over a period of nineteen consecutive weeks.[16] When predicting weekly trends on their own, individual forecasters averaged 56.6 percent accuracy. When predicting together as real-time swarms they increased their accuracy to 77 percent. Further, if the group had invested on the basis of these swarm-based forecasts, they would have netted a 13.3 percent return on investment (ROI) over the nineteen weeks, compared to the individual's 0.7 percent ROI.

Teaching Natural Language Processing Systems in Real Time

Zendesk isn't a really chill office desk or an alternative band. It's a customer service software provider that serves 150,000 customers in

160 countries and territories. As the company was building this global footprint, its huge volume of support documents for its offerings were written in English only. So the company's support team set a goal of having all of the articles translated into five target languages. After some initial investigation, they soon found themselves up against the dilemma faced by many enterprises (and governments) needing to translate mountains of complex documents: Using human translators yields high-quality translations but is prohibitively expensive; using machine translation is cost-effective, but yields low-quality results. Further, even highly talented human translators face the challenge of understanding industry-specific language. And for humans and machines alike, translation requires the ability to comprehend not one, but two, huge, constantly evolving linguistic social systems.

To complicate matters for Zendesk, their articles ranged from extremely popular, high-traffic content to seldom-viewed articles, all of which needed continual updating. In Lilt, a translation services pro-vider, they found a partner whose AI-assisted translation combined the efficiency and cost effectiveness of an advanced neural language machine translation (MT) model with the expertise of human translators.

In simple terms, the end-to-end translation pipeline works like this:[17] Zendesk designates which of its documents need a human-in-the-loop translator and which can go straight to the neural model for purely machine translation and then uploads them to Lilt. To facilitate the transfer of content, the system is connected directly to Zendesk's content management system. The documents that need a human touch are routed to a translator aligned with the client's industry. The translator uses the neural machine translator as a prompt for her translation but has the final say in the finished product—incorporating Zendesk's specific vocabulary and adding the nuanced contextual understanding that only a human can provide. Further, the translator's polishing of the machine translator's prose teaches the machine how to improve the quality of the suggestions it subsequently shows to all human translators in Lilt. The human + machine translations and pure machine translations are sent back to Zendesk and stored also in Lilt's centralized translation memory so they can be rapidly updated in the future.

The real-time teaching of the machine translator by the human translator continually increases throughput times. Further, because the machine translator engine is taught through translation feedback in real time, there's no need to externally retrain the engine. Most importantly, machine teaching imbues the translation with the social context for which language is a principal medium. The machine translator learns the context of a word and its nuanced meaning in each individual document, industry, and dialect (such as European French versus Canadian French).

Machine teaching also reduces the time and expense of machine training. Because data trained on a specific industry or dialect by knowledgeable humans is more effective than a generalist approach, Lilt is able to train machine translation tools with up to 400 times less data than tools that leverage large, generalist datasets. Focusing on a specific industry/dialect, it doesn't need to learn potentially fewer applicable words and phrases early on (but does gradually build a more general understanding over time). This contextual learning, rather than generalist, data-hungry correlations, allows the Lilt translation tool to provide specific, cheap, and accurate translations through understanding human teachers.

Shopping in Style on Etsy

At Etsy, the online marketplace for vintage and handmade goods, the motto is "keep commerce human." And it was to humans they turned first when they wanted to teach their search engine how to recognize what is the crux of many purchasing decisions—aesthetic style.[18] When considering an item for purchase, buyers look not only at functional aspects of an item's specification like its category, description, price, and ratings, but also at its stylistic and aesthetic aspects. Like language and the other collective contexts we have been discussing here, styles exist in a constantly evolving social context that humans take for granted and AI struggles with.

For Etsy, capturing style is particularly challenging. Unlike mass produced goods, which can be easily classified, most of the items listed for sale on Etsy are one-of-a-kind homemade creations. Many buyers and sellers, though they know what they like, are unable to adequately articulate their notions of style. Many items may borrow from a number of styles or exhibit no strong style at all. And there are some 50 million items on offer at any given time.

In the past, style-based recommendation systems have produced unexplainable style preferences for groups of users. The AI assumed that two items must be similar in style if they are frequently purchased together by the same group of users. Another approach uses low-level attributes like color and other visual elements to group items by style. Neither method has been able to understand how style affects purchase decisions.

Who better to school AI in subjective notions of style than Etsy's merchandising experts?

Based on their experience, the merchandisers developed a set of forty-two styles that captured buyers' taste across Etsy's fifteen top-level categories from jewelry to toys to crafts.[19] Some are familiar from the art world (art nouveau, art deco). Some evoke emotions (fun and humor, inspirational). Some refer to lifestyles (boho, farmhouse) and some to cultural trends (scandi, hygge). They even produced a list of 130,000 items distributed across their forty-two styles.

Etsy's technologists then turned to buyers who tend to use search terms related to style like "art deco sideboard." For each such query, Etsy assigned that style name to all the items the user clicked on, "favorited," or bought during that search.

From just one month of such queries, Etsy was able to collect a labeled dataset of 3 million instances against which to test its style classes. Etsy then trained a neural network to use textual and visual cues to best distinguish between the forty-two style classes for each item.

The result was style predictions for all 50 million active items on Etsy.com. Items from a single shop as well as items purchased or favorited by a user tend to have similar style. Etsy also found that incorporating a style module into the site's recommender system increased revenue.

In another test, the Etsy team quantified "strength of style"—how intensely an item exhibits one of the styles. For example, a piece of wall art that depicts an anchor, a sailboat, and a whale strongly represents the nautical style. Items with a strong style do better than items with a weak style or a style that is distributed over several styles at once. Says Mike Fisher, Etsy's CTO, "We can help sellers determine whether they have a strong style or not."[20]

The stylistic classes also track well in terms of seasonality. For example, sales of items deemed tropical peaked in the summer months; romantic items surged around Valentine's Day and other holidays associated with gift-giving. Inspirational style flourished during May and June, when many students graduate. The warm and cozy farmhouse style prospered in the fall, peaking in November. Sellers might use this information to tailor their products to appropriate styles at different times of the year.

When the pandemic struck and the supply chains of mass retailers broke down, many buyers turned to Etsy—the company's revenues doubled to $10 billion, and its market value rose to $25 billion.[21] One of the hottest selling items? Masks tailored to the aesthetic sensibilities of customers. Sales of masks went from virtually nothing at the beginning of April 2020 to $740 million the rest of the year, allowing buyers to find one, said Etsy CEO Josh Silverman, "that expressed their sense of taste and style." Buyers, he said, "discovered you can keep commerce human."[22]

Personal Expertise: Inherent Human Technology

For decades, AI researchers have struggled with how to imbue machines with the basic building blocks of human intelligence. But as we said in chapter 1, the human turn in intelligence is not about recreating human consciousness. Instead, it's about solving problems by mimicking the most powerful cognitive characteristics of humans and supplementing them with the most powerful abilities of computers.

The radically human turn in personal expertise is about directly leveraging, not mimicking, the innate and acquired intelligence of humans—to augment AI. This can be a more subtle kind of teaching, a kind where tacit skills—some that the teacher may not even know they possess—are subtly transferred to a learning system.

Putting the Whole Person in the Loop

In traditional human-in-the-loop (HITL) machine learning, people train, tune, and test algorithms. They label the data; the machine learns to make decisions or predictions based on the data; the humans tune the algorithm, score its outputs, and try to improve its performance—all in a virtuous circle. Though effective in training machine learning models, this narrow definition of HITL doesn't begin to encompass all the rich possibilities of machine teaching.

Like many robotics companies during the pandemic, Kindred AI saw its development rapidly accelerated by the pressing need for warehouse robots. But while many such companies were stalled by the need to perfect their AI before they could widely deploy their robots, Kindred's insertion of a "whole person" in the loop from the start enabled the company to ramp up quickly to meet the needs of one of its first significant customers, the Gap clothing retailer.

As Covid-19 spread across North America, Gap was forced to close many of its stores, including its Old Navy and Banana Republic outlets. Online orders skyrocketed, but there were fewer warehouse workers to fulfill them due to social distancing measures the company had put in place. For Kindred, that meant that what had been a pilot program at the Gap in 2019 suddenly turned into an order for 106 of the company's eight-foot-tall robot stations.[23]

Powered by reinforcement learning and proprietary grasping technology, Kindred's "SORT" machines help assemble multi-item orders. Items from a customer's checkout cart slide down a chute into a basin where a robotic arm, equipped with suction and a physical grip, scans the bar code and places it in a nearby bin. Once all the items in the order have been placed in a bin, a worker puts it on a conveyor for packing and delivery.

What distinguishes Kindred from other warehouse robot providers is its "robot pilots." They're stationed in a Toronto office monitoring fleets of robots and teaching them best practices.[24] A stereo camera on the robotic arm lets the pilots monitor the robots' behavior. When the robot makes a mistake or is stumped about how to grasp an item or where to place it, the pilot steps in to guide it. The machine begins to learn the pattern, receiving a reward signal each time it succeeds, eventually achieving a level of proficiency that no longer requires human assistance.

Early on, the company modified the movements of the arm and gripper so that it could learn to reach and grasp with the same fluidity that pilots can. Easily picking things up is one of those things people can do almost unthinkingly, like ride a bike, touch type, or sing. They are part of our "inherent technology"—what the philosopher Michael Polanyi dubbed "tacit knowledge."

Tacit knowledge, which is hard to verbalize, contrasts with explicit knowledge, which we can easily verbalize or write down. "We know more than we can tell," as Polanyi put it, which is why explicitly transferring tacit knowledge to another person or a machine is so challenging. Kindred's pilots need only be able to show the robots how to do something, not tell them. When Gap put in its rush order in May 2020,

Kindred deployed the additional robots at four of Gap's fulfillment centers around the country in a matter of weeks, months ahead of schedule. If online demand contracts once the brick-and-mortar stores fully reopen, Kindred's Smart Robots as a Service (SraaS) model, where customers pay-per-pick, enable easy scaling down of capacity. In addition, the pilot plus reinforcement learning model enables the system to be quickly repurposed to operate anywhere unstructured sets of small components need to be arranged, and the company is now looking toward the automotive, electronics, and manufacturing industries.

More-Efficient Knowledge Transfer

Thanks to machines that can absorb the tacit knowledge of practitioners and experts alike, future systems will require far less data for their construction and training, enabling them to capture the specialized knowledge of experts. It's a turn from data-hungry AI to more data-efficient AI, from systems built from the bottom-up to systems finessed from the top down.

At a competition organized by the University Hospital of Brest and the Faculty of Medicine and Telecom Bretagne in Brittany, France, competitors vied to see whose medical imaging system could most accurately recognize which tools a surgeon was using at each instant in minimally invasive cataract surgery.[25]

The winner was an AI machine vision system trained in six weeks on only fifty videos of cataract surgery—forty-eight operations by a renowned surgeon, one by a surgeon with one year of experience, and one by an intern. Accurate tool recognition systems enable medical personnel to rigorously analyze surgical procedures and look for ways to improve them. Such systems have potential applications in report generation, surgical training, and even real-time decision support for surgeons in the operating room of the future.

Harnessing Expertise in Your Organization

Machine teaching will take its place alongside the other six human-machine hybrid activities we identified in *Human + Machine*, keeping humans securely in the driver's seat while transforming AI into an even more powerful engine of innovation. Further filling out the "missing middle," the human turn from machine learning to machine teaching will create a variety of new, satisfying human-centered jobs. Most important for companies, machine teaching unleashes the often-untapped expertise throughout the organization, allowing a much broader swath of your people to use AI in new and sophisticated ways. Because machine teaching is customizable for your business situation, it opens the way to real innovation and advantage—you no longer are simply playing technology catch-up. In supervised learning scenarios, machine teaching is particularly useful when little or no labeled training data exists for the machine learning algorithms—as it often doesn't because an industry or company's needs are so specific.

To get the greatest value out of both systems and knowledge workers, organizations will need to reimagine the way specialists as well as nonspecialists interact with machines. You can begin by imbuing your domain experts with the digital fluency (detailed in chapter 6) to efficiently combine their expertise with company processes and technology. Such fluency will also equip them to develop creative ways to apply AI to the business. At the same time, companies should recognize the potential of people at all levels of the organization to be experts. Like our medical coders, AI-empowered personnel can transform tedious, low-level tasks into high-value knowledge work, increase employee engagement, and ease the burdens on your data scientists.

Meanwhile, the ease and efficiency with which AI techniques can harness the collective knowledge of human groups opens up new competitive possibilities for companies across the board—from industrial giants like Tesla to purveyors of fashion goods like Bustle. Think of it as the difference between market research, which seeks empirical data and observations about what people want, and the market directly teaching your products and services how to behave.

Finally, don't hesitate to put humans in the loop to directly impose their innate and acquired human abilities onto AI systems. A robot pilot, for example, or a human translator doesn't represent a failure of AI; it represents the highest and best use of human and machine, the former providing the near infinite and unsayable nuance of what we know and the latter supplying a superhuman efficiency. That is what it means for humans and machines to meet—and powerfully merge their abilities—in a middle soon to be no longer missing.

You should now have a fix on the three basic building blocks of AI-enabled business innovation in a world where innovation is being turned upside down: intelligence (I), data (D), and expertise (E). The remaining challenge is to tie them together through systems architecture (A), which produces innovation across the enterprise—the challenge to which we turn in chapter 4.

4

ARCHITECTURE

From Legacy to Living Systems

L.L.Bean is an iconic retailer with a century-old legacy that includes classic clothing, rugged outdoor gear, and a deep commitment to customer satisfaction. But in recent years, as the company embraced reaching out to customers across multiple channels—print, brick-and-mortar stores, website, app, and social media—it found itself hampered by an increasingly less valuable legacy: a cumbersome IT system, parts of which had been in use for twenty years.[1]

Much of the system consisted of on-site mainframes and distributed servers. Different systems, only loosely connected, supported each of the different customer channels, running on separate applications that performed in disparate ways. Providing a seamless customer experience across all channels was next to impossible. And instead of focusing on delivering customer value, IT personnel had to spend time managing the infrastructure.

Meanwhile, the percentage of consumers who use multiple channels for shopping had risen to 73 percent. Moreover, researchers found that multichannel shoppers spend an average of 4 percent more on every shopping trip to the store than single-channel customers and 10 percent more online. Multichannel shoppers are also more loyal than single-channel customers and more likely to recommend a favored retailer to friends and family.[2]

To compete successfully in the age of Amazon, L.L.Bean needed to offer customers a satisfying omnichannel experience that pure online retailers couldn't match. So they decoupled mission-critical applications from their legacy system and located them in Google's public cloud, where the company can now integrate data from multiple systems, handle peak website loads more efficiently, provide richer website and mobile experiences, and innovate and deliver new customer features faster.

Because the cloud-based architecture is being continually optimized in the background, the company's front-end team, instead of spending valuable time on infrastructure management, can use agile software development to experiment with new features and deploy them as soon as they're ready. And with the flexible front-end architecture in the cloud, decoupled from the legacy system, the company can easily, quickly, and cost-effectively scale up capacity in peak buying periods and scale down during lulls. This ability to flex quickly in response to changing conditions is one of the most consequential developments of all: from *scalability* to *elasticity*, one of the many potent advantages of approaching architecture as if it is a living system.

Leaving the Legacy Behind

Living systems use IT in different ways than legacy systems: they are boundaryless, adaptable, and radically human. Boundaryless systems break down barriers within the IT stack, and also between companies, using cloud-based platforms to harness network effects (see "Platforms Explained"). Adaptable systems move legacy systems to the cloud to reduce dependencies between systems, increase speed and efficiency, capitalize on the human intelligence of your talent, and meet the evolving needs of customers, as we will see later in the chapter. And, finally,

PLATFORMS EXPLAINED

For digitally born companies, the platform *is* the product. Think of Google's search advertising or Airbnb's booking system. The platform harnesses digital ecosystems and network effects across many industries and uses. For instance, Uber's ride-sharing platform also facilitates food delivery.

And now for an increasing set of companies across industries, platforms are becoming a strategic focus as they transform their products, services, and customer experiences in new ways. The platform acts as a revenue accelerator, brings agility to business, and can be customized to specific industry needs. For example, Nike offers a platform of digital services, such as metrics about your workout, that interoperate with its iconic shoes to enhance the customer experience.

Platforms are made of related, reusable, and integrated technology and business capabilities. Advanced architectures are enabling platforms to be crucial accelerators of innovation and are helping build new and lucrative relationships between businesses and their customers.

living systems are radically human in the ways they use agile methods, complex human intelligence, and nimble data strategies to deliver insights and trusted experiences. Such systems connect people across organizational silos, bringing together your business talent, your IT talent, and your ecosystem partners to innovate and co-create.

Leaders in both of our technology studies build systems that score significantly higher than the average on the attributes of boundarylessness, adaptability, and the radically human. More specifically, they do it through digital decoupling, strategic cloud adoption, integration of edge computing, and a holistic approach to the IT stack that melds strategy and technology at every layer. In fact, for these leaders, "architecture," with its implication of things set in stone, doesn't do justice to the dynamism of living systems that blur boundaries, afford agile adaptability, and create seamless human-machine integration.

Digital Decoupling

For many companies, the journey toward living systems begins with digital decoupling—using new technologies, data-access methods, and development methodologies to build new systems that execute alongside legacy systems.[3] These include open application programming interfaces (APIs), Agile DevOps, cloud migration factories, microservices, and robotic process automation (RPA) that enable greater flexibility. Using these and other approaches, organizations can gradually decouple their core systems, migrating critical customer-facing functionality and data to new service-based platforms. Instead of the periodic large-scale IT transformations that rigid architectures require, this decoupled approach provides stable and constantly evolving architecture capable of accomodating innovation and scaling to respond quickly to changing market conditions and the competitive landscape. And it is popular among tech innovators: 83 percent of leaders in our initial technology study agreed that it is important to digitally decouple data from legacy infrastructure, compared with just 37 percent of the laggards.[4]

You can start decoupling by moving data from legacy systems to "data lakes." Data lakes are centralized repositories that allow you to store all of your data just as it is, whether structured or unstructured. Meanwhile, your data warehouse is optimized to analyze relational data coming from transactional systems and line of business applications in order to provide a single source of truth for operational reporting and analysis.

Data lakes allow you to run many types of analytics, as varied as dashboards, visualizations, and big-data processing, in order to guide better decision making. Goldman Sachs used this principle to create Marquee, a new banking platform that pulls data about transactions, markets, research, and emails instantly into a data lake and applies machine-learning algorithms to derive insights.[5]

For established companies, decoupling data from legacy systems makes it easier to evolve toward living systems as fast or faster than agile, digital-native companies. They can then build on their enormous wealth of data, accumulated through systems built for another era, turning a potential disadvantage into a competitive edge.

Consider Smiths Group, a UK-based industrial technology business with 22,000 employees around the world.[6] The company makes a wide range of products from scanners at airports to medical devices in hospitals and connectivity solutions for satellites. Since its founding in 1851, the company grew organically and through acquisitions to five business divisions serving customers in 200 countries and territories. Each division used different reporting systems and data storage, for a combined total of 800 applications across the company. In some cases, Smiths Group employees had to manually extract data from many sources to produce reports or to attain an all-encompassing view of the company's data.

To gain centralized visibility into all its business data, Smiths deployed a comprehensive Microsoft Azure data lake solution, consolidating data from multiple business divisions and data sources, including enterprise resource planning tools, finance systems, and SAP applications. With the new system, the company was able to reduce the time it takes to create reports; eliminate the errors that plague manual reporting; and refocus employee time on making strategic, informed business decisions from data insights. "We now have the capability to rapidly drive value from our data," says Ahmed Adnani, director of applications and analytics. "The actionable insights from the data models we're creating will help us increase revenue, reduce costs, and minimize risk."[7]

The key to unlocking the full value of a data lake is to have effective applications for searching, analyzing, and deriving insights from the massive amount of structured and unstructured data in the lake. The right applications, in conjunction with the data lake, open up a wide range of new business uses. For instance, you can search across legal contracts and compliance documentation based on the content's metadata, ensuring compliance and avoiding legal risks. In financial services, you can securely bring disparate enterprise and client data together to solve business problems, ensure compliance, detect fraud, and minimize risk of insider threats. You can search across text transcripts from enterprise video content to efficiently gather business insights. Life sciences companies can accelerate pharmaceutical R&D and manufacturing processes through the ability to quickly search for molecules with the same or similar substructures. In industries of all kinds, this move to data lakes is an early step toward a living system.

One of the first companies to recognize the power of digitally decoupling from legacy architecture was Amazon—*more than two decades ago*. It was an insight they would eventually leverage into Amazon Web Services (AWS), making elastic infrastructure available to everyone through the cloud. But back in 1998, when the company sold only books online, the operation was powered by a giant "bookstore" application and giant database. Every development team worked on that single monolithic application, and every update had to be coordinated across all of the various development teams. Whenever they wanted to add a new feature for customers, like video streaming, they had to rewrite vast amounts of code (much of which had little to do with the new feature) on an application that had been specifically designed to run the bookstore. "This was a long, unwieldy process requiring complicated coordination, and it limited our ability to innovate fast and at scale," says CTO Werner Vogels.[8]

An integrated, monolithic structure made sense in an era when computation happened all in one place and a company bundled systems (such as sales, R&D, and supply chain) for operational and strategic purposes. As technology evolves, such bundling makes less and less business sense, and it actually prevents each system or application from providing the most value. When processes are tightly combined in a monolith, the entire architecture must be scaled up merely to handle a spike in demand for one process. And the failure of a single process can bring down an entire application until the local problem is fixed.

Guided by a blueprint for change it called its "Distributed Computing Manifesto," Amazon began to break the monolith into microservices—independent components that run an application's processes as a service. Each service performs a single function (such as the online shopping cart). It runs independently of other services and can be updated, deployed, and scaled to meet specific demands like much larger volume during a sale. (Microservices, for which there is no hard and fast definition, can be seen as a more fine-grained extension of service-oriented architecture [SOA], the earlier attempt in the 2000s to address the challenges of a monolithic architecture through fairly large services, rather than narrowly scoped functionality.)

Amazon also broke down its functional hierarchies into its now famous "two-pizza teams" (said to be small enough to be fed by two pies). Each of these small, autonomous teams focused on a particular product or feature and was given authority over its portion of what had been part of the monolith. Teams were able to quickly make decisions and deploy new features without having to coordinate with all the other teams, enabling Amazon to go from deploying dozens of features each year to deploying millions.

To complete its journey to what Vogels calls "modern applications," Amazon developed an automated release pipeline and moved toward serverless operation. Automated release pipelines replaced a single manual release pipeline, enabling development teams to release new services independently. This solved the coordination problems posed by new releases, but raised the question of how to ensure consistent quality across all teams. The solution was to create best-practice templates for software delivery and reduce the possibility of human error in the delivery workflow. Teams regularly merge their code changes into a central repository, where they undergo testing and automatic builds. Teams can make changes multiple times a day and have them flow into production without any human touch.

Serverless operation frees developers from managing infrastructure. Despite its name, serverless computing doesn't mean no servers are involved, as in peer-to-peer computing. It means that the servers, located in the cloud, are out-of-sight/out-of-mind for a company's software developers. The cloud provider allocates machine resources, does capacity planning, performs maintenance, and charges customers for the actual amount of resources they use. Meanwhile, developers can concentrate on business logic and innovations that set them apart from competition. "We anticipate that there will soon be a whole generation of developers who have never touched a server and only write business logic," says Vogels.

Building applications using microservices, decoupled data stores, and serverless components help achieve the maximum agility and continuous adaptability that characterizes living systems. Ride-hailing service Uber provides a prime example of the evolution from a monolithic application to microservices. When the company began life in only one city, San Francisco, and had only one offering, UberBlack, a monolithic architecture made sense. It handled the core business functions—connecting riders with drivers, billing, and payments. But as the company expanded geographically and introduced new products, the monolith increasingly became a liability.[9]

Its components, which now included more cities, products, promotions, vehicles, and background checks, were tightly coupled and needed continuous integration as the company grew. As Uber engineers acknowledge, adding new features, fixing bugs, and resolving "technical debt" (the price companies pay for maintaining older, inflexible technologies) all in a single software repository became extremely difficult.[10] The huge codebase made it difficult to separate issues and, as the company grew from scores to hundreds of engineers with multiple teams owning pieces of the technology stack, the monolithic architecture made it difficult for teams to operate independently. Says Uber engineering manager Einas Haddad, "Tribal knowledge was required before attempting to make a single change."[11]

Beginning around 2012, Uber moved to the development of microservices dedicated to specific, well-encapsulated domains, each written in its own language or framework with its own database when required. The change brought numerous operational benefits. Systems became more flexible. System reliability improved—a service could go down without bringing everything else down with it. The architecture, by clearly defining the role of different components, made it clear why a particular service should or should not exist. It became clearer who was responsible for each service. Clear lines of ownership enabled various product and platform teams to execute autonomously and rapidly. Now, with more than 2,200 critical microservices and thousands instead of hundreds of engineers, Uber is moving to a further refinement of microservices it calls Domain-Oriented Microservice Architecture (DOMA).[12]

The Cloud Continuum

Few IT architectures can become living systems without making use of the cloud. Over the past few years, the cloud has earned a reputation for driving cost savings. Indeed, in another global survey we conducted of about 4,000 global business and IT leaders, we found that nearly 65 percent of respondents saw up to 10 percent in cost savings, on average, from moving to the cloud.[13] But our research revealed something else that was new and surprising. A small subset of the companies we surveyed—about 12–15 percent of respondents depending on the region—are seeing substantial gains from *innovating* in the cloud, benefiting even amid recent global disruptions. For instance, they are two to three times more likely to re-engineer knowledge work, are up to three times more likely to use the cloud to target at least two sustainability goals, and are targeting improvements in up to fifty business outcomes.

In all, these companies are using the cloud differently—transforming how they interact with customers, partners, and employees; how they make and market their products, services, and experience; how they build and operate their IT systems; and how they reimagine the role of data and computing. And in doing so, they are establishing a lead over other companies.

Such companies have made a conceptual leap in terms of architecture that the laggards have not. They realize that today's cloud is not simply a destination for cost savings, or even, at an architectural level, a single entity. Rather, it exists within and through a range of technologies—the cloud continuum—that spans from centralized cloud services residing on public servers to localized edge-computing services residing close to mobile devices. It includes technologies that often exist between these completely centralized and completely decentralized poles, including IoT, 5G, and hybrid clouds that mix public and private capabilities. These leading companies recognize the cloud continuum is the key to not only remaining relevant but to supercharging innovation.

Consider how Alibaba Group's financial arm, Ant Financial, uses cloud and AI to offer a wide variety of services in mobile payments, banking, insurance, and wealth management.[14] Ant can achieve significant scale in its cloud-based, AI-driven innovations. For instance, the company has developed an AI system that assesses credit risk in seconds to target loans to underserved people, who may not have bank accounts. Another capability, which allows users to snap a photo after an accident, uses computer vision and machine learning algorithms to assess the damage, automatically file a claim with the insurer, list nearby repair shops, and even estimate repair costs.

As AI becomes more central to businesses of all kinds, innovation along the cloud continuum will take on new urgency. For example, leaders adopt AI at a rate of 98 percent. But before implementing it, they set up complementary technologies such as data lakes and cloud services. Says Lori Beer, global chief information officer of JPMorgan Chase, who is leading the bank's ambitious adoption of cloud services, "It was AI and machine learning that drove our thinking to do more of a public-cloud-first mindset."[15]

Three powerful trends in AI are rapidly making reliance on exclusively earth-bound legacy systems increasingly untenable. First, the old world of rules-based programs is giving way to a new world of AI systems run on models that require exponentially more data-processing power. Second, there has been explosive growth in the scale and variety of computing resources available to companies, which puts companies that fail to take advantage of these new capabilities increasingly at a competitive disadvantage. Third, with the wide spread of edge computing, which can disperse AI to the IoT and billions of devices, there's a need to orchestrate systems through the cloud in agile and adaptable cloud-to-edge architectures. In the face of these trends, companies will increasingly shift the balance of power in their architectures—making their legacy infrastructure much leaner and their adoption of the cloud continuum much broader.

More Data-Processing Power Is Needed Than Ever Before

Since 2012, the data-processing power needed to train and run AI has been doubling every 3.5 months. That's seven times the growth rate of data-processing power for traditional programming. In just one recent eighteen-month period, the cloud computing power requirements to run leading AI models increased a thousand-fold. Consider, for instance, the exponential growth in the size of state-of-the art natural language processing (NLP) models. Going well beyond speech recognition, NLP aims to make sense of human languages in a way that adds great value to human-computer verbal interaction. The more data these models are trained on, the better they perform, making major improvements as the size of the training set reaches into billions of examples.

In 2018, researchers at Google AI Language open-sourced BERT (Bidirectional Encoder Representations from Transformers), the most advanced NLP model at the time. BERT relies on a transformer—an attention mechanism that learns contextual relationships between words in a text. The model obtained new state-of-the-art results on eleven natural language processing tasks, including natural language inference, sentiment analysis, question answering, paraphrase detection, and linguistic acceptability.[16] The core BERT model consisted of 340 million parameters (the values that a neural network tries to optimize during training).

OpenAI's GPT-2 (Generative Pretrained Transformer 2), unveiled in 2019, considerably upped the ante—to 1.5 *billion* parameters. When prompted with an opening sentence, GPT-2 can generate convincing text in a variety of styles.

In May 2020, GPT-3 debuted, weighing in at a whopping 175 billion parameters. Researchers who were given access to GPT-3 via a private beta were able to induce it to produce short stories, songs, press releases, technical manuals, text in the style of a particular writer, guitar tabs, and even computer code.[17] GPT-2 and GPT-3 are so powerful that OpenAI initially deemed them too dangerous to release because they could potentially be used for dubious purposes, including generating plausible sounding "fake news."

When we were writing *Human + Machine*, we didn't expect the breakthrough that these transformers represent would come so soon. While *Human + Machine* looked at the first generation of AI, we are now on the cusp of a new generation of powerful combinations of algorithms and the enormous data-processing power of the cloud. This next generation of cloud-AI will do at least three things for workers. First, it will enhance creative work, through smarter apps that can, for instance, anticipate the needs of designers, salespeople, and others. Second, it will augment language-based tasks, including insurance claims analysis, marketing campaign development, and scientific research. Third, it will lower the barriers for scaling digital innovations, making it even easier for nontechnical staff to use everyday natural language rather than programming languages to build apps and solutions (a development already under way, as we saw in chapter 3 with the turn from machine learning to machine teaching).

Legacy systems simply can't handle the data-handling requirements of these and other emerging AI technologies. The cloud, however, provides access to virtually unlimited computing power as well as the elasticity that provides both affordability and the strategic agility that distinguishes living systems. But when we look at our data and client work, we see that nearly 75 percent of companies' computing power is tied to legacy systems, which are woefully underpowered. We estimate that a much smaller percentage of companies today have the computing infrastructure capable of competing in the world of next-generation living systems.

The cloud is also more environmentally friendly than in-house data centers, offering a substantial boost for the sustainability goals discussed in chapter 9. Research by Jonathan Koomey and Eric Masanet, two leading scientists in the field of technology, energy use, and the environment, has debunked doomsday scenarios that assume cloud computing centers will inevitably eat up more and more energy as they grow, generating more greenhouse gases.[18] In fact, from 2010 to 2018, the workloads hosted by the cloud data centers of the big providers and in-house company data centers together increased 2,600 percent and energy consumption increased 500 percent. But energy consumption for *all* data centers rose less than 10 percent during that period. Why so little? Because, say the researchers, in 2010, an estimated 79 percent of data center computing was done in traditional computer centers, but by 2018, 89 percent of data center computing took place in much more efficient centers run by the big cloud providers.

More Computing Resources Are Available Than Ever Before

The ten-fold growth in total available computing resources over the past decade has increasingly been driven by innovations in "built for purpose" AI chip designs, 5G, and sensor and mesh networks. In many applications of AI, like NLP, more computing resources translate to better performance. For companies that have decoupled to the cloud, that means a big advantage—an exponentially greater ability to capture the full potential of AI than companies tied to legacy systems.

Cloud AI services allow companies to punch above their weight, accessing the scale of huge computing resources when needed, while keeping their in-house infrastructure lean. Consider Uklon, a Ukrainian ride-hailing service that began in Kyiv and is expanding into other cities. Founded in 2010, it has since grown to become the biggest such service in Ukraine, despite competition from global player Uber and new entrants from Russia. Using cloud-based machine learning, Uklon offers customers a unique pricing service no one else in the market can match.

Because there are no standard fares for Ukrainian cabs, potential customers bid during peak demand periods to secure a driver. Customers have to come up with a price they think is fair and negotiate with the driver until agreement is reached. Uklon has automated that process through an app that suggests the optimal fare to bid. The suggested fare, based on factors like time of day, traffic conditions, distance, and previous fares accepted, are generated by a customized Uklon algorithm running on the Microsoft Azure cloud service. Customers can accept the suggested fare or tweak the price in hopes of a driver accepting the lower offer. "We needed to increase the number of completed bookings our drivers see at even the busiest times of the day," says chief technology officer Vitaliy Diatlenko.[19] With the cloud-based AI continually refining the suggested fares, customers immediately accept the suggestion 75 percent of the time, and average successful taxi bookings at peak times have risen 18 percent.

Large cloud providers now offer a wide range of services based on AI and machine learning, including language-oriented, vision-oriented, and automated machine-learning services. Within these major categories, there are many discrete and narrower services that can be used alone or in conjunction with other services to create distinctive applications. For instance, the wide array of language services includes speech to text, text to speech, language recognition, natural language understanding, natural language generation, chatbot frameworks, translation, text analytics, and sentiment analysis.

The cloud will play an increasingly larger role in application development.[20] Gartner estimates that, by 2023, 40 percent of development teams will be using automated machine learning services to build models that add AI capabilities to their applications, up from less than 2 percent in 2019. By 2025, says Gartner, AI will automate 50 percent of data scientist activities, freeing them to do higher-value work and easing the current talent shortage. By 2023, AI will combine with human programmers to create "centaurs" that perform 50 percent of programmer workloads, doubling the productivity of stand-alone programmers.

The cloud is also seeing a multiplication of hosting methods and locations as it gets more sophisticated in its capabilities. As companies develop their application and data strategies, they are increasingly adopting a multi–cloud provider approach (using multiple public providers), with the placement of applications and data workloads in a hybrid, distributed fashion across public and private clouds—that is, either operated in external cloud data centers or walled off in dedicated company-specific servers. This approach balances the business need for increased agility and innovation with optimal performance, service levels, security, and cost-effectiveness. Hybrid deployments combine the public cloud's benefits of innovation, speed, agility, and scale with private cloud's benefits of control, regulatory compliance, and leverage of existing investments.

An example of the hybrid cloud can be found in Bank Leumi, an Israeli bank founded in 1902. In a push to become a bank based in mobile environments, the firm decided in 2017 to build on its IT infrastructure investments by moving to a hybrid cloud model. Using technologies and services provided by Dell EMC and VMWare, Bank Leumi now sees the rollout of code in a matter of hours rather than weeks, while also saving on costs. Combining home-grown server solutions with public cloud offerings was just the approach Bank Leumi needed to move fast and be responsive in the mobile banking world.

The lines between public and private clouds are blurring. In the past, betting on a hyper-scaler meant picking public over private. That is no longer the case. To support regulatory, performance, and other requirements, the hyper-scaler cloud services providers are now offering private cloud carveouts in public environments. Examples include VMware on AWS (VMC), Azure VMware Services (AVS), and Google's SAP, Oracle, and Bare Metal solutions, and more.

At the same time, the hyper-scalers have been working on private cloud extensions, platform as a service (PaaS) and infrastructure as a service (IaaS) solutions that push customers' data centers even closer to manufacturing and other operational technology use cases. Examples include Microsoft's Azure Stack, AWS Outposts, Google's Anthos, and Alibaba's Apsara. Additionally, platforms like Red Hat's Openshift and Cloud Foundry have created hybrid environments thanks to a software layer that enables connectivity across disparate technology platforms and have created what are essentially hybrid environments by introducing a heterogeneous technology layer at the foundational level, enabling connectivity across disparate technology platforms. This blurring of public and private under a hybrid cloud umbrella is likely to accelerate in the future.

Integrating Cloud and Edge

Architectures that combine the cloud with edge computing stand to generate even more opportunities than cloud alone. Edge computing runs our digital world—managing and monitoring manufacturing operations, powering robots, piloting driverless vehicles, enabling the "smart home," and running the billions of devices that make up the IoT. It moves much of the information processing out to the edge of networks while still harnessing the enormous computing resources of the cloud and the power of AI.

The global market for edge AI chips in 2019 was valued at $1.8 billion and is expected to grow at a compound annual growth rate of 21.3 percent from 2020 to 2027 due to increasing use of social media and e-commerce platforms that demand efficient processors for quick execution of machine learning tasks.[21]

While the cloud provides elasticity and agility at the back end, edge computing brings more intelligence to the front end, where networks meet with the physical world through sensors, smartphones, robots, drones, virtual reality devices, cameras, autonomous vehicles, and the IoT. For example, augmented reality combines the real world with a digital overlay, such as the Pokémon GO augmented reality game for mobile phones, while virtual reality offers a fully immersive digital environment such as the virtual reality headset offered by Microsoft called HoloLens. Applications range from gaming and entertainment to training, education, and healthcare. In each case, providing a novel and advanced human experience is central to the design.

Placing more intelligence at the edge creates real-time value by increasing speed and reducing latency at the point where a decision or action is needed. It brings predictive analytics to local devices. It eases bandwidth issues, as edge computing deals with data at the point of capture, instead of transmitting huge volumes of raw data back to the cloud. It offers innovative ways to protect the privacy of sensitive data. And when systems interact directly with people, edge computing can provide more immediate and immersive experiences. As it is combined with other emerging technologies, edge computing also vastly increases a company's operational and strategic capabilities. (See "The Next Wave of Frontier Technologies.")

Moving Analytics to the Edge

Fugro, the world's leading geo-data company, offers a helpful example of the ability to speed up inference at the edge and ease bandwidth issues with the cloud.[22] Fugro provides geotechnical, survey, subsea, and geosciences services to clients in the renewables, oil and gas, power, and infrastructure sectors, supporting them in the design, construction, and operation of their assets.

To understand how a structure such as a wind farm might behave in extreme climates, a team of oceanographers, meteorologists, and hydrographers collects environmental metadata on water depth,

THE NEXT WAVE OF FRONTIER TECHNOLOGIES

A host of technologies have emerged that will enable future innovation. The following is a field guide to what's here and what's next.

BLOCKCHAIN. Blockchain, which is part of a class of technology known as distributed ledgers, enables new kinds of digital ownership and trust. In simple terms, blockchain maintains and records data in a distributed way that allows organizations and individuals to confidently share access to the same data in real time, while mitigating concerns around security, privacy, and control. In one of its common uses, blockchain allows people to exchange money without intermediaries such as banks or other financial institutions. (Bitcoin and Ethereum are examples of blockchain-based crypto-currencies.) Blockchain is moving well beyond the initial crypto-currency applications and has large implications for businesses and governments as it is applied to government-issued currencies, supply chains, digital identity, and other applications.

Blockchain-based, nonfungible tokens, or NFTs, for instance, can be used to verify that a specific person is the owner of an original digital artwork. If the value of the art goes up and the buyer wants to resell it, he or she can conduct a sale and record it on the public, secure distributed ledger. And depending on the contract between the artist and the original buyer, the artist might even recoup a percentage of the secondary sale and potentially retain more control over the terms of a sale. As blockchain enables new forms of trust and transparency in the digital world such as these, it will lead to novel economies and systems of digital value that have previously been unimaginable.

THE METAVERSE. At one time just a science fiction concept, the metaverse is moving into more mainstream discussion, thanks in part to attention from some of the biggest technology players. The technology building blocks of the metaverse include virtual and augmented reality, along with blockchain-enabled digital identity and commerce, as well as AI, which powers deep, immersive experiences. A core idea of the metaverse is that digital worlds, previously cordoned off, will become interoperable, allowing more freedom to roam across disparate virtual environments. In the metaverse, you can do more than play *Fortnite* with friends. While in the comfort of your home, you can have an immersive shopping experience at your favorite retailer, where your virtual avatar can find the right fit based on your dimensions. You can also take an interactive class with a virtual professor.

Afterward, you might meet up with a friend who lives across the world for a virtual spin class. Then you could take in a virtual concert or take a walk together in a virtual park where the trees are pink and the sky is green. These kinds of activities, available in some ways today but not yet well-integrated, will become increasingly accessible as more companies realize the value of building digital spaces within a shared metaverse.

QUANTUM COMPUTING. Once the purview of research scientists, quantum computing is finally making its way out of the lab and into practical business applications. While still in its early days, quantum computing promises exponential improvements in computational speed and processing over traditional computing. It harnesses strange subatomic principles of quantum physics like entanglement and superposition. Applications can be found in areas as diverse as healthcare and financial services, supply chain management, research and development, and, naturally, technology.

A number of exciting commercial developments are expected, even though no off-the-shelf quantum solutions exist yet, and the research to make these machines broadly usable is ongoing. A few leading companies are already helping make quantum hardware available for purchase and shared use; others are working to offer cloud-based platforms and software applications that provide customers with access to quantum computing power. Broader business adoption is expected within the next two to five years, with the market for quantum computing projected to reach $65 billion by 2030. As quantum computing extends its reach, it may help people find solutions to problems that were previously inaccessible—cures for diseases, optimized shipping routes, uncrackable cryptography, simulations to fight climate change, and other complex human challenges over the decades to come.

wind, waves, currents, and temperature before design and construction begin. The company analyzes this geo-data to derive insights that produce the most cost-effective, sustainable designs and help clients manage their assets throughout their lifecycle.

Marine geo-data can be collected in various ways—by dispatching vessels that analyze the ocean floor or transmitting time series data from satellites and sensors located inside ocean buoys or other structures. Because the company often works in remote areas, it must depend on satellites with sometimes spotty links and limited ability to handle large amounts of data. A satellite outage of just an hour could mean missing a critical environmental event that affects a client's operations.

In the past when an outage occurred, Fugro would send a vessel and crew to the affected sensor. They manually collected and uploaded the data to on-premises servers aboard the vessel, transferred the data to an external hard drive when the ship got back to port, and then took it to the company's onshore offices for analysis. All of this was slow and costly.

To streamline the process, the company is deploying a cloud continuum solution across nearly thirty oceangoing vessels. After migrating the on-premises servers to the cloud, it deployed a fully managed service to run workloads on the vessels. Time series data is ingested, queried, stored, and processed at the edge. Fugro's technology spends far less time in communication with the cloud, saving significant time and costs associated with latency and bandwidth. With in-built AI and machine learning capabilities, Fugro can conduct real-time scoring for improved analysis at the edge. "We bring advanced functionality such as machine learning and real-time analysis of temporal data where we need it most: locally, on the asset," says Richard Corless, Fugro's lead cloud architect.[23]

With the company's vessels and onshore assets connected through a cloud architecture, Fugro has reduced the time needed to process and deliver monthly data reports from offshore locations to client dashboards from two weeks to eight minutes. New software can be remotely deployed on a vessel almost instantly, instead of being laboriously built from scratch by a team of developers each time. And vessels must no longer return to port to upgrade software.

"Now that we can collect and act on data in near real time from anywhere in the world," says Pim Peereboom, global project manager of integrated marine management at Fugro, "we can make our work faster, safer, and more efficient, no matter where we are or what the project scope is."[24]

Moving more processing to the edge can also reduce latency—delays in response time—in critical domains like industrial safety systems and autonomous vehicles, where processing, inference, and action must take place in real time. Analytics on the edge can detect problems with a wind turbine, an aircraft engine, or an MRI, and then AI can make instant adjustments to prevent damage or optimize performance.

Schneider Electric employs a cloud architecture designed to reduce latency and bring predictive analytics to thousands of oil and gas pumps spread over large geographic areas for energy companies. Schneider's Realift Rod Pump Control allows companies to monitor and configure pump settings and operations remotely, enabling settings and performance adjustments and shutdowns of failing devices.

"In some critical systems or critical processes—whether at an oil pump or in a manufacturing plant—you may have to make a decision in a matter of milliseconds, and someone's life could be at stake," says Matt Boujonnier, analytics application architect for Schneider. "By building machine learning algorithms into our applications and deploying analytics at the edge, we reduce any communication latency to the cloud or a central system, and that critical decision can happen right away."[25] With intelligence embedded at the edge, companies can also predict abnormal operating conditions before they happen and take action, reducing unplanned downtime, which decreases costs, increases production, and increases the agility of maintenance services.

"Traditionally, machine learning is something that has only run in the cloud, but for many IoT scenarios that isn't good enough, because you want to run your application as close as possible to any events," says Boujonnier. "Now we have the flexibility to run it in the cloud or at the edge—wherever we need it to be."[26]

The Multi-Access Edge Meets 5G

Even more of the cloud will be brought to the edge by multi-access edge computing (MEC) technology, in conjunction with 5G networks, unleashing a new wave of innovation in applications and business models. It is hard to overestimate the potential of genuine 5G when it is fully implemented. With bandwidth measured not in megabits but rather in gigabits per second, 5G networks will be as much as 100 times faster than today's mobile technology.[27] Their speed, capacity, and dramatically reduced power consumption and communications response times will make possible an astonishing range of innovative new products and services. The economic and social benefits could be enormous.

A pioneer in using MEC in conjunction with 5G was Verizon, one of the world's leading providers of technology, communications, information, and entertainment products and services. The company was an early adopter of 5G multi-access edge computing using a service that extends the AWS infrastructure, including computing power and storage services, to the edge of Verizon's network.

This combination of 5G bandwidth and cloud-to-edge services enables Verizon's enterprise customers, entrepreneurs, and independent software vendors to build large-scale, super-low-latency apps that serve mobile end users and devices. For example, some football fans are already able to watch up to seven instant replays live from the stands at a crowded game on their smartphones through Verizon's Ultra Wideband 5G service, and many concert-goers may one day enjoy immersive new augmented reality experiences at live events.

The parts of an application that require ultra-low latency are deployed to the edge of the network and connect to the full range of AWS cloud services. Bringing those services to the edge minimizes the network hops required to connect to an application from a 5G connected device. Previously, application data had to travel from the device, to the mobile network, to networking devices, and then to the internet to get to the application's servers, often in remote locations. With infrastructure that embeds computing power and storage located in the company's datacenters at the edge, connected devices reach application servers without leaving the network.[28]

Areas where the single-digit millisecond latency can be applied will be limited only by the imagination of developers. For example, it could bring customers breathtakingly immersive experiences on "extended reality" devices, remote gaming, and live streaming. And it will bring real-time analytics and inference at the edge in areas where low-latency is critical, like autonomous vehicles, robotic manufacturing systems, and smart cities.

Computing Power, Data Privacy

When privacy is a priority, new privacy-preserving machine-learning (PPML) techniques can also bring the power of the cloud to the edge. Those techniques include federated learning, secure multiparty computation, differential privacy, encrypted computation, and more. In federated learning, for example, training data is stored locally on edge devices. Each device downloads the machine-learning model from the cloud, updates the model, and sends it back, where it will then be averaged with other updates from other sources. Thus, each client helps train the model while still storing data locally.

PPML opens up new possibilities in fields like healthcare. AI has proven to be potentially lifesaving and essential for progress against disease. Standard machine-learning approaches centralize training data in the cloud, where enormous computing power can be brought to bear to create a predictive model. But in healthcare, patient information must be maintained locally to ensure privacy, precluding the traditional approach to training. Enter federated learning.

Developed by Google, federated learning elegantly meets the challenge of helping advance medicine while keeping patient data local and private.[29] The current model for predicting a particular disease is downloaded to a smartphone or other edge device at a medical facility. The model learns from the patient data on the device and then summarizes the changes as a small, focused update. The update to the model is sent to the cloud, using encrypted communication, where it is immediately averaged with other user updates to improve the shared model. All of the individual patient data used to train the model remains on the local device.

The technique also holds great promise for drug development, which can take years and cost upward of a billion dollars to bring a new drug to market. To speed the discovery of potentially lifesaving compounds, ten of the world's most prominent pharmaceutical companies, including AstraZeneca, Bayer AG, GlaxoSmithKline, and Novartis, have embarked on a collaborative federated learning project called "MEL-LODDY," short for machine learning ledger orchestration for drug discovery. Says Mathieu Galtier, chief product officer of Owkin, a French-American AI company that is coordinating the project, "The goal is to harness the collective knowledge of the consortium in a platform containing, amongst others, multi-task predictive machine learning algorithms incorporating an extended privacy management system, to identify the most effective compounds for drug development, while protecting the intellectual property rights of the consortium contributors."[30]

The companies will train their algorithms on each other's chemical compound libraries, while protecting each contributor's intellectual property, such as the exact chemistry of the compounds. With access to millions more compounds, the companies hope to improve the ability of their algorithms to identify the most promising compounds to become drug candidates. Bayer AG's library, for example, contains about 4.5 million compounds, but the project will give the company access to 10 million more, as well as billions of data points about the biological effects of those compounds.[31] (Bayer also plans to engage seven hospitals and research organizations for a second federated learning project dealing with cancers caused by a rare genetic mutation.) By sharing the data, while preserving the essential intellectual property that underlies it, the companies can accelerate the identification of promising compounds, reduce failure rates in development, and preserve a route to patentable discoveries.

Currently, the project focuses exclusively on preclinical data, which involves studies conducted before a drug candidate is tested in humans. If MELLODDY proves successful, participants could develop a similar platform using patient data from clinical studies. The Mayo Clinic has already taken a step in that direction with the creation of its Clinical Data Analytics Platform.[32]

Based on federated-learning architecture, the platform will apply advanced data analytics on de-identified data from Mayo Clinic and other organizations, as well as the vast information in the scientific literature, to expand treatment options for some of the most serious and complex diseases. Working with nference, a Cambridge, Massachusetts, augmented intelligence company, participants will build a common artificial and machine learning model without sharing datasets. It will focus on identifying targets and biomarkers for new drugs, optimal matching of patients with therapeutic regimens, and real-world data and evidence applications, such as label expansion, post-marketing surveillance, and drug purposing.

"Platform business models have been a force of disruption in many sectors, and the rapid digitalization of health care is affording us an unprecedented opportunity to solve complex medical problems and improve lives of people on a global scale," says John Halamka, MD, Mayo Clinic platform president.[33]

Stack Strategically, Stack Holistically

As many of these examples demonstrate, technology and business strategy are converging, often thanks to developments within various layers of the technology stack—that is, the architectures, technologies, and partners companies choose for IT implementation. But to tackle the most ambitious challenges and position the enterprise to be flexible and future-adaptive, businesses also need to think holistically and strategically across layers. These imperatives will involve some of the most important decisions that companies make.

NVIDIA demonstrated the value of this approach during the pandemic. As Covid-19 flared around the globe, NVIDIA launched Clara

Guardian, a smart hospital solution that enabled hospitals to respond rapidly to an unprecedented time.[34] Installed in more than 10,000 hospital rooms, the system made it possible for healthcare workers to remotely monitor and detect changes to patient vital signs, enforce the wearing of personal protective equipment (PPE), direct employees and visitors away from high-risk areas of the hospital, have contactless patient interaction through a voice-powered AI agent, and more.[35]

This feat would have been impossible without innovation and cohesion at every layer of the technology architecture. The system's smart sensors were able to stream data and generate insights about body temperatures, movement, social distancing, and mask detection. Pre-trained data models could use that data to assist with a diagnosis or predict if a patient was going to go to the ICU. Edge AI chips and GPUs provided much-needed horsepower to the system, while simultaneously supporting intelligent human-computer interactions like voice-powered assistance and dynamic wayfinding in facilities. The system allowed hospitals to respond and reorient to ever-changing needs in a time when speed was critical. And it's not just a Covid-19 solution, but one that will grow in value over time as hospitals repurpose parts of the system and uncover new use cases, allowing them to reap benefits long into the future.[36]

As enterprises reimagine the possibilities of technology-powered products and services, they will soon find they are playing a more active role in the relationship between people and technology than ever before. The convergence between business and technology means it's highly likely that the first time a customer interacts with a near-human AI agent, puts on a pair of virtual reality goggles, or learns about blockchain, it will be linked to a company's cutting-edge offering.

Some 80 percent of respondents in our initial study believe that systems of the future will provide seamless interaction with humans, and 78 percent believe these systems will adapt to suit human styles of work.[37] Since intelligent technologies are going to be pervasive in the workplace, as in our daily lives, it is paramount to design these systems to be radically human to get the maximum returns. Using technologies such as natural language processing, computer vision, voice recognition, and machine learning, radically human systems are making human interaction with them easier and more efficient. Companies can now reimagine systems to empower new human + machine relationships with natural conversation, simple touches, and abundant personalization.

The way to this future will be determined according to the technology strategy choices leaders make. Effective leaders will ramp down and digitally decouple legacy systems, while ramping up and cloud-enabling the boundarylessness, adaptability, and radically human features that characterize living systems.

Leaders are also strategically adopting sophisticated cloud services, taking advantage of the increasing multitude of ways to organize and orchestrate networked architectures in order to increase speed, flexibility, and responsiveness. For example, more than 90 percent of leaders in North America in our cloud continuum survey use the cloud to enhance collaboration among employees and support ambitious projects that cut across business functions and geographies. They use the cloud to make work more interesting and data-driven by reducing rote tasks and manual maintenance work, and use cloud-based tools to make technology approachable.

Leaders are also beginning to integrate edge computing into cloud architectures, ensuring that what happens locally informs what's known centrally, and vice versa. The edge becomes the path to insight on the cloud, and the cloud becomes the vehicle for disseminating that knowledge to the edge.

Finally, leaders will build a holistic approach to IT that melds strategy and technology across multiple layers of applications and systems. The great convergence of strategy and technology happens within and across IT systems, and has ignited a new era of business, where competition has become a battle between systems. Organizations that successfully combine their business and technology strategies, and work to find their most valuable combination of technologies across the technology stack, will find themselves able to develop truly one-of-a-kind offerings with unprecedented agility, capturing new markets no matter how fast the world changes.

In the next chapter, we'll take an in-depth look at ways organizations are bringing it all together into effective, future-looking business strategy (S), the capstone of the IDEAS framework. That strategy—how you integrate your tech investments and take advantage of the radically human turn in approaches to intelligence (I), data (D), expertise (E), and architecture (A)—will ultimately determine how prepared you are to pre-empt disruption and seize the future.

STRATEGY

We're All Tech Companies Now

Nowhere is the human—and human agency—more central than in strategy. That is where the capacity to make a difference in performance is limited only by the imagination of humans—especially those in the C-suite. They are responsible for negotiating a future in which radically human technologies will set the terms of competition and further separate leaders from laggards. That is what we mean when we say that all companies, in every industry, are now technology companies and all CEOs must now be tech CEOs.

The challenge lies in the fact that technology, business strategy, and execution are becoming so closely intertwined as to be nearly indistinguishable. All three elements evolve together almost simultaneously, thanks to the flexibility and agility conferred by radically human approaches to intelligence, data, expertise, and architecture. Of course, this convergence of IT, strategy, and execution has not come overnight. It has been coming in stages—each typified by specific technologies and business strategies, as we'll see next.

The Three Stages of Human-Machine Interaction

The response of companies to intelligent technologies has unfolded in three stages. The first stage was *machine-centric*. The dominant response to new technology was to reengineer (akin to the reengineering that occurred in the 1990s when desktop computing became widespread in business). AI and other emerging technologies were used to automate repetitive tasks. Humans had to adapt to machines (and were often replaced by them). Strategy and execution were sequential, spread over steps like assess, identify, design, and implement.

The second stage of human-machine interaction was *collaborative*. Humans and machines adapted to each other, the phenomenon we examined in *Human + Machine*. As a new generation of intelligent technologies and techniques emerged, companies sought to reimagine their traditional business processes in order to take advantage of collaborative teams of humans working alongside machines. Nevertheless, strategy and execution remained separate. First, a process was reimagined in light of AI, machine learning, and the like, and then tested in small experiments. If it passed the test, it was then implemented at scale across the enterprise—again, a sequential approach that separates strategy and execution.

The third stage, underway now, is the *human-centric*. Machines adapt to humans. The agility and adaptability of radically human technologies guided by humans enable savvy companies to interrelate technology, strategy formulation, and execution in an organic whole. The three elements grow and change synchronously, often very rapidly (see figure 5-1, "The Evolution of Technology").

Consider how Starbucks handled the Covid crisis. In March 2020, the scale of the challenge was only beginning to emerge. In response, even at that early date, CEO Kevin Johnson told investors and analysts on an earnings call that the company was moving aggressively to further differentiate the brand from competitors.[1] Starbucks already had

FIGURE 5.1

The Evolution of Technology
A Subset of Examples of How Technology Is Advancing

	MACHINE-CENTRIC The machine can do what it's programmed to do	**COLLABORATIVE** Humans train machines; machines augment humans	**HUMAN-CENTRIC** Machines adapt to humans, and humans teach machines
 INTELLIGENCE	**Industrial Robot** Uses sensors to guide preprogrammed actions behind safety gates	**Deep Learning** Employs neural networks to learn from large datasets	**Emotional AI** Responds to human emotions and increases relevance
 DATA	**Business Intelligence 1.0** Produces reports from database queries and batch processes	**Big Data** Uncovers actionable patterns from extremely large datasets	**Synthetic Data** Mimics original data, with strong privacy safeguards
 EXPERTISE	**Traditional Programming** Uses computer code to instruct machines	**Data Science** Extracts insights from data to solve problems	**Machine Teaching** Enables nontechnical experts to train AI systems
 ARCHITECTURE	**Monolithic** Works as a homogeneous, static integrated system	**Layered** Handles functions autonomously at separate levels	**Living System** Assembles heterogenous, adaptive capabilities dynamically like LEGO blocks
 STRATEGY	**Reengineer** Fosters sequential change from analysis to execution	**Reimagine** Rethinks processes, then sequentially experiments, adapts, and scales	**Interrelate** Synchronizes human-guided technologies, strategy, and execution

113

a history of experimentation with electronic payments, mobile apps, pickup-only stores, and third-party delivery networks that put it ahead of most other retailers.[2] So when the pandemic struck, the company was able to immediately introduce new digital capabilities that allowed them to switch quickly to 90 percent of their orders being remote with pickup at stores.

Meanwhile, APIs and microservices architecture allowed Starbucks to partner quickly with Uber Eats to have new means of delivery and new modes of service for its customers. Driven by technology, this ability of third-stage companies to simultaneously formulate strategy and execute on it greatly accelerates the speed with which they can evolve, act in the marketplace, and grow—and greatly increases the threat to companies that lack that ability.

A Grocer Wants to Disrupt Your Industry

Ocado, the world's largest online grocery retailer with no physical stores, makes no bones about being a technology company. For more than two decades, Ocado has been developing some of the world's most advanced capabilities in AI, machine learning, robotics, cloud technologies, IoT, simulation and modeling, and digital twins—invaluable IP that includes more than 150 patents, with hundreds more pending.

That IP was developed in one of the most demanding operating environments imaginable—grocery. It is the world's largest retail category. It is also one of the most complex, with constantly varying product ranges with diverse shelf lives and temperature requirements—unlike, say, books. Take that complexity online, where customers spread over an entire country demand accurate and reliable order fulfillment at an attractive price point, and the complexity grows exponentially.

Ocado's customer fulfillment centers (CFCs) boast some of the most advanced grocery picking technology in the world.[3] A typical CFC can be as large or larger than a soccer field. Inside, a "hive" of hundreds of robots, communicating with each other over a 4G network, sits atop a three-story aluminum grid playing three-dimensional chess.

Using swarm technology, the dishwasher-size robots wheel around at nearly nine miles per hour on rails above crates of grocery products. The crates are placed without regard to product category. Instead, they are organized by an algorithm based on frequency of purchase. Robots equipped with claws lift a crate and place it in their interior cavity. They can then either move the crate to another location or drop it down a chute to a picking station. At the picking stations, employees refer to a screen in front of them, select the items in an order, and put them in a shopping bag, which is placed in another crate. Both crates are then sent back to the grid to be refilled with items or routed to the shipping dock. A fifty-item order can be fulfilled in as little as five minutes.

"It's all very much 'just in time' processing," says Anne Neatham, commercial director with Ocado Technology's office of the COO. "If you've ordered a pen, a box of pens will be brought out at just the right time to go past the picker, so they can pick a pen for a specific box with all of your groceries in it."[4]

Two modular data centers are located at each CFC to control the robots. Like much edge architecture, the on-site centers are intended to reduce latency. Otherwise, the robots' elaborate dance would degenerate into constant collisions.

In the midst of these impressive technological achievements, Ocado saw an even bigger opportunity. Instead of remaining an online grocer only, Ocado would provide a smart platform that other grocery retailers around the world could use to replicate Ocado's online model profitably and scalably in their own regions. Thus was born the Ocado Smart Platform, a combination of end-to-end e-commerce fulfillment, logistics, and swarm robotics technology that other retailers could use to create their own CFCs.

To execute this dramatic pivot, Ocado looked to the cloud. "When we started to build our Ocado Smart Platform, it was clear that we were going to have to be able to build completely new environments for our retail customers, pretty much at the flick of a switch," says Paul Clarke, CTO of the Ocado Group, "and we didn't really want to be building data centers in other countries—that was the point at which we decided to adopt a cloud-first strategy."[5]

Running in the AWS cloud, the Ocado Smart Platform enables retailers to operate their entire online e-commerce business. They can take advantage of features like real-time stock projection, intelligent van routing, and last-minute order processing. And they can offer customers mobile access to the site both online and offline via an app.

The cloud provides Ocado with an elastic, event-driven architecture that responds to spikes in customer demand in a cost-efficient way. It also enhances development agility. Ocado's engineers can test out new initiatives without making upfront infrastructure commitments and get ideas from concept to production in under an hour.[6] The company can also integrate data from hundreds of microservices into a data lake that powers AI capabilities across the infrastructure.

The leap from legacy systems to living systems was long. "It's a complete end to end rewrite; it's a complete refresh of all our technology stack," says Clarke. "I don't think there's a single line of code in common between our existing platform and the new one."[7]

Grocery retailers around the world have signed on. Over the next several years, Kroger plans to build twenty automated CFCs with Ocado. The platform has also been adopted by Sobeys in Canada, ICA in Sweden, Groupe Casino in France, Preu in Spain, and Aeon in Japan. In 2020, Ocado CEO Tim Steiner described what he saw as a shift in the center of gravity at the company: "We are now truly a technology-led global software and robotics platform business."[8]

Like many sectors, online grocery shopping was fast-forwarded to the future by the Covid pandemic, as people sheltered at home and grocery chains around the world rushed to step up their online business in response. "As a result of Covid-19, we have seen years of growth in the online grocery market condensed into a matter of months; and

we won't be going back," Steiner says. "We are confident that accelerated growth in the online channel will continue, leading to a permanent redrawing of the landscape of the grocery industry worldwide."[9]

Most observers believe that the widespread change in grocery shopping habits is here to stay, potentially boosting the attractiveness
of the Ocado Smart Platform. But even if those grocery habits fade
post-pandemic, Ocado's deeper technology strategy transcends any
particular industry. Its robots perform basic tasks—lifting, moving,
sorting—that can be applied in many industries and operating environments. Soon, the robots may be able to do more. The company has
recently embarked on a project to develop "soft hands" that can pick
up virtually any delicate object (like fresh fruit) without damaging it,
a skill that would be welcome in many manufacturing environments.[10]

The scalable and modular design of CFCs enables Ocado's customers to size disparate warehouses for different regions and flex when
necessary. The cloud-edge architecture, consisting of loosely coupled
microservices and APIs, gives customers the ability to alter their IT
infrastructure nimbly, instead of painfully and laboriously transforming it, only to watch it quickly become obsolete. Few companies have
married technology, strategy, and execution as comprehensively as
Ocado and still fewer have made the resulting advantages widely available to other players.

Technology-Integrated Strategies
for the Age of IDEA

Like Ocado, other companies have adopted this new approach to technology and have woven radically human intelligence, data, expertise,
and architecture into distinctive strategies as varied as the industries
in which the firms compete. No one size fits all. But three prominent
strategies illustrate the wide range of possibilities that radically human
technologies have opened up.

These three strategies—Forever Beta, Minimum Viable IDEA (MVI), and Co-lab—create distinct advantages for companies and customers alike. Forever Beta strategies offer software-enabled products and services that continually evolve and improve after they've been purchased so that customers see them grow in value and utility over time, rather than fade. MVI strategies use one or more elements of the IDEAS framework to precisely target weak links in a traditional industry and provide a superior customer experience that can be quickly scaled to make rapid inroads in the market. Co-lab strategies produce superior results in the sciences or other knowledge-intensive environments through human-guided, machine-driven discovery.

Strategy 1: Forever Beta

With a broad wink to readers, Elon Musk posted "The Secret Tesla Motors Master Plan (just between you and me)" on the then-fledgling car company's website back in 2006. It was Henry Ford turned upside down. Instead of starting at the low end of the market with a universally affordable model and one day expanding into the luxury market, Musk declared that "the strategy of Tesla is to enter at the high end of the market, where customers are prepared to pay a premium, and then drive down market as fast as possible to higher unit volume and lower prices with each successive model."[11] As Musk acknowledged, it was a strategy typically pursued with technology products, not cars.

In 2008 came the Tesla Roadster, which proved that an electric vehicle (EV) could deliver high performance and sleek design with sufficient battery life to stay on the road for 250 miles before needing to recharge. At its release, the Roadster cost $100,000. Then came the steady march down market. In 2012, the Roadster was discontinued and the Model S, a luxury sedan with a price tag of $76,000, a range of 300 miles, and reduced charging time, went into full production.

In 2016, the company announced its Model 3 sedan, which by the beginning of 2020 started at a price of $38,000.

Having achieved its entry into the mass market, the company then began to expand into the more expensive SUV market with the Model X, a mid-size crossover that sells for more than $80,000, and the Model Y, introduced in 2019, a compact crossover that lists for about $49,000. The company was also in various stages of development for a semi-tractor trailer, with self-driving features, and a futuristic, headline-grabbing pickup called the Cybertruck.

What's notably absent in that product timeline is yearly updates of each model, as car buyers have long been accustomed to from other automakers. That's because Tesla puts out a model and then continually improves it after the fact. Tesla owners see their existing cars continually transformed through updates that advance the vehicle's autonomous driving capabilities, improve performance, and enhance safety features.

Through cloud/edge connectivity with the cars, Tesla monitors performance and provides remote diagnosis and repair. For example, a motor problem involving occasional overheating was diagnosed and repaired by a software patch.[12] As we saw in the chapter on expertise and machine teaching, Tesla drivers are in a constant feedback loop with the company, helping train Tesla's neural network merely by driving. The result is an ownership experience that sees the car continually grow in value and utility. This experience is designed to be an intrinsic part of the usefulness and differentiation of the product for customers, who are, in effect, highly privileged beta users of each new improvement. Heading into 2020, Tesla was the number one automaker in the world in terms of total return, sales growth, and long-term shareholder value, despite building fewer than 500,000 vehicles per year.[13]

Samsung, too, is continually enhancing the value and utility of products for customers. For example, the company is always expanding the capabilities of common items like TVs and refrigerators by integrating

119

connected products from disparate companies with its SmartThings app. Through software updates, devices like the Family Hub smart refrigerator continue to improve after the customer has purchased it.[14]

Machine teaching plays a vital role in this continuous improvement. The fridge comes equipped with interior cameras that snap a picture and identify the food inside every time you close the door. You can check on what you have on hand through the app or on a touchscreen on the door. When the fridge makes a mistake—for example, misidentifying an avocado as a bell pepper—you can correct it, teaching it to get better.

Signify, the new company name of Philips Lighting, keeps the latest and greatest technology in its customers' hands through Signify circular lighting. It's an enterprise solution where Signify offers lighting based on the uptime and energy needs provided by its customers. The company maintains the materials, lightbulbs, and sensors, swapping out older pieces for new in order to deliver a consistent experience. This also allows Signify to reuse, refurbish, and recycle as much as possible, helping both the company and its clients to meet sustainability goals with better energy efficiency and reduced digital waste.

Signify shouldered responsibility for the lighting throughout the power plants that provide all of the electricity for Dubai, resulting in a savings of 68 percent in lighting-related energy consumption.[15] The company is essentially providing lighting-as-a-service, including all future technology updates. This deemphasizes individual devices and focuses on continually providing the optimal experience, shifting the business model from selling products to selling and continuously delivering desired outcomes.

This strategy takes on even more power when joined to Signify's IoT platform.[16] Called Interact, the platform supports the company's expanding from lighting products and systems to new, data-enabled services. The highly scalable, cloud-based platform uses machine learning to make sense of data from disparate sources. Sensors embedded in a customer's connected lighting system can collect data and share it with other management systems through secure APIs, offering new insights about how a building, a business, or even a city can improve its ways of working. For example, the system might collect data from an enterprise's buildings, combine it, and analyze it to understand and anticipate how people use office space. This could lead to more efficient, better designed buildings.

Customers can also use the Interact APIs to share their data with business partners or third-party software developers, tapping into Signify's cloud-based services to create additional software and data-enabled innovations. And consistent with the strategy, existing connected lighting customers can be seamlessly transitioned to Interact through software updates, giving them access to the more extensive services available through the platform.

Companies like Signify, Samsung, Tesla, and others are extending the value of their products and services by embedding intelligence into physical devices and designing flexible products and services that can support new capabilities as they become possible, marrying strategy and execution. Ultimately, they will form stronger relationships with customers, built on an understanding that the devices they purchase today will appreciate in value tomorrow. In the past, what you bought was what you got. But as we see with these companies, the evolving digital experience is now an intrinsic part of the product. Customers may own a physical product, but the company administers the digital side—effectively retaining ownership over part of what makes the product valuable and, in effect, delivering value-as-a-service.

Strategy 2: Minimum Viable IDEA

Lemonade, a New York–based insurance company co-founded by Daniel Schreiber and Shai Wininger, offers coverage to renters, condo owners, homeowners, and pet owners. Their AI-powered app streamlines getting quotes and settling claims, sometimes in seconds. But, says

Wininger, "Lemonade is a tech company doing insurance, not an insurer doing an app."[17]

Lemonade has combined AI chatbots, machine learning, and the cloud to focus with laser-like precision on the features of traditional insurance that make the industry widely disliked among consumers. And, for the element of expertise, they found a stunningly creative way to put a human in the loop.

With only a general understanding of how the insurance industry worked, co-founders Schreiber and Wininger started with some ideas about how it *ought* to work—without the endless paperwork, glacial bureaucratic processes, haggling over claims, and mutual distrust between insurers and customers that is built into the traditional insurance business model. Although AI was at the heart of the company from the beginning, Lemonade is not one of the "insure-tech" vendors springing up to provide existing insurers with advanced technology. Rather it is a vertically integrated insurance company that, in its words, "set out to replace brokers and bureaucracy with bots and machine learning, aiming for zero paperwork and instant everything."[18]

Consider the company's claims process. Users tap the "Claim" button in the app and simply tell the chatbot, named Maya, what happened. There are no forms to fill out, no waiting in a phone queue, no being handed off from one department to another. The company's AI runs its anti-fraud algorithms and if the claim is instantly approved—as some 30 percent are—the AI pays it immediately. If not, the claim is escalated to a human who contacts the insured as soon as possible.

In one instance, says the company, a claim was settled in seconds.[19] A young man had his coat stolen on a subzero December night in New York. Six days later, having given up hope of it turning up, he pulled out his iPhone at 5:43 p.m. and opened the Lemonade app. He entered the details: a Canada Goose Langford Parka, purchased at Saks Fifth Avenue for $979. He then spoke into a camera and described what happened, which took about a minute. At 5:49, he tapped "Submit." Three seconds later his claim was paid.

The process is so frictionless thanks, in part, to a financial model that resolves what Lemonade's founders saw as an inherent conflict of interest for insurance companies: every dollar of a customer's claim that a company denies is another dollar of profit for the company. This sets up an adversarial relationship that incentivizes the insurer to do everything possible to deny or reduce the amount of a claim. It also motivates the customer to inflate claims. This spiral of distrust harms the industry's reputation and spurs even otherwise honest people to cheat.

Lemonade simply takes a flat percentage of each premium. It returns the unclaimed remainder in an annual "Giveback Day," when the money is donated to worthy causes policyholders care about. Policyholders who choose the same cause are pooled in a virtual peer group. The premium money collected from each peer group is used to pay for the group's claims. Whatever money is left goes to that group's cause. On Giveback Day in 2020, the company donated more than $1.1 million to thirty-four nonprofit organizations, including UNICEF, Direct Covid Relief Response, the Malala Fund, Born This Way, and others.[20]

The humans in the loop in the claims process are the customers themselves. When they enter a claim, they know that Lemonade has no incentive to unreasonably deny or reduce it. Just as important, they know that every dollar by which they inflate a claim means less money for a cause they care deeply about. This dynamic not only puts a human in the loop, but puts what is uniquely and radically human at the center—moral conscience. Lemonade even has a chief behavioral officer, famed behavioral economist Dan Ariely. "Long story short: instead of fighting with our customers over the same coin, we join our customers in fighting for a common cause," he says. "That changes everything! It eliminates conflicts of interests, and creates a partnership between Lemonade, our customers, and their chosen nonprofit."[21]

Lemonade's precisely targeted MVI strategy also enables what the company calls "precision underwriting."[22] Although Lemonade's bot is designed with underwriting algorithms in place, allowing most customers to get premium quotes instantly, Lemonade is able to collect about a hundred-fold more datapoints per customer than traditional insurers, who collect only about forty datapoints on the typical insurance form. A population that appears to be monolithic at forty datapoints turns out to consist of several differing subgroups when looked at through the lens of exponentially more datapoints. Each of those subgroups can yield markedly different loss ratios (the total paid out in claims divided by the total premiums paid). The lower the loss ratio, the more profitable the insurance company. As the company grows and accumulates data, these subgroups yield their own component subgroups, enabling increasingly precise underwriting and more favorable loss ratios. The company's performance history seems to bear out the cumulative power of precision underwriting. In the first quarter (Q1) of 2017, the company paid out $3.68 for every dollar it earned, for a disastrous loss ratio of 368 percent. Since then, that figure has dropped steadily and steeply; by the second quarter (Q2) of 2020, it stood at 67 percent.

Telecom Giant Nurtures Its Inner Unicorns

Telefónica, headquartered in Madrid, is one of the world's largest telecommunications companies, with annual revenues exceeding €48 billion in 2019. But when its chair and CEO, José María Álvarez-Pallete, in a letter to stakeholders, unveiled a sweeping new strategy in late 2019, parts of the announcement read like a manifesto for MVI strategy.[23] "If in the past the low penetration of voice and data services assured future growth," he wrote, "the current maturity of the markets and the appearance of new competitors subject to different rules demand a highly focused and alternative strategic approach in order to continue growing. We must recognize that the model that has allowed us to get this far successfully is close to being exhausted."

One of the new strategic moves was the launch of Telefónica Tech, to focus on three distinct businesses: cybersecurity, IoT and big data, and cloud. "With this move," wrote Álvarez-Pallete, "we want to boost growth in these services which are already collectively growing revenue by over 30 percent annually and can be considered unicorns, gaining market share with recognition as leaders."[24]

For instance, the cybersecurity "unicorn," called ElevenPaths, declares that it combines "the freshness and energy of a start-up with the knowledge, power and strength of a global Telco to provide innovative solutions spanning prevention, detection, and response to daily threats in our digital world."[25]

Telefónica Tech soon deepened the focus of ElevenPaths by acquiring two other companies and integrating them with it. Govertis, acquired in August 2020, is a cybersecurity consulting firm that specializes solely in governance, risk and compliance, and electronic digital asset management. Its solution is designed to unify the legal and technological aspects of cybersecurity.[26] One month after buying Govertis, Telefónica acquired iHackLabs, a company specializing in cybersecurity training.[27] iHackLabs teaches and trains cybersecurity professionals through cloud-based platforms and labs, using a SaaS model that simulates real cyber-threat situations, like ransomware and denial-of-service attacks, tailored to companies in numerous sectors.

Now the company is extending its precision innovation strategy through Telefónica Tech Ventures, launched in October 2020 under the auspices of ElevenPaths to make investments in cybersecurity-related startups. The investments are "geared towards startups with high disruptive potential in areas such as threat intelligence, cloud security, data protection and the application of automations and artificial intelligence in defense of any organization."[28]

The effort began with a portfolio of nine investments in startups, with plans for fifteen more such investments in the ensuing three years. For example, one of the original nine startups powers cyber-threat intelligence centers for law enforcement and defense agencies. Another tracks down and eliminates illegal copies of their clients' assets. Yet another specializes in employee cyber risk management. The startups will complement the ElevenPaths product portfolio, will integrate new capabilities into the company, and could become candidates for acquisition.

Telefónica's three "unicorns," and the extension of its MVI strategy through Telefónica Tech Ventures, point up a significant advantage for established companies. They have the resources to stand up multiple MVIs, unlike upstarts for whom everything is riding on a single play.

Strategy 3: Co-lab

Co-lab strategies show us the kind of rapid and superior discovery that's possible when processes are designed to enable the best from both people and machines together. Companies that pursue this strategy use elements of the IDEA model in the service of a hyper-efficient, machine-driven science guided by humans. Freed by automation and machine learning to leverage their knowledge at the highest levels and to the fullest degree, specialists and knowledge workers, driving these powerful technology platforms, exponentially increase productivity, multiply value, and erect high barriers to entry.

Consider Exscientia, a UK-based startup with an AI-driven drug discovery platform it calls Centaur Chemist. The term derives from chess grandmaster Gary Kasparov's "Centaur chess" events, where human players were assisted by computer chess technology. With Centaur Chemist, as with Centaur chess, machines provide a level of computing ability that humans can't match, but humans remain firmly in control. And in both cases, the result is a process that outperforms experts or machines acting alone. As a company scientist put it to a gathering at the British Embassy in Tokyo, "Artificial intelligence will not replace chemists. But chemists who don't use AI will be replaced by those who do."[29]

To identify a disease to target, Exscientia initially applies deep learning algorithms to narrow down the almost limitless number of potential candidates. Then the company's experts devise a discovery strategy that is carried out by the Centaur Chemist's "active learning" system, which relies on highly data-efficient algorithms. Typically, in drug discovery, little is known about new targets for therapies, and there is scant data that could be used in big dataset, machine-learning approaches.

Says Exscientia, "We recognized several years ago that progressing new targets would require a blend of innovative approaches, with a particular focus on what we call the small data problem, where predictive models cannot initially be built. In these situations, we have to start a project efficiently with limited seed data, whether it be from literature and patents, or more likely a small internal screening campaign." The active learning algorithm "learns" its way into a drug discovery dataset with these limited data points.[30]

The company's approach has paid off. Since its founding in 2012, Exscientia has secured multiple pharma and biotech drug discovery collaborations with companies including Celgene, GSK, Sanofi, Bayer, and Evotec—collaborations estimated to be worth over $1 billion in total development milestones and royalties.

Now the company is at the center of the pharma ecosystem in Europe. Exscientia is leading small-molecule drug design activities in the Corona Accelerated R&D in Europe (CARE) consortium. Co-led by Johnson & Johnson and Takeda, CARE is the largest undertaking of its kind dedicated to discovering and developing treatment options for Covid-19 and future coronaviruses.[31] The public funding for these projects comes from the Innovative Medicines Initiative (IMI), which is funded by the EU Commission. The five-year project brings together thirty-seven partners from Belgium, China, Denmark, France, Germany, the Netherlands, Poland, Spain, Switzerland, the United Kingdom, and the United States, including Bayer AG, Merck, Novartis, Pfizer, and the Bill & Melinda Gates Foundation. To accelerate the preclinical phase of drug discovery, Exscientia is using its AI platform to generate and optimize the design of new medicines, essentially acting as the fountainhead for drugs that could save millions of lives in future coronavirus outbreaks.

Bühler Finds the Toxic Needle in the Haystack

According to the World Health Organization (WHO), 600 million people a year fall ill from consuming contaminated food ingredients.[32] Producing safe food is a vital concern for the milling industry; eliminating contaminated grains efficiently without losing healthy grains is the key to financial viability. The Swiss firm Bühler AG, a world leader in food-processing equipment, worked with Microsoft to transform the grain-sorting process into a hyper-efficient, human-guided, machine-driven science.

Maize, a diet staple for humans and animals in many regions of the world, is particularly susceptible to a family of toxins called aflatoxins. Some 500 million people, mostly in the poorer regions of the world, are at risk of chronic exposure to aflatoxins, which are estimated to cause up to 155,000 cases of liver cancer every year and contribute to stunting the growth of millions of children.[33]

Aflatoxins often can't be seen, smelled, or tasted. And because they're not destroyed by heat, cooking aflatoxin-contaminated food doesn't make it safe. Since consumers can't tell if their food is tainted, the responsibility for ensuring safety falls entirely on growers, harvesters, and processors. Just two contaminated kernels in 10,000 are enough to make a whole lot unfit for purpose.[34] Alongside health risks, the economic impact on farmers and food processors can be significant, sometimes compelling them to discard entire lots because they couldn't be precisely sorted.

Combining cutting-edge technologies from Bühler with Microsoft cloud and AI, Bühler created a unique optical-sorting technology called LumoVision. It identifies aflatoxins based on direct indicators of contamination, rather than just sampling, while simultaneously using real-time, cloud-based data to monitor and analyze contamination risk.[35]

Contaminated maize kernels exhibit a specific bright green color under UV light. To detect this florescence, LumoVision's proprietary, highly sensitive cameras analyze the color each kernel exhibits as it passes under powerful UV lighting in the sorter. Within milliseconds of detection, air nozzles deploy to blow contaminated kernels out of the product stream. The machine processes up to fifteen tons of product an hour, eliminating up to 90 percent of contamination—a significant improvement on current solutions.

This is not a classic Big Data approach, where tera/petabytes of data are stored and analyzed later to uncover insights. Instead, the key variable is speed. Once the detection model is trained, the monitoring data doesn't need to be stored, only checked for anomalies in real time. This approach reduces yield loss to below 5 percent, compared with up to 25 percent for other solutions. Now Bühler has used this more efficient approach to data, deep domain expertise, and cloud-edge architecture to scale its Co-lab strategy to other services.

Co-Lab Meets the Pandemic Head-On

On Sunday, November 8, 2020, Pfizer CEO Dr. Albert Bourla hurried to company headquarters. He was going to hear for the first time the clinical trial results for the Covid-19 vaccine his company had created in collaboration with the German firm BioNTech.[36] A week later, Moderna chief executive Stéphane Bancel anxiously awaited similar news about his company's vaccine.

The stakes couldn't have been higher. By November 2020, more than 46 million people around the world had contracted Covid-19. Some 1.3 million had been killed by it. And the pandemic was about to enter a second wave more deadly than the first.

The results for both vaccines were strikingly similar—about 95 percent effective in preventing Covid. When Dr. Bourla got the news about his vaccine, he couldn't believe he had heard correctly and asked that it be repeated; when Bancel got the news about Moderna's drug, he embraced his family, and together, they cried tears of joy.[37]

Besides the two companies crossing the finish line at almost the same time, there were other similarities. Both the Moderna and Pfizer/BioNTech vaccines used messenger RNA (mRNA) to make their vaccines. The mRNA molecule contains instructions to cells for making the coronavirus protein to trigger the immune system without causing infection. Despite the fact that there had never been an mRNA vaccine approved by the U.S. Food and Drug Administration, both vaccines were brought to fruition in months, not the four to five years successful vaccines typically take.[38]

Even more striking, from our point of view, was that in the midst of writing this book, we were presented with perhaps the most consequential confirmation of our thesis imaginable. Both the Pfizer/BioNTech and Moderna efforts employed virtually all aspects of the IDEAS framework, and both companies molded them into a strategy—Co-lab in this instance—that vaulted them into the future.

Moderna was hiding in plain sight. Before the coronavirus appeared, the company had provided a comprehensive, detailed account of its operations, its technology, and its strategy in a public document called "How Building Digital Biotech Is Mission-Critical to Moderna."[39]

Moderna had built a core mRNA platform technology with the intent of having all of its medicines work the same way—directing cells in the body to make proteins to prevent or fight disease. Addressing many diseases simultaneously required a digital model that would transform how medicines were designed and manufactured. So, from the company's founding in September 2010 through 2019, Moderna invested more than $100 million in digital technologies, robotics/automation, analytics, data science, and AI.

Their technology strategy comprised six "digitization building blocks":

- *Cloud enablement* for its computational power, elasticity, and freedom from the limitations of computing technology

- *Integration* of data and processes between systems to break down silos and continue to synchronize operations as they grow

- *IoT* data from instruments and environments to provide real-time guidance to scientists and engineers, as well as providing supply chain and manufacturing compliance and traceability

- *Automation*, especially robotics, to increase operational accuracy, repeatability, and throughput

- *Analytics* to harness the power of its data

- *AI* to enable breakthroughs in analytics and predictive modeling, accelerating the learning cycle, and providing otherwise inaccessible insights into research and production data

Two core "engines" are at the heart of the operation. A "research engine" is designed to move many mRNA research programs simultaneously from concept to development candidate nomination, providing ease of scalability. An "early development engine" then advances development candidates through clinical studies to human proof-of-concept.

Expertise plays a key role in the process. Moderna scientists turn their ideas into mRNA designs using a suite of tools that allows them to build novel mRNA sequences. Embedded AI algorithms, embodying years of accumulated knowledge around the interactions of mRNA sequence with both production yields and protein, convert acid sequences into nucleotide sequences and optimize a sequence for production. As soon as raw data is saved to the cloud by the sequencers, a fully automated pipeline triggers AWS servers to run an analysis algorithm and then shut down, minimizing costs.

To improve its analysis of sequences, the company has also developed a convolutional neural network (CNN), trained on only 20,000 labeled data files generated from expert operators. Though reliant on expertise, the algorithm exceeds human performance, increases the consistency and quality of the mRNA, and saves many hours of manual human analysis.

In 2018, the company launched a fully digital manufacturing site in Norwood, Massachusetts, fully integrated and without silos of legacy systems or data. At the center are expert human operators to accelerate execution and scale rapidly while maintaining flexibility. Digital changes required to support a new product can be accomplished in only a few days. Rather than using product-specific records, processes, and equipment like traditional pharma companies, Moderna's platform enables experts to create "product-agnostic" manufacturing processes. More than 90 percent of operations are controlled from the cloud. "Balancing resiliency with limited on-site computing," says the company, "gives us a template to deploy additional sites in the future faster with lower capital investment."

Moderna was focused on oncology drugs. But so confident were they in the adaptability and broad applicability of the principles underlying their approach, that when the virus struck, the company went all-in on developing a vaccine. And with their technology platform they were able to make this strategic shift and execute on it with breathtaking speed.

The story with BioNTech was similar: a technology-first mRNA platform that was ready for the critical moment when it came, strikingly illustrating the power of the Co-lab strategy to produce superior results through human-guided, machine-driven discovery and merge strategy and execution.

IDEA + S

Forever Beta, Minimum Viable IDEA, and Co-lab hardly exhaust the strategies that will emerge from the radically human turn in intelligent technologies. If the history of technology has taught us anything, it is that new tools give rise to unforeseen strategic dynamics that prove extraordinary powerful. Think, for example, of the phenomenon of network effects that drove the strategies of social media companies.

Of course, technology-driven strategies aren't self-generating. They require farseeing leaders who discern possibilities that others don't. Ocado didn't start out to be a provider of smart online retail systems, but in the combination of AI, platformization in architecture, and swarm robotics, company leaders eventually saw a strategic opportunity that transcends the grocery business. Similarly, Cloud/edge technologies and machine teaching made way for the Forever Beta strategies dreamed up by companies as disparate as Tesla, Samsung, and Signify.

For Lemonade, it wasn't just a combination of mobile apps and cloud-driven analytics that enabled the company to deliver the kind of precisely targeted, superior service that typifies MVIs. It was the insight of the company founders that the key to success lay in making the customer the human in the loop. In Co-lab strategies like those of Exscientia, Bühler, Moderna, and Pfizer/BioNTech, we see some of the most complex and advanced interlinking of intelligence, data, expertise, and architecture to be found anywhere, guided from the first by visionary leaders—seen, for example, in Moderna's public document describing exactly how it intended to weave together intelligent technologies that would apply not just to cancer but to other diseases as well.

In addition to imagination, the path to IDEA-driven technology enabling the near merging of strategy and execution requires two somewhat contradictory postures: forethought and speed. Technology investments must be sequenced logically and carefully. Yet, it has never been truer that "he who hesitates is lost." Pre-pandemic, the leading technology-first companies showed the way in carefully considered technology adoption. During the pandemic, many companies had to play catch-up, with widely varying degrees of success. And some—like Moderna and Pfizer/BioNTech and, in other industries, companies like Ocado and Starbucks—came into their own, as a result of their pre-pandemic forethought. Following the pandemic and the demonstrable success of radically human, IDEAS-based innovation, the task will be to move forward with all deliberate speed. The future has arrived far sooner than expected. It requires wise and rapid mastery of new approaches to innovation that are only just beginning to emerge and leaders who, no matter their industry, are able to see opportunity at the new, radically human nexus of people and technology.

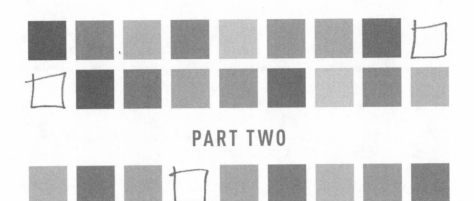

COMPETING IN
THE RADICALLY
HUMAN FUTURE

In part one, we explored the latest developments in intelligence, data, expertise, architecture, and strategy—IDEAS—that farseeing leaders will use to transform their companies. Taken together these turns toward the radically human in technology will remake business. In intelligence, machines are more closely mimicking the way humans reason, feel, and behave. Data on a more human scale is making more agile and more targeted applications possible for more companies; it is also complementing massive data systems to produce unprecedented levels of precision and power. Machine teaching is enabling humans to directly impose their professional, collective, and inherent expertise onto AI-powered applications. More agile and adaptable living IT systems, leveraging the cloud/edge and digital decoupling, are supplanting monolithic legacy systems. None of this is theoretical—some or all of these elements are already at work in strategies like Forever Beta, Minimum Viable IDEA, and Co-lab, with more to come as the technology continues to evolve.

Part two turns to how these new technologies and platforms will drive differentiation in four key areas that will be critical for companies to compete successfully in the radically human future: talent, trust, experiences, and sustainability.

Why these four? Since at least the turn of this century, many companies have sought to differentiate themselves along some or all of these dimensions. That's not news. What's new—and what is giving executives pause—is that these issues have taken on an unprecedented degree of urgency. In some cases, intelligent technologies have themselves contributed to that urgency. With trust, for example, AI has created some of the suspicion with which customers and employees alike regard technological innovations. The rise of new technologies has also put pressure on talent. For if, as we've argued, all companies are now tech companies, all employees are now tech employees whose skills with intelligent technologies will be major difference makers. These technologies also provide customers and employees with digitally driven experiences that transcend traditional notions of customer experience or employer brand—and threaten to leave purveyors of prosaic experiences far behind. It should be noted, too, that like the technology, these differentiators are themselves radically human. Talent—people— are the most radically human resource of all. Trust is the basis of human bonds, as well as commerce. Memorable experiences point beyond the transactional to the personally transformative. Sustainability speaks to the very survival of the human species.

Many executives are fully aware of the pressures. In our prepandemic study respondents reported that in the absence of retraining their employees, 52 percent of their IT workforce's skills, and nearly half—47 percent—of their non-IT workforce's skills would be obsolete in three years.[1] In chapter 6, we will see how leading companies are responding by putting intelligent technologies in the hands of diverse people at every level, investing in innovative "digital fluency" training, and using technology to achieve productivity anywhere through new ways of combining office and remote work. These companies are redeveloping existing talent, attracting new talent, and refashioning deeprooted cultures to turn the workforce from passive users of intelligent systems to active producers of such systems, with exponentially more valuable and profitable results.

Trust is similarly taking on renewed urgency. IDC predicts that by 2023, 50 percent of the *Forbes* Global 2000 will name a chief trust officer, who orchestrates trust across functions including security, finance, HR, risk, sales, production, and legal.[2] But trust must also be rethought in light of ubiquitous technologies that tap into deep wells of anxiety about our relationship to them. In chapter 7, we will see what can be done to imbue these technologies with the essentials of trust: humanity, fairness, transparency, privacy, and security. Privacy is now Apple's foremost differentiator. Goldman Sachs-based startup CYFIRMA is using predictive analytics to detect cyber threats before they become cyberattacks.[3] Manhattan-based AI startup Pymetrics is one of a number of tech startups trying to overhaul the hiring process with the help of AI—but in a way that's free of human bias and genuinely fair to both the jobseeker and the employer. These companies and others, in making trust an integral component of their business model, strategies, and the technology itself, are turning trustworthiness into operational reality.

As we saw in chapter 4 on architecture, technology has now made it possible for companies to provide customers and employees alike with a vast array of new experiences—new experiences of products and services as well as new experiences of work. In chapter 8, we look at the ways leading companies are drawing on IDEAS to design radically human experiences that tap into some of the most compelling human aspirations and interests: (1) *empowering* experiences that fulfill our need for mastery; (2) *rewarding* experiences that provide personal growth, fun, or satisfying collaboration; (3) *tuned-in* experiences that offer effortless engagement; and (4) *responsible* experiences that connect us with something larger than ourselves. Companies that continue to think of experience merely in terms of customer touchpoints are likely to fall behind in the marketplace and miss the boat entirely in terms of employees.

For a planet under mortal threat, perhaps no issue is more urgent than sustainability. As predictions of climate change have become reality, companies are deploying new technologies to outperform less responsible actors and meet rising expectations of customers, partners, and the wider society. In chapter 9, we will encounter companies in industries, from automobiles to textiles to mining and more, that are putting sustainability front and center, using intelligent technologies and living systems featuring cloud/edge architecture to help them make good on their promises.

In the radically human future of commerce and technology, companies that excel on these key differentiators will separate themselves from the pack. Some already are, as you will find in the pages that follow, and where you will learn how your company can, too.

TALENT

Humans + Radically Human Technology

by Christie Smith

Within days of Covid-19 lockdown restrictions being put in place, Deutsche Telekom's (DT) networks faced an onslaught of traffic. The number of digital conferences increased 322 percent. The number of people watching Netflix soared 3,074 percent. Yet DT's communications networks remained stable and secure, and the company was able to move 16,000 service and call-center employees into their home offices within a very short time.

Why?

Because in 2016 the company had decided to modernize its IT estate and invest in technological and cultural innovation.[1] The initiative was aimed at, among other things, opening up access to technology across the enterprise, improving employees' digital skills, and creating a flexible, resilient organization that turned out to be ready for work-from-anywhere when the need arose.

Companies that thrived, rather than merely survived, during the pandemic know that maintaining a rigid division between technologists and nontechnical people underuses the most radically human and readily available resource of all: their talent. Putting IDEAS to work in ways big and small, they take three bold steps to unlock the full potential of their people + radically human technology, taking differentiation on talent to a new level of distinctiveness: (1) they democratize technology by putting it in the hands of employees of all kinds at all levels, (2) they invest in innovative technology-skilling programs to take their people beyond digital literacy to digital fluency, and (3) they leverage the combination of democratized technology and a culture of digital fluency to enable productivity from anywhere at a time when how and where work gets done is undergoing a massive shift.

Democratizing Technology

Equality among employees is about diversity, inclusion, and equal access to opportunities, including technology, to do their jobs better and to innovate. In a survey of more than 30,000 employees, we found that "innovation mindset" (an individual's willingness and ability to be innovative at work) is six times higher in the most-equal cultures than in the least-equal ones."[2]

Uneven access to technology can have a corrosive effect on morale and business performance. In many companies, we find a growing divide between teams with ready access to intelligent technologies and teams without. The latter find themselves behind the eight ball both in terms of productivity and skill development. Consider the disparities among software programmers. Some might spend 60 percent of their day performing automatable tasks. Programmers who leverage AI tools to handle those activities code faster. They also become expert at collaborating with AI systems and less prone to errors. This divide becomes critical as the market today doesn't tolerate slow engineering delivery cycles. It demands modern engineering practices with quick build-measure-learn cycles that the technology have-nots cannot produce.

Technology democratization ensures that as many of your people as possible are empowered to become drivers of change, igniting grass-roots innovation by equipping every employee with the tools and skills to build technology solutions at the point of need.

Natural language processing, low-code platforms, and robotic process automation (RPA) are just a few of the capabilities and services making technology more accessible. They each have different and unique applications, but all are putting innovative power into the hands of nonspecialists with as little friction as possible, letting people optimize their work or fix pain points on their own.

Takeda, a global biopharmaceutical leader, is empowering its people to focus on higher-value activities, supporting better patient outcomes by scaling automation throughout the company. At the time of publishing, the company has trained over 2,200 people and democratized the development of over 500 bots.[3] At LexisNexis Risk Solutions, a project manager used an RPA management tool from UiPath to house and manage automation ideas, reuse bots when possible, and demonstrate ROI to leadership.[4] In one instance, his work uncovered a backlog of records that needed to be cleared. His team used eleven robots to clear 31,000 of them in a single day. These successes have also helped evangelize RPA among other peers, scaling the automation and value creation beyond the project manager and his own team.

Technology democratization could not come at a more critical time for businesses. As companies seek to compress digital transformation into a rapid timeframe and reorient for new circumstances, they can't afford to wait and hire someone tomorrow to build the solution they need today. In the first months of the pandemic, healthcare provider Geisinger saw a 50 percent decline in outpatient visits and a sudden surge in in-patient and ICU needs.[5] The company faced a major challenge trying to get the right healthcare professionals to the right places at the right time. By using Quickbase low-code development they were able to build an app to help coordinate and assign the thousands of healthcare workers in their network in just two days.

With the massive shift to cloud under way, many companies for whom democratization is new territory may already have access to these tools through existing cloud solutions. Amazon's Honeycode, for instance, is an AWS service that lets people build mobile and web apps without writing a single line of code.[6] Salesforce's Lightning App Builder is a point-and-click tool for creating custom pages on the Salesforce app.[7] For the many organizations migrating their people to Microsoft Teams, Power Apps can be directly embedded.[8] These tools, and many others, offer an opportunity to bridge the gap between complex technology and workers at every level of the organization.

When access to powerful technology spreads throughout an organization, every employee can be an active and vital part of digital transformation. People can decide for themselves what to automate, allowing them to focus on the things they do—and like doing—best. They can help to improve both the customer and the employee experience—not by gathering feedback to send to a team of tech experts for consideration, but by putting technology to work themselves.

Schneider Electric is one company demonstrating a vision of this future. The organization has made RPA a significant part of its digital transformation effort, deploying more than 220 bots as part of the process.[9] But the company had the foresight to realize bots might create silos, break other parts of the system, or fail to meet expectations. To combat this, they established a global RPA team to review use cases submitted by business leaders and act as a backstop to ensure that the use cases are strategic and part of end-to-end transformation strategy. The group has rejected more bots than they have approved at this point, but the extra process helps to guarantee that approved bots will remain useful for a long time.

At Google, employees are able to use new technology tools—even if they aren't yet supported by the organization—if they have a strong business need.[10] This doesn't give them free rein to use whatever whenever. Teams that adopt new tools must put in the work to support their new technical stack and must be conscious of potential issues like difficulty communicating and collaborating between teams. Google recognized the value in providing freedom to the people closest to the work in question, so rather than create policies about what technology not to use, it adopted a more inclusive framework for how workers can choose their own technical stack.

Democracy Requires Diversity

Democratization also means democratizing talent. It's not enough to put intelligent technologies in the hands of a workforce that isn't diverse and inclusive. Many organizations are falling short, partly because only 28 percent of the science and engineering workforce is female and only 2.5 percent is composed of Black women.[11] This isn't just a problem on equity grounds: $2 trillion is at stake with US gross domestic product (GDP) alone as women exit the workplace in historic numbers. Additionally, there is an anticipated $11 trillion cost to the G20 countries over the decade if we don't get equitable skilling right.[12]

To improve performance on diversity and gender, many companies have turned to AI, with mixed results. It was hoped that AI applications for hiring would help eliminate human biases from hiring decisions. But, as we will see in the chapter on trust, such applications often reproduced the biases of their human creators. On the other hand, AI can also be a powerful tool for eliminating biases. The intelligent text editor Textio revises job descriptions to better attract underrepresented groups. The company Atlassian leveraged Textio and increased the percentage of female recruits from 10 percent to 57 percent.[13] Unilever used an AI-based interactive game from Pymetrics, a company we will also meet in the next chapter. The tool helped Unilever double the number of applicants hired after the final round of interviews, increase revenue by hiring higher quality employees, and up the diversity of its overall applicant pool.[14]

Indeed, AI-generated insights now have the power to reveal biased behavior or language in real time and correct it, while boosting equity and a company's bottom line. Pipeline Equity is an AI-based startup that uses a data-driven analytics platform to assess, address, and take actions against the gender biases costing the United States nearly $2 trillion each year. And better yet, this technology calculates an uptick in revenue for each equity achievement located and corrected.

Another game-changing phenomenon is the move away from old models of hiring and staffing to ones that help build a skills-based economy. Walmart and Unilever are creating more equitable skilling opportunities by leveraging an AI startup called SkyHive. The technology uses quantum labor analysis to determine labor market supply and demand. SkyHive looks at declining and emerging jobs as collections of individual skills and analyzes how much these skills overlap between jobs, while highlighting the specific skills an individual needs to move from a declining role to an emerging one.[15] (Full disclosure: Accenture is an investor in SkyHive and in Pipeline Equity, a startup whose SaaS platform uses AI to address the gender equity gap, and we use the services of both companies extensively.)

Before SkyHive, people self-identified, on average, eleven skills they needed to complete their jobs. Research has shown us that women and people of color are far more likely to underestimate their skills, especially in the STEM fields.[16] Once the AI solution was introduced, that average number of skills jumped to thirty-four. The data also shows that a person might need to acquire only a few additional skills to switch disciplines—which wouldn't have been possible if AI hadn't identified the skills people didn't realize they already had.

Making the Culture Safe for Ideas

For the democratization of technology and the democratization of talent to yield results—in innovation, in competitiveness, in a superior employee brand—leaders must create an environment that is open to new ideas from everyone, even if some ideas fail. For people to feel free to take initiative, speak up, and push the limits of the possible, they must feel psychologically safe. The notion of psychological safety among employees springs from the pioneering research of Harvard organization behavior expert Amy Edmondson, who defined it as "a shared belief held by members of a team that the team is safe for interpersonal risk taking."[17] A psychologically safe and equitable environment is necessary to allow *everyone* to execute on and create lasting value from the abundant opportunities that humans + radically human technology offers.

After years of extensive research into the ingredients of high-performing teams, Google concluded the most significant predictor of team success was how psychologically safe people felt with their coworkers.[18] Interestingly, neither co-location of teammates nor seniority drove team effectiveness. High performance can be achieved only if people feel free to open themselves up to each other for the exchange of ideas, take risks, and learn from failures.

To help establish psychological safety, companies are increasingly turning to AI and people analytics. A top-three global chemical company was facing a well-known problem: previous attempts at transformation and restructuring had led to declining trust, motivation, and engagement among employees. Using InsightScan, a people analytics platform that measures psychological safety, leadership discovered that team members were worried about negative consequences for speaking up. Based on the insights gained from the platform, leaders were coached on behaviors that would lead to more psychologically safe environments. The result? Employee engagement jumped by over 10 percent by the year's end.

Research shows that when employees feel psychologically safe and can act fearlessly at work, productivity increases by 50 percent, turnover drops 27 percent, workers are 40 percent less likely to experience burnout, and companies become 11 times more innovative compared to their peers.[19] For companies that have grasped the implications of democratization, the question is no longer just "who can I hire?" but "how can I empower?"

From Digital Literacy to Digital Fluency

Increasingly rapid technological change renders jobs and roles obsolete faster than ever. As we've noted, in our pre-pandemic study (encompassing more than 8,300 companies) respondents reported that in the absence of retraining their employees, 52 percent of their IT workforce's skills, and nearly half—47 percent—of their non-IT workforce's skills would be obsolete in three years.[20] In response, as we found in our second study, leaders were using experiential learning at three times the rate of laggards (73 percent versus 24 percent); leaders launched apprenticeship programs at more than double the rate of laggards (79 percent to 36 percent); and 87 percent of leaders were using AI and advanced analytics to personalize learning, predict skills needs, and match workers' skill requirements with appropriate training versus 35 percent of laggards.[21] The pandemic kicked training by leaders into even higher gear: 70 percent looked to aggressively increase funding on training (versus 52 percent of laggards).

From startups hoping to quickly establish themselves among more seasoned competitors to legacy organizations working to complete their digital transformations, smart companies are establishing programs that put the skills gap behind them. What was historically seen as an HR-only responsibility is now shouldered across the C-suite. CEOs feel the weight of this responsibility to reskill: 54 percent of them ranked a workforce skills shortage as the number one barrier to achieving value from digital transformation efforts.[22]

At a basic level, employees need digital literacy—an elementary understanding of what technologies are at their disposal and how they work. Traditionally, companies have settled for digital literacy through traditional in-classroom or online training. But fostering basic literacy alone has resulted in uneven adoption, understanding, and utilization of digital capabilities. Moreover, the impact of the pandemic has forced a shift in demand from digital literacy to digital fluency—immersion in the language, techniques, and application of intelligent technologies. Think of it as the difference between someone who has a phrasebook understanding of a foreign language and someone who can communicate confidently with a native speaker. When the workers closest to customers, clients, or internal problems are digitally fluent, they can deliver more customized responses and offerings, with greater agility than ever.

Our firm has created what we call a Technology Quotient (TQ) program, a global learning initiative to help employees across the firm raise their "TQ" through training and competitions. We think of TQ in terms of a worker's enthusiasm toward a technology, their competency to work with the technology, and the value they see the technology adding to their work. The program helps employees understand and articulate important technology concepts as well as their business value and applications. It covers everything from mature strategies like DevOps and cloud to more cutting-edge technologies like blockchain and AI and is built for any role or skill level. The aim is to have every employee become conversant in technology and see technology as part of the solution to the most pressing client needs.

IOOF, an Australian wealth management firm, has created a program to immerse its people in low-code development. The company wanted to explore new digital innovation opportunities but most of their highly skilled developers were busy working on a multiyear project.[23] So the company's CIO launched a low-code competition, paired developers with less technical colleagues, and gave participants two weeks off to experiment with OutSystems, its low-code platform of choice. Already, the company says this experiment has proven valuable. Employees with outdated skills didn't need to spend years retraining, and the low-code apps they created are fulfilling mission-critical needs. One has evolved into a full-scale production system.

A number of companies are finding that there are creative ways to give domain experts a working knowledge of AI so they can apply it in their areas of expertise. At global financial services firm Morningstar, teams of employees build miniature self-driving cars and race them against other contestants in Amazon's DeepRacer league. The league was created by Amazon Web Services (AWS) to teach participants skills in reinforcement learning. Using Amazon SageMaker software, participants create and train algorithms to race a 1/18th scale AWS Deep-Racer car around a 17×26-foot track. Participants compete for prizes at AWS events around the world and in virtual events and tournaments by entering time trials on special tracks in the AWS Deep-Racer simulator.

"The DeepRacer League gives them the opportunity to discover reinforcement learning in a hands-on fashion and then proceed to build, train, and tune reinforcement learning models and deploy them into their autonomous model racing cars," said Swami Sivasubramanian, vice president, Amazon Machine Learning at the inception of the program.[24]

Beginning in January 2019, more than 450 Morningstar equity analysts, quantitative researchers, and software developers formed nearly 100 racing teams in 10 countries. In addition to using virtual race tracks within the AWS DeepRacer simulator, teams could use physical tracks available across Morningstar offices from Chicago to Mumbai. Within months, one of the teams developed an idea for a tool based on reinforcement learning that would look for patterns in regulatory filings in order to accurately identify relevant information. Another team saw a way to use reinforcement learning to automatically find and fix broken links to the websites of financial institutions. The company expected to have dozens of such projects up and running by the end of 2020.[25] Says Morningstar's chief technology officer James Rhodes, "It provides hands-on training across the company and accelerates Morningstar's practical application of machine learning across our investing products, services, and processes."[26]

Digital Fluency and the Logic of the Radically Human

Achieving digital fluency requires a genuine belief in employees' abilities and an investment to match. Nationwide Insurance announced they would spend $160 million over five years to provide "future capabilities" training for their 28,000 employees in the United States. Done right, the propagation of digital fluency throughout the organization can transform what employees—and the business as a whole—can do.

Consider Capital One. When it became an entirely innovation-driven digital company, it undertook a complementary transformation in its approach to talent and culture. Capital One sought not only to replace the technology stack, but also to inculcate digital fluency in the workforce. For instance, when the company embarked on its cloud-first strategy, it also instituted a cloud-computing training program. Capital One Tech College offers a learning program built by engineers for engineers. To ensure that everyone is cloud-fluent, online courses and in-person workshops are offered to employees—tech and nontech alike—across more than a dozen disciplines.

In 2017, the company launched Capital One Developer Academy (CODA) to create a pathway into technology for noncomputer scientists from diverse backgrounds. In the six-month, intensive training program, nontech employees learn to code by working alongside engineers. After completing the program, participants join a two-year rotational Technology Development Program as full-time software engineers. At the same time, Capital One launched separate programs in technology, analytics, and design thinking to provide opportunities for their associates to reskill and upskill themselves in roles that are outside of banking but are critical for building a multidisciplinary culture of experimentation with technology.

Meanwhile, Capital One Lab, an innovation arm that brings a startup mindset into the culture, fosters customer-centered design thinking in new processes, products, and services. Through Capital One Ventures, the bank stays abreast of innovation at startups and taps into that innovation through collaboration. Today, the bank engages in advanced technological exercise such as chaos testing, resilience, and agility—activities that have traditionally been the domain of big tech companies.

This tech-first culture, where digital fluency is a top priority, also helps attract top talent. "Talented software engineers want to work where they see other great software engineers," says CIO Rob Alexander. "They want to work with modern technologies, and they do not want to work on legacy applications platforms, or slow bureaucratic ways of working, which are often the case that you might find in large banking or other large institutions. We took on those two challenges, which is how do we build a team, a critical mass of great software engineers that will attract others, and change our technology operating model in a way that allows us to evolve like the best technology companies."[27]

Not surprisingly, Capital One has consistently ranked as one of the best places to work.[28] Without the company's thriving development and training programs, and the push for experimentation and working across business units, it's likely that, paradoxically, technology alone would not have transformed the bank into a technology company. That is the logic of the radically human. It's also a lesson in how to genuinely differentiate an organization on the dimension of talent in an age of radically human technology.

Productivity Anywhere

The year 2020 saw the biggest workforce and workplace transformation in living memory. To keep employees safe during the pandemic, companies allowed legions of their people to work from home. To keep the business functioning and employees productive, companies doubled down on technology solutions. Almost overnight, billions of people around the world changed their mode of working. As of 2019, only 5.4 percent of employees in the twenty-seven member countries of the EU usually worked from home—a share that had remained roughly constant for a decade. At the outbreak of the pandemic, the figure jumped to 40 percent.[29] Research conducted by Stanford University in May 2020 found nearly twice as many people, in the United States alone, working from home than working on-site—accounting for more than two-thirds of economic activity.[30]

Initially, many companies regarded this massive shift as a short-term solution to a temporary problem. But employees soon came to like working at home. Consider Fujitsu.[31] Just prior to the onset of the pandemic, 74 percent of the company's workers indicated in a survey that they thought the office was the best place to work. By March, 80,000 of the company's Japan-based workers were working from home; in May, only 15 percent of Fujitsu employees preferred the office.

Nearly one year after the Stanford study, 90 percent of office workers in midtown and lower Manhattan, the two largest central business districts in the United States, were continuing to work remotely.[32] Another national survey of commercial landlords conducted at the same time by a real-estate technology platform found that only 18 percent of respondents envisioned a return to the traditional five-days-a-week, on-site model of work.[33] Meanwhile, the appearance of the more contagious Delta variant of the Covid virus prolonged the necessity of remote work. Many companies in the tech, finance, and media sectors have indicated that they will continue to have employees work remotely some or all of the time, but so have companies like Novartis, Ford, and Siemens.[34]

While many workers enjoy the freedom of remote working, research shows that finding the optimal balance between what works well on site *and* what works well remotely is what people really want. They want the environment that's best suited for them. For some, that means going back to the office; for some, it means going 100 percent remote; still others prefer a mix.

When people can work from anywhere, they can do their jobs in different or even brand-new ways that will outlast the pandemic. For instance, at the University of Liverpool, scientists worked with a robot chemist to continue their research during lockdowns.[35] The robot found ways to speed up reactions inside solar cells and could run experiments autonomously, even when no one was present. The researchers won't stop using these robots just because they can go back into the lab themselves. They'll expand what they can do, like running experiments 24/7 or having robots handle toxic substances.

Businesses must accommodate rather than fight this new reality. They need to toss out convention and reimagine how their workforce model can best support and enable their people to be more productive— how remote employees and on-premises employees collaborate, what work is better done in which locations, and what the purpose of physical offices will become.

To be effective, people need a sense of autonomy. Back in the 1970s, work psychologists discovered that giving people a sense of autonomy in their work tasks resulted in higher levels of responsibility and performance. Less control ultimately generates more value. Fujitsu's new "Work Life Shift" program seeks to maximize creativity and efficiency by letting the company's workers determine the best work situation for themselves.[36] All employees will be able to work from home permanently and to work flexible hours. But while Fujitsu is halving its total office space in Japan, the company is actually expanding satellite offices in different parts of the country. The new model will give employees the freedom to choose where they want to work—whether that's their home or one of these smaller offices.

Companies must also change the way they manage and evaluate employees. Even though research has definitively shown that the most productive people take breaks to achieve higher levels of performance, many work cultures are built upon a "busyness" mindset.[37] But in productivity-anywhere workforces, it's no longer about staying busy and visible, but about delivering valuable outcomes.

Consider one global biotechnology company. With a flexible approach to how, where, and when work happens, the company created an outcomes-focused culture to allow people more freedom in how they achieve results. A digital worker toolkit centered on a collaborative platform enabled asynchronous communication to flow more easily. Behavioral nudges drove better meeting etiquette and empowered employees to manage their time. The result: the company has successfully shifted away from a "presenteeism" culture, where meetings are the primary way for employees to demonstrate their value. The pressure to always be "on" has lessened, thanks to increased trust and flexibility. The solution prioritizes results, supports collaboration, enables flexibility across teams, and draws the boundaries people need to take breaks, allowing for meaningful connection and reflection throughout the day. It's no surprise that higher company performance followed.

Platform technologies such as Microsoft Viva are making a focus on outcomes even more accessible to companies today. The AI-powered platform helps create a centralized experience regardless of where people work. A digital system of shared understanding and connection is made visible on the platform to ensure people are in sync about what others are doing, get access to valuable knowledge in real time, and gain insights into why they are doing certain things.

With more people working from home, Humana, a leading healthcare company, used the Microsoft Viva employee experience platform to help transition its 26,000 employees at speed.[38] Humana uses Viva insights "to help the company gain privacy-protected insights into work patterns, collaboration overload, manager effectiveness, and organizational resiliency." These insights empower Humana to work smarter and help balance productivity and well-being in a hybrid model.

Productivity anywhere also lets companies rethink how they recruit new employees. Almost every major company already runs its business globally but still sees itself tied to geographies. Opening up to the idea of geographically distributed employees will finally give companies access to a truly global and genuinely diverse talent pool. And it will give employees the freedom to live anywhere they wish and avoid having to uproot their families to pursue work opportunities. Facebook, for example, is transitioning more of its workforce to remote work as a way to expand and diversify its talent pool. Mark Zuckerberg has cited this newfound ability to recruit people from more locations and the ability to retain people who might leave the company because they want to move to a different area.[39]

Companies must also manage the potential disconnect between in-person and remote workers. Workers in different roles will benefit from the best work environment for their particular needs, but without careful implementation, in-office and remote workers could struggle to collaborate, become demoralized, or feel unsupported. Quora, for instance, is adopting a remote-first approach while also keeping its California headquarters open as a co-working space. To avoid distant workers' voices being minimized in favor of those in physical office spaces, all employees attending meetings will be required to appear on their own video screen.[40]

Organizations are also addressing the tricky new question of how to ingrain their mission and values into new hires who have never experienced the in-person work environment. Verizon, which transitioned 90 percent of its workforce to a work-from-home model in mid-March 2020, was hiring for 950 new home-based customer service roles.[41] Leaning on its experience transitioning existing workers to a remote model at the beginning of the pandemic, the company has redesigned its new hire training programs to be digital, self-guided, and video-based and to include work-from-home-specific training as well as training from current employees.

Twitter, which was among the first major organizations to announce permanent remote work, is transforming its workforce culture in even more ways.[42] While remote working will help the company meet its goal to hire more diverse employees from all parts of the United States, leaders have also identified areas where improvement is needed. To avoid meeting fatigue, executives formally cut down on video calls. They have also decided to rethink their performance review system to prevent bias against remote workers, and they are looking for ways to recreate "water cooler" connections and social engagement.

The benefits of productivity anywhere to your operations and your employer brand are many: truly global access to diverse talent; having a workforce that's constantly "on" by virtue of coverage across time zones; resilience against future disruptions; even delivering on sustainability goals by right-sizing company office spaces and cutting down on polluting, energy-consuming employee commutes. Most importantly, embracing productivity anywhere is an opportunity to reimagine what you do and what you can offer to the employees who help you deliver it—to turn human resources into radically human resources—differentiating your company from those still engaged in the old-fashioned war for talent.

The concrete business benefits of productivity-anywhere workforces are well documented. Accenture research has found that 63 percent of high-growth organizations have enabled productivity-anywhere workforces. On the flip side, 69 percent of organizations with negative or no-growth projections are still focused on where people should work—favoring either completely on site or remote workforce models. And 85 percent of people who feel they can be productive anywhere also plan to work for their current organization for a long time.[43]

Getting Started

Capitalizing on humans + radically human technologies to differentiate your organization on the dimension of talent is a moving target. Best practices are still evolving. But one thing is certain: waiting to act isn't an option. You will need to constantly experiment with new solutions, thinking beyond traditional HR categories and taking some concrete steps to democratize technology, build a digitally fluent culture, and achieve productivity anywhere.

To begin democratizing technology, evaluate your existing access to technology. Identify what tools you may already have access to, or what additional investments need to be made, to power grassroots innovation. Then pick one area of the enterprise and experiment. For instance, give sales development representatives the tools needed to design their own apps or customer service agents the ability to automate workflows.

To democratize talent, use the career-enhancing promise of democratized technology and the flexibility of productivity anywhere to create a powerfully differentiated employer brand that attracts diverse employees. Leverage both the power of debiased hiring technology to help ensure genuine diversity and create psychological safety to maintain it and reap its benefits in innovation.

To fully harness the powerful logic of radically human technology—that it is humans who confer technological leadership—invest in digital fluency programs across your organization. Immerse employees in available technologies. Teach them how to use those technologies to design solutions at the point of need.

For the dawning age of productivity anywhere, identify where you have made rapid, pandemic-driven digital transformations; address any security concerns; and consider how you can make hybrid models seamless and sustainable. Remember, you are undertaking one of the most massive workforce experiments since the dawn of the industrial era. Evaluate how it's going. Invest in workplace analytics tools, and develop a set of key performance indicators to gain a deeper understanding of how employees are responding to remote work.

Reimagine how your company's physical space is utilized. Plan for optimizing offices to account for a growing remote contingent, and imagine how the enterprise can transform those spaces. You should also explore creating capabilities and environments that foster immersive digital collaboration and unite on-site and at-home employees in shared experiences, ensuring that the informal advantages of workplaces are virtualized as well.

What technology democratization, digital fluency training, and productivity anywhere have in common is a deep trust in the radically human possibilities of employees. The issue of trust has never been more prominent for individuals or so problematical for organizations. Trust is not only the invisible motor of commerce, but also the basis of our most radically human instincts, determining how we respond to everything from other individuals to enterprises large and small. As we will see in the next chapter, how your company and your technology embody and interact with this most fundamental of human responses will play a large part in your ability to compete.

7

TRUST

Appealing to Our Most
Radically Human Instinct

Never have people been more alert—in a more deeply personal way—
to matters of trust. Throughout the coronavirus pandemic, virtually
every individual in the world had to gauge how much they trusted
every other individual they came in contact with, including members
of their own families. Masks—and their absence—became visible signs
of how much others could be trusted to care about one's welfare.

From this human center, concerns rippled outward to businesses
and institutions. How much trust could be placed in the Covid-related
practices of restaurants, retailers, theaters, hotels, airlines, museums,
schools? What about vaccines and vaccine makers? Meanwhile, trust
was being eroded by public discourse that routinely dismissed facts, evidence, and science itself, undermining the very notion of truth. And
in the commercial world, a rising tide of mistrust had been building
for years, driven by a succession of corporate scandals and malfeasance,
including the worldwide financial meltdown of 2008, massive breaches
of customer data by numerous companies, insider trading, and more.

Capitalism runs on trust—call it "the invisible handshake"—a point
made forcefully almost 250 years ago by Adam Smith (and often

overlooked by his simplifiers). When trust declines, transaction costs rise, either in the form of measures we must take to protect ourselves against unethical or harmful behavior or measures governments must take to regulate such behavior.[1]

What's more, we judge companies just as we do human beings. Over the past several decades, social psychologists have deduced that our ancient ancestors, in order to survive, developed an unconscious ability to make two important judgments very quickly about other people.[2] First, what are their intentions toward me—do they mean to help me or hurt me? Second, how capable are they of carrying out that perceived intention. The researchers call these two dimensions, respectively, *warmth* and *competence*. Today, we instantly judge other people that way, trusting and admiring those we perceive as warm and competent. Princeton professor Susan T. Fiske, one of the founders of this research, and brand expert Chris Malone, joined forces to determine whether—and to what extent—we judge companies in the same way. In a series of ten separate studies encompassing forty-five of some of the world's best-known companies, they found that "companies and brands were judged so strongly along the lines of warmth and competence dimensions that these judgments explained nearly 50 percent of all purchase intent, loyalty, and likelihood to recommend a brand or product."[3] In short, trust is one of the most radical—in the sense of deeply rooted—differentiators of all.

Five Essentials of Trust for the Digital Age

Much of our current mistrust stems from the technologies we have been discussing throughout this book. Algorithms take credulous website visitors down rabbit holes of hatred, disinformation, and bizarre conspiracy theories. Machine learning reinforces biases in hiring, policing, and access to credit. The data that enables AI to advance human health and well-being can be used to discriminate against the unwell. Social media platforms have become weaponized by malign governments meddling in other countries' elections. Internet giants and advertisers engage in relentless cyber tracking—some observers call it surveillance[4]—looking for ways to mine and monetize the massive amounts of data they collect on billions of individuals every day.

Companies that cannot be trusted suffer consequences in real financial terms. In 2018, the *Economist* looked at eight of the most notable corporate crises since 2010. All eight firms suffered a drop in their share prices after a crisis struck, with the median share price down by 33 percent at the lowest point. Although most of the companies made up their absolute losses over time, comparison with the performance of their peers tells a story of massive value forgone. On that basis, the median firm was worth 30 percent less than it would have been had the crisis not occurred. The *Economist* estimated that the eight companies forfeited a total of $300 billion.[5]

By contrast, leading companies are seizing this opportunity by turning this moment of truth into a "moment of trust," embracing the power of exponential technology change to completely reimagine and rebuild the future of business and human experience post-Covid.[6] These organizations are making trust a fundamental feature of their offerings. They are adopting and adapting elements of the IDEAS framework, each of which is underpinned by trust. They are acutely aware that they must be able to trust the algorithms that power intelligence, the data that feeds their technology, the expertise that drives machine teaching, and the security of constantly adaptable architecture. And they then weave those elements into a strategy that makes trust one of the most powerful differentiators of all. In the process, they are turning what have historically been liabilities to be shored up or minimized into advantages to be proudly seized in the marketplace—addressing five essentials of trust in our digital age: humanity, fairness, transparency, privacy, and security.

Humanity: The Experience of Trust

In our thoroughly digitized daily activities, we all live in varying degrees of trust or mistrust with AI-powered platforms, devices, websites, business systems, and online government processes. One of the great boosters of trust in AI-powered entities is their connection to the human element.

As we've seen with online insurer Lemonade, the human element can be direct and simple. Customers filing a claim simply look into the camera and tell the story of their loss and either settle instantly or get immediately bumped up to a human for assistance. In the case of Etsy, the aesthetic sensibilities of human beings help power the choices of products that AI lays out for customers. In the cases of the many companies where humans teach machines—the "Expertise" in IDEAS— the human element may sometimes be less visible, but no less important to the success of the companies that employ it to win trust.

The next frontier in building experiential trust is to teach machines how to *cooperate* with humans and other machines. In a 2021 ground-breaking commentary in *Nature* about the emerging field of "cooperative AI," leading AI experts described the challenge this way:

> AI needs social understanding and cooperative intelligence to integrate well into society. The coming years might give rise to diverse ecologies of AI systems that interact in rapid and complex ways with each other and with humans: on pavements and roads, in consumer and financial markets, in e-mail communication and social media, in cybersecurity and physical security. Autonomous vehicles or smart cities that do not engage well with humans will fail to deliver their benefits, and might even disrupt stable human relationships.[7]

According to the authors, researchers will need to focus on three areas to foster cooperative AI:

- **AI-AI cooperation.** Teach AI how to learn to play cooperative board games like *Diplomacy* the way humans do, with all their messy alliances and coalitions, negotiations and bargaining, deception and trust-building, and ad hoc teamwork and communications.

- **Human-AI cooperation.** Teach robots how to work alongside humans in factories and in hospitals, and how to reach alignment with others who have conflicting interests. AI assistants would complement human intelligence and depend on humans for skills where people have a comparative advantage. They would build trust that machines won't replace humans once humans train them: "AI won't replace radiologists, but radiologists who use AI will replace radiologists who don't use AI for human collaboration," says Stanford University radiologist Curtis Langlotz.[8]

- **AI for human-to-human collaboration.** Teach AI how to foster cooperation rather than conflict among humans in areas like scientific research, social media, and recommendation algorithms. That capability fosters healthy communities and enduring values.

Human-AI cooperation, and specifically AI augmentation of human capability, were of course the thrust of our previous book *Human + Machine*. We argued that human judgment is a critical part of engendering trust in AI, if we are going to be able to harness its full power in a world of widespread "algorithm aversion."[9] The opposite of algorithm aversion is "algorithm appreciation," to use a recently coined term.[10] Appreciation for AI blossoms when elements of radical humanity rise to the surface. In turn, strategies that foster a more natural, human level of interaction with AI have the potential to fuel new layers of trust among customers, employees, and many others.

For example, "conversational AI," systems that learn from user interaction, offer one way to increase trust in the impersonal world of

AI-powered bots. Alexa announced in late 2020 that its voice assistant could now decipher requests that it has not previously been trained to understand.[11] Most existing conversational AI systems tend to break down when they encounter new situations.

Beyond conversational AI, fully immersive and humanlike "digital personas" are taking shape—3D holograms that look and seem like real people and can answer users' unscripted questions. These personas add or subtract trust based on people's perceptions of how "real" they are. For example, Accenture Labs created a 3D hologram of celebrated Indian artist M. F. Husain for the Museum of Art and Photography in Bangalore, India.[12] The historical figure passed away in 2011, so the artist's face was superimposed on archival video interviews with Husain. Experts ensured that the simulated answers would be viewed as trustworthy, and the persona received the approval of the artist's estate and family members. Speech synthesis, AI, and deep learning technologies trained the persona to speak like the artist, as well as to detect and respond to users' emotions. Such lifelike interactions strengthen trust, particularly when the persona echoes the real person along so many dimensions.

Surprisingly, a greater appreciation for human imperfection is also critical. An AI chess program called Maia, based on technology originally developed by Alphabet's DeepMind unit, does not strive to be superhuman. Instead, it takes into account all the ways humans screw up in chess, and designs systems with human fallibility in mind.[13] It has an ability to look ahead and anticipate human actions *and* errors, as well as a specific individual's most *likely* moves, not just all the *possible* moves like IBM's Deep Blue system that has defeated chess champions.

A focus on human imperfection gives Maia a better ability to interact with humans: sometimes it can teach them, sometimes it can assist them, and other times it can negotiate with them. For example, it could train doctors to read medical images more accurately, by understanding how doctors themselves disagree when looking at the same image.

Human brains are by no means completely reliable. People sometimes can't even trust their own eyes—and thanks to AI, we are beginning to learn why. An artificial brain called MotionNet can simulate the human perception of motion, a highly complex process that is notoriously difficult to observe in the real world.[14] Using a virtual model of human perception, researchers are able to show how people underestimate the speed they are driving in conditions of low visibility like fog. The system models how neurons in our brains make objects look like they are moving more slowly than they really are in these situations—a mistake that can have fatal consequences on the highway.

These radically human flavors of machine intelligence have a much greater chance of instilling confidence in humans that systems are boosting their abilities rather than replacing them. And that basic human decency can produce marked improvements in trust.

Fairness: Debiasing AI

On a Thursday in January 2020, Robert Williams of Farmington Hills, Michigan, unwillingly had an AI milestone thrust upon him. He became the first documented example in the United States of someone wrongfully arrested based on a false hit produced by facial recognition technology.[15]

With his wife and two daughters, ages five and two, looking on in fear, police arrested him for allegedly stealing $3,800 worth of watches from a trendy retail boutique in Detroit. He was detained for thirty hours and spent the night on the floor of a jail cell. The technology had mistakenly matched footage of the perpetrator from the store's security camera to Williams' driver's license photo on file with the state.

It has been well-documented that many visual recognition systems, trained mostly on white examples, have difficulty distinguishing darker-skinned people, and even greater difficulty if the subject is a dark-skinned female.[16] Researchers at the Georgia Institute of Technology have also found that object-detection systems, like those used in autonomous vehicles, are better at detecting people with lighter skin tones.[17] Self-driving cars might be less likely to register the presence of darker-skinned pedestrians and crash into them as a result.

Or consider gender bias. An online-translation program that, when asked to translate the phrase "She is a doctor and he is a babysitter" into Turkish and then translate it back to English, spits out: "He is a doctor and she is a babysitter." Medical-imaging diagnostic systems, trained on a preponderance of male data, can lead to inadequate care for female patients.

Microsoft and Boston University researchers discovered that word-embedding algorithms took on the social biases lurking in the vast amounts of text they had been fed from Google News, Wikipedia, and other online sources.[18] The GPT-3 AI algorithm, created by Open AI in San Francisco and trained on around 200 billion words, excels at writing poetry and news stories better than any AI so far, but it also excels at spouting pure gibberish and generating radicalizing texts that outperform those written by real Nazis, conspiracy theorists, and white supremacists. The AI fundamentally does not "understand" what it's saying.[19]

Bias in training data or in an algorithm can also have serious business consequences. For instance, a bank installed an AI system to assist in mortgage underwriting only to find that it had created a rule to deny loans in low-income zip codes—a violation of bank "redlining" regulations.

When AI focused on back-office applications, bias could certainly creep in, but the potential damage was not nearly so extensive. Now AI is being used extensively both in management decision support and customer-facing applications. At the click of a button, automated algorithmic decision making can have an impact on huge populations, making the risk of biased AI much worse.

With biased AI, companies risk making strategic wrong turns, offending customers, alienating employees, and damaging reputations.

Worse, biased AI is morally wrong. In June 2020, around the time the story of Robert Williams' false arrest broke nationally, Amazon, Microsoft, and IBM announced they would suspend or end their facial-recognition offerings for law enforcement. Meanwhile, a number of companies are tackling the problem of bias head-on.[20]

Consider bias in automated hiring. Over the last several decades, companies have been using algorithms to sort through thousands of job applications to find just the right candidate for and achieve bias-free hiring. But many of these algorithms have unfortunately perpetuated inequities in the hiring process.

This is where Pymetrics comes in. The Manhattan-based AI startup is one of a number of tech startups trying to overhaul the hiring process with the help of AI. Co-founded in 2013 by Frida Polli, a cognitive scientist who has held fellowships with Harvard Medical School and Massachusetts Institute of Technology, Pymetrics harnesses a blend of neuroscience-based tests and machine learning to pair job candidates with the right openings.

One way that Pymetrics does this is through a series of online tests. Companies that partner with Pymetrics have their current employees take an assessment designed to measure attributes such as memory, attention span, altruism, skepticism, and appetite for risk. Pymetrics then pinpoints patterns among the top performers in various roles. For example, a salesperson might lean toward being more high-risk/high-reward, while a software developer might be more process and detail oriented. All this information feeds into the Pymetrics algorithm to evaluate job candidates who take the same test as they apply for different roles within the company. In one instance, a company hired a former hairdresser for a sales position with no prior sales experience. The new hire ended up being a top performer. "It's those types of diamonds in the rough, or people you wouldn't be considering otherwise," Polli says.[21]

The Pymetrics test involves a series of short computer games that were developed based on cognitive-science literature. In one game, for example, candidates try to inflate a balloon without popping it. But these tests are not really *tests*. As Pymetrics stresses, there are no right or wrong answers. If the results suggest a candidate isn't necessarily a natural planner, the conclusion is not that they're "disorganized." Rather, they're "improvisational." The goal is not to rank order the candidates but to determine a jobseeker's cognitive and behavioral traits that make her well suited for the position. Candidates don't get to see how their scores stack up against what their potential employers are looking for, but they do see how they score along the spectrum of each trait. The test is available in twenty languages and is offered in different versions for people with dyslexia, ADHD, and colorblindness, for example.[22] Companies such as Nielsen, LinkedIn, Kraft Heinz, Mastercard, McDonald's, and Accenture have already implemented Pymetrics as a part of their job application process.

But algorithms, in the end, are written by people, and sometimes those people can be biased, whether they're conscious of it or not. That's why Pymetrics developed a bias-detection tool called Audit AI that detects bias in algorithms. It was originally developed to root out bias in the company's own algorithms, which ultimately are used to determine if a candidate is a good fit for a job. Recently, however, Pymetrics open-sourced the tool to help others audit the output of virtually any machine learning technique. Audit AI determines whether a specific statistic or trait fed into an algorithm is being favored or disadvantaged at a statistically significant, systematic rate, leading to adverse impacts on people underrepresented in the data set.

As any executive responsible for diversity and inclusion can attest, rooting out bias and unfairness can be wickedly difficult. Bias is insidious, often unconscious, and sometimes so deeply embedded in processes as to be invisible. Though the initial faith that AI could easily solve the problem has proved naïve, more recent developments in bias detection suggest that the solution lies in more—not less—AI to achieve the fairness that is essential for trust.

Transparency: Peering into the Black Box

The core of the transparency challenge is explainability—the notorious "black box" problem that bedevils machine learning. Systems that employ deep learning are especially opaque. As we saw in chapter 1, it's almost impossible to explain how their algorithms, working with enormous numbers of parameters and layers of abstraction, reach their conclusions. And as we also observed, such systems aren't going away, despite the welcome new approaches to intelligence and data we've been discussing throughout.

Executives across industries have been clamoring for greater explainability. When possible, they want their nontechnical business managers and data scientists alike to be able to understand all the processes and reasoning behind an algorithmic decision. Knowing "why" and "how" can be extraordinarily helpful in preventing ethical and regulatory breaches and justifying decisions to stakeholders, especially as enterprise-level AI algorithms become widespread.[23]

Knowing the "why" and "how" can also help mitigate issues of fairness. Apple came under fire in 2019 when a software developer vented on Twitter about the different credit limits he and his wife were offered with the company's credit card. "My wife and I filed joint tax returns, live in a community-property state, and have been married for a long time," the developer tweeted. "Yet Apple's black box algorithm thinks I deserve 20× the credit limit she does."[24] Financial services regulators in New York State took note and promised to investigate. Had Apple fully understood the algorithm's behavior, the problem might have been avoided.

Explainability doesn't come easily. The power of machine learning lies in doing what people cannot—detecting patterns that sometimes defy human logic or intuition. How can we begin to understand, much less explain, what is really happening with machine learning at a granular level? Even if one could explain how a model is working in language that a data scientist could grasp, explaining it to nontechnical decision makers in plain language can seem like an impossible task.

Nevertheless, some organizations and industries are tackling the black box issue head-on, investing heavily to develop new capabilities to audit and explain machine learning systems. Explainable AI—or XAI for short—are emerging systems with the ability to explain their rationale for decisions, characterize the strengths and weaknesses of their decision-making process, and convey an understanding of how they will behave in the future.

NVIDIA is one such company trying to the push the frontiers of Explainable AI. The chipmaker recently developed a car that can be controlled entirely by a deep-learning algorithm. The company handed out no rulebooks or instructions; it programmed the vehicle's computer to match input from several video cameras with the behavior of a human driver and teach itself how to drive. The computer learned by observing. But a question nagged at NVIDIA. How was the computer doing this? And why?

To answer those questions, NVIDIA engineers tried to get the vehicle to explain its driving style—visually. NVIDIA's researchers developed a neural network architecture to allow the system to highlight the parts of a video picture that contributed most strongly to the behavior of the car's deep neural network.[25] The results showed that the network focused on the edges of roads, lane markings, and parked cars—the same things a good human driver would pay attention to.[26] Interestingly, NVIDIA never directly told the network to care about these things.

"Think about why you recognize a face in a photo, and then try to break that down into a set of specific rules that you can program—you can't do it," says Urs Muller, chief architect for self-driving cars at NVIDIA.[27] "The question thus becomes: 'Do we want to limit our solutions to only the things we can define with rules?'"

Meanwhile, other large companies, including Google and IBM, are investing in the capability to audit and explain machine learning systems. IBM has developed a cloud-based AI tool that shows users which major factors determined an AI-based recommendation, and in the process is hoping to identify in real time issues like inherent bias.[28]

One effort to create Explainable AI is happening at the governmental level: DARPA is currently funding a program whose goal is to interpret the deep learning that powers drones and intelligence-mining operations.

DARPA's Explainable AI is trying to address two discrete problems. The first is to better understand why machine-learning models sometimes behave in unanticipated ways. The second is to determine how AI systems can better communicate what they do with humans.

According to Dave Gunning, program manager for the DARPA initiative, they hope that Explainable AI methods will be able to help generate both "local" and "global" explanations. "Local" explanations would lay out individual decisions made by an AI system, while "global" explanations would detail the general logic behind the behavior of the AI model.[29]

A part of the solution is "more deep learning," says Gunning.[30] There would be one deep learning system trained to make the decisions and then a second deep learning system to generate the explanation. Regardless of the approach, Explainable AI will be vitally important for building trust in a technology that is revolutionizing everything from pharmaceuticals to plant operations.

Privacy: "A Fundamental Human Right"

Back in 2015, Apple CEO Tim Cook famously declared, "Privacy is a fundamental human right."[31] As each new product comes out—a credit card, a news service, a premium TV channel service, or a new app in the App Store—Apple emphasizes how each product was built from the ground up with consumer privacy in mind. What's more, Apple explicitly links maintaining privacy to innovation.

For instance, the privacy features of Apple devices are a virtual blueprint of technology innovation strategy that draws on key elements of an IDEAS approach. Take the photos app. Many such apps and services process and organize your photos in the cloud. The Apple photos app uses machine learning to organize photos right on your Mac, iPhone, or iPad, rendering the sharing of photos with Apple unnecessary. This approach to architecture brings the power of the cloud to the edge through the Apple Neural Engine in a chip on the device. The chip performs 100 billion operations per photo to recognize faces and places without ever leaving your device.

The iPhone is one of the most effective data collection and retention devices on the planet. Smartphones have the power to gather massive amounts of data about us—from where we've been and the routes we took to get there to what websites we've visited and apps we've used (and probably will visit and use in the future). But with each new release of Apple's iOS, the company's developers make it harder and harder for third parties to gather data from users and profit from it. Apple's Safari browser, for example, was the first browser to block third-party cookies by default. Safari also lets you manage whether websites can gain access to your camera and microphone, a unique feature.

For iOS 11 and MacOS High Sierra, Apple introduced Intelligent Tracking Prevention, a feature designed to prevent advertisers from tracking users' clicks and searches. For iOS 12, Apple took privacy protection one step further, wresting the unique characteristics of our devices away from advertisers' tracking software.[32] All told, the iPhone has built-in privacy features that other web browsers don't offer. In addition to advanced security features such as security code autofill, password reuse auditing, and automatic password generation, iOS 13 offers a new privacy setting that shows users what apps are using their Bluetooth data and giving them the ability to shut off those apps' access to their Bluetooth connection.[33]

To be sure, Apple still collects user data. Like many tech companies, Apple uses AI to collect personal details about users as they engage with the company's devices and software. The aim is to improve the user experience. But to prevent unconstrained gathering of user data, Apple employs what is called local differential privacy,[34] among other privacy-preserving machine learning (PPML) techniques we touched on in chapter 4. To mask the individual user's identity, statistical noise is injected into data before that data ever leaves the device. But if many people are submitting the same data, the statistical noise that has been added averages out over large numbers of data points and Apple can glean meaningful, but anonymized, information. The company learns what large groups of users are doing without learning anything about individuals.

Apple maintains privacy throughout the data collection and analysis process. It removes device identifiers from the data, which it transmits over an encrypted channel. The Apple analysis system takes in the differentially private contributions, dropping IP addresses and other metadata. The privatized records show only the relevant statistics, and only then are the aggregate statistics shared with relevant Apple teams.

As a company that sells physical products at a high premium, Apple can afford to have an ethos of protecting privacy. Its business model doesn't hinge on collecting and monetizing consumer data. But we are starting to see other companies take bold stances on privacy protection, passing up opportunities to monetize information about their customers.

Consider the case of Sonos. Our homes have become the latest frontier in trust. In the age of smart speakers equipped with voice assistants, app-activated thermostats, and internet-connected home devices, companies are harvesting more and more data that could prove valuable to product designers, advertisers, governments, and law enforcement. A range of interest groups, from civil liberties organizations to consumer advocates and children's privacy watchdogs, have raised sharp questions about this potential erosion of privacy.

With this in mind, Sonos in 2019 introduced a new internet-connected speaker—the Sonos One SL—that doesn't have an internal microphone. The Sonos SL can't react to voice commands in the way other smart speakers can, nor can it listen to what people are saying in the privacy of their homes. "There is a group of people who just don't want microphones in their house," Sonos' chief executive officer Patrick Spence explained. "We thought it was a good opportunity to . . . give peace of mind to people that want it."[35]

There is also the case of Simcam, an in-home security system that uses an "intelligent edge" approach to AI to provide privacy. A key point of value for a home security system is its cameras' ability to detect events or objects and trigger a security response. The Simcam camera performs all facial recognition on the device itself, rather than sending data to the cloud for analysis. Simcam's cameras use Intel's Movidius Visual Processing Unit (VPU), and analysis is run locally using Intel's hardware. This gives customers control and privacy—and fosters trust.

How seriously do people take technology-related privacy? A survey conducted by the Future of Humanity Institute, housed at the University of Oxford, queried more than 2,000 Americans on their attitudes to AI. Among thirteen AI governance issues, two of the top four concerns of those surveyed were "preventing AI-assisted surveillance from violating privacy and civil liberties" and "protecting data privacy."[36]

Security: As Fragile as Trust Itself

On November 24, 2014, hackers, likely sponsored by the government of North Korea, began releasing a trove of confidential information about Sony Pictures, including personal information about employees and their families, embarrassing internal emails, executives' salaries, copies of then-unreleased films, and more.[37] Malware rendered many employees' computers inoperable and wiped the company's computer infrastructure. In December, the hackers demanded that Sony withdraw its upcoming film *The Interview*, a comedy starring James Franco and Seth Rogen about a plot to assassinate North Korean leader Kim Jong-un, and threatened terrorist attacks on theaters that screened it. Sony curtailed wide release of the film. A number of former Sony employees sued the company for failing to protect their personal information.

During the crisis, the studio called in FireEye, one of the world's leading cybersecurity firms. After Russian hackers breached several US federal agencies in 2015, the government likewise turned to FireEye. So did Equifax, the consumer credit reporting company, when information on nearly 150 million people was compromised in 2017. But in late 2020, in one of the great ironies of the internet age, FireEye itself was hacked. A "nation with top-tier offensive capabilities" stole the company's cybersecurity tools.[38] The tools, which FireEye uses to look for vulnerabilities in its clients' systems, mimic the world's most sophisticated hacking tools.

It turns out that the internet is as fragile as trust itself. The number of external links an organization has with others, and the volume and sources of data that flow through those connections, continues to grow exponentially. The number of vulnerabilities has grown accordingly.

This includes fish tanks. A casino in North America had an internet-connected fish tank that fed the fish automatically and monitored their environment. Hackers used the fish tank's internet connection to break into its feeding monitor and then use this as an entry point into the company's systems. The data was then sent to hackers in Finland.[39]

These attacks erode trust and threaten the entire internet-enabled digital economy. In 2007, there were 1.2 billion internet users; by 2020, there were nearly 5 billion—more than 63 percent of the global population.[40] The total installed base of IoT connected devices is projected to amount to 21.5 billion units worldwide by 2025.[41] And that figure includes only active nodes, devices, or gateways that concentrate the end-sensors, rather than consumer devices such as computers and cellphones. Every connected device, or "endpoint," is a potential vulnerability.

And when vulnerabilities get exploited, the results can be disastrous. For example, the 2017 NotPetya cyberattack cost shipping company

Maersk more than $300 million, and the damages to all other companies affected totaled more than $10 billion.[42] That same year, the WannaCry cyberattack on the United Kingdom National Health Service (NHS) ultimately cost almost £100 million.[43] In one recent attack believed to be sponsored by Russia, hackers managed to install malware in an update of SolarWind's Orion network-monitoring software, which was then downloaded by thousands of clients—compromising top federal agencies as well as hundreds of private companies.

Covid-19 accelerated these trends. As social distancing measures took effect, cyberattacks increased globally, driven by virtual work, overwhelmed IT departments, and millions of untrained users of remote-work technology.[44] Additionally, some organizations, faced with disruptions in their supply chains, resorted to alternative suppliers whose vulnerable cybersecurity practices opened up new avenues of attack.

The continued growth of the digital economy depends on the ability of companies to protect their operations and their customers' digital information. Security can't be an "add-on" feature for products and services. Fortunately, some promising AI technologies will enable companies to make security a prominent part of their value propositions.

Consider the use of predictive analytics by the Goldman Sachs-based startup CYFIRMA, which uses predictive analysis for cybersecurity. Led by Kumar Ritesh, a former member of the British intelligence service, CYFIRMA is using virtual agents to gather intelligence on potential cyberattacks that are being coordinated in underground forums before they occur. Cyber threat intelligence feeds may include data such as IP blacklists, malware hashes and signatures, malicious and phishing URLs, vulnerability lists, indicators of compromise (IOCs) such as IP addresses that suggest a breach has occurred, and command and control (C2) domains that are used to orchestrate attacks.[45] But to Ritesh, most threat intelligence is too reactive. "If intelligence is not predictive, it's not intelligence," he told TechTarget.[46]

With the cybersecurity market growing at a rate of 10 percent a year,[47] Ritesh saw an opportunity to enter the fray with a highly differentiated offering. Ritesh and his team created hundreds of virtual AI agents to silently—and covertly—listen in on conversations going on between cyber criminals in the deep and dark webs, hackers' forums, peer-to-peer groups, and other underground communities. The agents' job is to listen for any mention of a client's name, industry, or geolocation. When there's a "hit," the virtual agents capture those bits of data and funnel them back into the cloud-based, AI-powered platform.

Human cybersecurity experts train the models as well as read and react to cyber-threat situations as they develop. Instead of the data-hungry approaches to intelligence that drive machine learning, CYFIRMA is pursuing a data-efficient, highly contextualized approach that more closely resembles human intelligence. Instead of relying on ever-bigger data to build AI systems, they are leveraging smaller, highly focused, and limited datasets.

People lose trust in a company's data security for myriad reasons. For instance, many companies too often find themselves in a defensive crouch and react mode, which is often too little, too late. The approach taken by CYFIRMA upends the approach to threat intelligence and takes a more offensive, aggressive, preventive approach to cybercrime, using the same technologies that comprise companies' data integrity.

Operationalizing Trust

Humanity, fairness, transparency, privacy, security—it is these five attributes that companies must put into practice in the digital age, when intelligent technologies have the capacity to do good as well as harm on a vast scale. It's no longer a matter of making promises of trust in corporate communications or urging employees to do nothing that would compromise the company's good name. The explosion of intelligent technologies has made addressing trust a matter of operationalizing it throughout the organization. With these technologies deeply woven into your company's processes, products, and services, trust is not only an ethical concern, but a technical challenge. To excel at cementing trust with stakeholders, you can begin by making sure that the radically human essentials of trust permeate each element of IDEAS as you adopt and deploy its new approaches to technology:

- **Intelligence.** AI that mimics human ways of thinking and feeling makes employees comfortable using it and puts customers at ease when they encounter it directly. In addition, provably unbiased algorithms and explainable results are mutually reinforcing, inspiring confidence in your trustworthiness among employees, customers, regulators, and citizens alike.

- **Data.** As with unbiased algorithms and explainable results, the way you treat stakeholder data is another opportunity to marry trust with technology. The more that stakeholders trust you to keep their personal information secure and private, the more such information they are likely to share with you, strengthening their bond with your organization.

- **Expertise.** When non-technical people and employees at all levels of the organization have the power to directly impose their knowledge on AI and other intelligent systems, they not only come to trust the technology but trust that the company values their unique abilities.

- **Architecture.** System architecture designed to be adaptable and accessible across business functions ensures greater fairness among employees. For customers and members of your wider business ecosystem, security is paramount. As cyberattacks continue and grow increasingly sophisticated, security remains challenging for many organizations. Organizations that master it have the opportunity to powerfully differentiate themselves along this indispensable dimension of trust.

- **Strategy**. Strategies that employ intelligent technologies to deliver value in novel ways such as Forever Beta, MVI, and Co-lab, can exponentially increase their appeal by making trust a fundamental feature of the offering.

The common thread in these practices is the mutually reinforcing dynamic between trust and technology, humans and machines, values and value. The more trustworthy the technology, the more enthusiastically it will be embraced, creating a virtuous circle of adoption and innovation among employees and partners, of purchase and loyalty among customers, and of support and confidence among investors.

Ignoring trust or treating it as a nice-to-have is not an option in the digital age. New technologies raise issues of trust as never before, and platformization has put technology at the center of company operations. To truly differentiate on trust, you have to deliver. Trustworthiness may be a value you proclaim, but for stakeholders it's an experience, rooted in our most radically human instincts and it is that experience, not what you say, that will determine whether they trust you.

In chapter 8, we widen the lens to look at a wide array of experiences that intelligent technologies have made possible for individuals, customers, and employees. Leading organizations are redesigning digital experiences with new models that amplify personal agency, turn passive audiences into active participants, and transform one-way experiences into true collaborations. But people don't want their experiences overly determined for them without their knowledge. They are asking enterprises to be their partners—to work with them to create experiences, help them reach their goals, and give them the option to change the experience when a company gets it wrong. As we will see, it's a new model that goes beyond traditional customization to sharing of power and control in the relationship, offering nearly unlimited possibilities for differentiation.

8

EXPERIENCES

The Difference Radically
Human-Centered Design Makes

In 2015, NASA announced a zero-g coffee cup designed so astronauts could smell the coffee they're drinking rather than just sipping scent-free from a pouch with a straw. The new design is a clear plastic vessel that looks a little like a boot with a spout that doesn't form a full tube so that it's open along its length at the top. This way, when an astronaut slurps through the spout, the coffee, adhering to the edges of the cup and being pulled toward the astronaut's mouth, is exposed to air where volatile molecules that carry that wake-you-up smell pass close enough to the nose so that the astronaut can catch a whiff.[1]

The difference between the scent-free pouch and the aroma-enriched cup is the difference between efficiency-first engineering and radically human-centered design. Efficiency-first engineering is not to be scorned. It has been the basis of technological progress for centuries. But it frequently leaves the human out of account, producing experiences that can seem soulless, or even worse, alienating. As we have said, yesterday's rigid systems forced humans to adapt to technology. In contrast, today's living systems, relying heavily on AI, *adapt to humans.*

Radically human-centered design gives us the ability to "stop and smell the coffee" (literally, in NASA's case), providing richly human experiences. As with talent and trust, the upsetting of assumptions about intelligence, data, expertise, and architecture—and their convergence in strategy—has opened up dramatically new possibilities for experiences for customers and employees alike.

Companies are getting the message, as a recent survey conducted by Accenture indicates. Encompassing more than 1,550 top executives worldwide, 25 percent of whom were CEOs, and covering twenty-one countries and twenty-two industries, the research was designed to study the way that business leaders considered their customers' experiences and how their companies' capabilities contributed to experiences and business outcomes. Seventy-seven percent of CEOs said their company will fundamentally change the way it engages and interacts with its customers.[2]

Getting Started

By designing radically human experiences that leverage the IDEAS framework, companies are pushing past traditional notions of customer experience to a more expansive notion of experiences that includes employees, and sharply differentiates the company from the competition. The business of experiences goes far beyond familiar customer touchpoints, includes employees, and sharply differentiates the company from the competition. The difference shows up on the bottom line: our researchers found that, on average, companies that have adopted a more expansive approach to experiences grow their profitability year-on-year by at least six-fold over their industry peers.[3]

The journey begins with three R's: replatforming, reframing, and reach.

Replatforming means fully committing to the cloud—not merely lifting and shifting some of your IT functions. From games to vehicle autonomy to customer interactions and much more, the cloud's computational power and flexibility make it possible to deliver experiences at scale and to continually improve the quality and depth of those experiences. Cloud-edge architectures provide the crucial ability to marry that computational power to the edge devices like smartphones, smart speakers, and smart vehicles through which people can access experiences. Our researchers found that 58 percent of today's leading companies say they can define and deliver new digital capabilities with agility (versus just 25 percent of their peers), a feat that would be almost impossible without the right kinds of platforms.[4]

Reframing requires shifting your organization's mindset about technology. Technology should not be seen as a mere facilitator of more efficient transactions and smooth touchpoints, but the driver of innovation. For example, the capabilities offered by cloud hyperscalers include programs that nontechnical employees can use to create innovative customer experiences as well as innovative internal processes, meanwhile increasing their own experience of agency and empowerment. As we found in our technology surveys, leaders direct a greater percentage of their IT budget toward innovation, and they accelerate their investments in innovation faster than other organizations. So do the leapfroggers, those previously middling companies that made giant strides during the pandemic.

Reach means moving beyond traditional business priorities to exceptional customer and employee experiences and new value propositions. Those companies that differentiate themselves on experiences don't think only in terms of smoothing the traditional "customer journey" from initial interest to conversion and loyalty. They also seek to do more by delivering engaging and meaningful experiences inside and outside the organization. Replatforming and reframing are the prerequisites for differentiating on experiences, but it is reach—moving decisively beyond customer experience to a more inclusive and expanded notion of experiences, for customers and employees alike—that will drive the most successful companies that choose to compete in this arena.

Four Types of Radically Human Experiences for the Digital Age

Experiences enabled by human-centered, IDEAS-enabled design can be as varied as the industries in which they're found. A great experience is defined not by what you offer but by how well you enable people to achieve the outcomes most important to them. Four types of such experiences suggest the wide range of possibilities:

- *Empowering experiences* give people access to activities that might otherwise be out of reach.

- *Rewarding experiences* foster personal growth, deliver fun, and are often satisfyingly collaborative.

- *Tuned-in experiences* are engaging and effortless. They feel "just-right," attuned to the individual's needs, attitude, or sensibility.

- *Responsible experiences* point beyond the individual to what is best for the community and the larger world.

Alone or in combination, these types of experiences tap into some of our most compelling human aspirations and interests: desires for mastery, growth, effortless engagement, and connection with something larger than ourselves. There can also be significant overlap among these tech-enabled experiences. A *tuned-in* tech experience with, for instance, a chatbot that knows just what to say, can also be *empowering* in that it enables an activity that might not have been possible otherwise, and *responsible* in that it respects an individual's privacy.

Empowering Experiences

The humble curb cut—the small ramp built into the curb of a sidewalk—illustrates the potential of human-centered design to democratize access to activities and opportunities that might otherwise be out of reach for many people. Mandated by the Americans with Disabilities Act (ADA), curb cuts make it easier for people using wheelchairs to pass from sidewalk to road. And as often happens with human-centered designs, the benefits of curb cuts soon became apparent for parents with strollers and people with grocery carts or luggage. When the determination to empower people is married to IDEAS-based innovation, the results can be truly inspiring and, as with curb cuts, often prove useful for people for whom they were not originally intended.

Driving Longer and More Safely

Demographically, Japan is one of the world's oldest countries. Thirty percent of its population is over sixty-five years of age. Prior to the pandemic, Japan saw a rash of automobile accidents involving older drivers. Subsequently, many older drivers gave up their licenses. Hundreds of thousands did so in 2019 alone. But when the pandemic arrived and public transportation ceased to be a safe option for travel, many of those former drivers found themselves suddenly and truly isolated.

Fortunately, companies are now considering ways that cars themselves can safely keep older motorists driving longer—empowering them to retain their geographic mobility. Toyota, for one, is offering an upgrade to its Safety Sense technology designed to minimize or prevent front collisions and keep drivers in their lanes. It uses bumper and windscreen-mounted high-resolution cameras to detect oncoming cars, pedestrians, and bicyclists in daylight hours. Image-recognition

AI gives audio and visual alerts if there's danger. Failure to respond to the alerts triggers the automatic brakes.

"A society in which the elderly can drive safely is crucial for their active social participation and healthier, fuller lives," says Toyota. "Our ultimate goal is, of course, to have zero casualties from traffic accidents."[5]

Web for All

In 2019, Apple released a film called *See*, a sci-fi drama set in the future where almost all humans are blind. The online trailer for the film features audio descriptions of the trailer's visuals.[6] In the opening scene, you'll not only hear dramatic music, but also hear a description of the scene as it unfolds. Audio description is a feature available for supported content on most Apple products, empowering blind or visually impaired users to enjoy a more robust audio experience of visual content like movies, TV shows, and commercials.

For someone who is visually impaired, navigating the internet for basic needs, let alone enjoying movies or other entertainment, is almost always a challenge. But, as audio descriptions illustrate, the means exist to make it easier. Thanks to disability activists, more companies have begun to pay attention to making the web more accessible. When the Americans with Disabilities Act was passed in 1990, it didn't explicitly address the digital sphere. But recent lawsuits have challenged companies to make websites accessible to people who are blind and use screen readers and those with motor impairments who use a simplified keyboard. A more accessible web means screen readers can read and convert content to audio, empowering people with disabilities to, for instance, listen to a menu or explore a retail site and order online.

The mission of the startup Evinced is to help companies revamp websites so that they are accessible to people with disabilities.[7] This process has previously been done manually, usually with the help of consultants using a patchwork of tools—an approach that doesn't scale.

Meanwhile, many automated accessibility testing tools are woefully inadequate, returning high accessibility scores when, in fact, many major problems remain.[8]

Evinced has created a new kind of automatic testing engine and validations that use AI and computer vision to take into account how a web page actually appears rather than evaluating only its underlying code. For example, someone who is visually impaired may not even know that a drop-down menu is available. Evinced's technology tools create a semantic structural model of a page partially based on its visual design, rather than relying on JavaScript to evaluate code syntax and functionality rendered in the browser.[9] Backed by Microsoft's venture fund M12, and Capital One Ventures, Evinced can license its products to build new platforms or assess existing ones for compliance.

Companies that find and fix the problems in web architectures that aren't designed for all can not only deliver an empowering experience, but also achieve a substantial payoff. According to Forrester, people with disabilities collectively account for $1 trillion of annual disposable income worldwide.[10] And when you consider that research shows friends and family of people with disabilities often prefer to do business with brands that care about accessibility, that amount grows to $8 trillion.

Giving Employees Agency

The employee experience is just as critical as the customer experience. McDonald's knows this well, which is why the fast-food giant is giving employees more control over their workplace experience. The company is rolling out digital ordering kiosks in its drive-throughs across the United States, featuring personalized menus and recommendations based on weather, time of day, trending menu items, and customers' past purchases. But McDonald's is relying on employees to make the tech work better for customers.

Rather than having the company prescribe the menu based on centralized data, employees are given the freedom to change menu displays based on local circumstances. They can use live traffic data and observational insights to identify peak times, and switch the menu recommendations to promote simpler items, easing the burden on employees and restaurant operations. At first glance, this might seem like typical customization. But what McDonald's does differently is make the individual—in this case the employee—an active and necessary contributor to the experience.

This is an important strategy, given fears of job replacement surrounding AI investments. McDonald's has repeatedly said, in fact, that adding AI-powered kiosks will not result in mass layoffs, but instead will transition back-of-the-house positions to more customer service roles such as "concierges" and even table service.

The move by McDonald's represents a powerful shift from the norm. Throughout the digital age, companies have built customization and technology services on top of their offerings, adding value to the customer experience. However, this has increasingly committed companies to the same limited path: inadvertently taking control away from people in the name of greater curation. But companies like McDonald's know that competing on experiences is as much about employees as it is about customers.

Munters is another organization that has reimagined the employee experience.[11] The maker of energy-efficient air treatment and cooling systems for industrial and agricultural applications found that onsite client visits were difficult during the pandemic. So, they enabled engineers to use mixed reality, powered by Vuzix Smart Glasses, to collaborate remotely with clients via real-time video, images, gestures, real objects, and more. The glasses could be plugged into their enterprise resource planning (ERP) and asset management systems by technology partner IFS Cloud, powered by Azure. Today, this experience is used by more than 200 Munters engineers worldwide.

The Canada Mortgage and Housing Corporation (CMHC), Canada's national housing agency, is another case in point.[12] Believing that homes provide the foundation and stability for people to participate more fully in society, the CMHC aims to see that by 2030, everyone in Canada will have a home they can afford and that meets their needs. But outdated systems—including nearly 1,000 software applications—were preventing CMHC from adapting to the digital age and limited the effectiveness of its employees. The organization's subsequent business and technology transformation (undertaken with the help of our firm) illustrates how replatforming and reframing not only leads to improved client experiences but more rewarding experiences for employees.

For example, the elimination of siloes—including between commercial and non-commercial operations—enabled more employees to track and measure overall client relationships. As a result, employees can now assess if a client could be better served by another product or service than the one for which they originally approached CMHC. New processes replaced manual work, such as for underwriting mortgage insurance, while the company's workforce became more collaborative and fully mobile. They were also given more autonomy and flexibility to innovate and be productive. And a new set of technologies built on a cloud platform provides real-time insights on clients and the housing market.

CMHC's cross-functional initiatives also supported the launch of thirteen new housing programs as part of the country's first-ever National Housing Strategy. This effort to strengthen the middle class and cut chronic homelessness in half provides an experience for employees that is not only empowering, but also rewarding, illustrating the often-overlapping nature of meaningful experiences facilitated by today's technology.

Rewarding Experiences

You don't need to be a formally trained musician to write and produce a song. OpenAI's MuseNet is an AI that collaborates with people to make music. It works this way: you give the software a starting sample, a target style, and instrument preferences. MuseNet then uses what it has learned from thousands of musical files to make suggestions about what should come next in the song. You then give it feedback, and the process continues until a new musical composition has been created.

Collaborating with AI (and, by extension, with musicians whose music trained the AI) can be a rewarding experience for young musicians—it can stretch novices beyond their prior capabilities and produce a finished product that wouldn't have been possible otherwise. It's fun, it's collaborative, and it fosters personal growth.

Hybrid Worlds

In March 2020, sales for Nintendo's popular Switch console more than doubled compared to sales the previous year.[13] This phenomenal growth was spurred, in part, by the release of the exceedingly popular and soothing game *Animal Crossing: New Horizons*. The world-exploring game became an instant balm for many who felt the real world becoming increasingly dangerous. In the midst of a global pandemic, *Animal Crossing* offered a locus of control and a calm place to focus attention. Similarly, Peloton, the at-home fitness company that offers streaming classes, saw a 172 percent surge in sales during 2020 as more than 1 million people signed up.[14]

Creative digital worlds like *Animal Crossing* and mixed-reality worlds like those of an at-home gym with expert instruction provide rewarding experiences. Peloton, for instance, recognized the importance of integrating social elements with its digital/real-world workouts: you can see other users in live classes and see friends in competitions.[15] Obé

Fitness, another at-home exercise streaming platform, has also seen a boom in membership over the past two years, with users "congregating" to chat before and after classes and in some cases even staying for after-workout, on-screen cocktails.[16]

All three of these companies are leveraging architecture to provide scalable, simultaneous digital or hybrid experiences to their customers. In the cases of Peloton and Obé Fitness, experts work in real time to foster community among customers as well as to instruct them. In early 2021, Peloton also acquired three AI companies, giving it the capability to further enhance its customer's workout and everyday experiences through smart wearables, voice assistants, and interactive workout mats.[17]

Epic Games, creator of the popular shooter game *Fortnite*, is another well-known leader in using advanced architecture to provide seamless online experiences to customers. The company's software framework, called the Unreal Engine, can support more than 8 million unique users simultaneously. In addition, the company's analytics pipeline streams gigabytes of data to the cloud, leveraging tools like Amazon Kinesis, Apache Spark, and Tableau to capture (and make sense of) up to forty gigabytes of game data every minute. This data feeds into Epic's multi-terabyte databases, from which developers glean key insights into customer behaviors, engagement, and satisfaction.

The Unreal Engine is a powerful tool that's useful beyond the gaming industry—a key part of Epic's strategy. The architecture firm HOK uses the Unreal Engine to showcase interactive designs to clients, offering a dynamic, immersive environment that integrates elements from multiple sources to make the world feel more real. Finnish airline Finnair has used the software framework to build a digital twin of the Helsinki Airport. The company used this precise rendering to build virtual reality experiences, such as situational awareness training for ground crews, and to familiarize airplane staff with cabin layouts and key functions.[18]

In a similar mixed-reality vein, retailers are beginning to offer virtual fitting rooms. The apparel company Men's Wearhouse has unveiled "Next-Gen" store locations in Shenandoah, Texas, and Buford, Georgia.

These stores feature an AI system that takes two photos to determine a customer's size and then allows him to visualize fabrics and a variety of style combinations. The stores are also equipped with interactive touchscreens that let customers pick their style, fit, and color from in-store and online inventory and easily add clothing to their "virtual fitting room," with store associates bringing them items to try on.

"We know that menswear retail is changing rapidly, driven by customers who are digitally connected, in control, and expecting zero friction as they engage in digital and physical environments—often simultaneously," says the company's chief customer officer Carrie Ask.[19]

Today, you can even build your own augmented-reality (AR) world to suit your needs—even if you don't have coding skills. No-code development platforms—drag-and-drop interfaces that anyone, technical or not, can use to create custom apps—can boost productivity within organizations, enabling more people in your organization to create the large volumes of content needed to offer customers more options for customizing their experiences. And these platforms can help customers design and personalize apps or experiences themselves. Amazon Sumerian lets people build their own AR, virtual reality, or 3D applications without any programming or 3D graphics expertise. Anyone with Sumerian can build immersive environments and experiences, like classrooms or building tours, and can populate them with 3D objects and animated characters.[20] For both employees and customers, these tools enable users to directly impose their expertise—the E in IDEAS—to create highly personalized, rewarding experiences.

Tuned-In Experiences

Since the dawn of toolmaking, humans have aimed to make tools as useful and as helpful as possible, compatible with our bodies and our needs and wants. Nearly three millennia ago, in the *Odyssey*, Homer described sea-faring vessels that were controlled by some sort of centralized system with access to a vast data archive of "virtual" maps and navigation charts of the entire ancient world. The ships were unsinkable, unflagging, and could weather any storm. Autonomous, but connected to the humans who use them, these ships, according to King Alcinous, "understand what we are thinking about and want."[21]

It's a fascinating premonition of things to come. We now have GPS systems built into cars as well as autonomous features that keep people safer and allow for longer journeys. Advanced "vessels" like these are a boon, but they also create human-oriented design challenges like motion sickness. Vehicle autonomy allows drivers and passengers to shift their attention to activities like reading, but it's well known that if your attention strays from watching the twists and turns of the road, you're more likely to experience nausea or vomiting. At Volvo, engineers are experimenting with an audio cue that hits passenger's ears about a second before the vehicle turns or accelerates. Unlike an obtrusive voice prompt, the cue resembles the sounds an automobile engine makes. It is intended to subtly prepare passengers for the change in motion, prompting them to change posture. Trials show that when the audio cues were used passengers felt less sick.[22]

Autonomous vehicles are still a nascent technology, and motion sickness might seem like a small problem. But Volvo knows that because new technologies like driverless cars often meet stiff resistance, considering small comforts can go a long way in advancing adoption. The technologies that take off in the future will be those designed to be tuned-in to their users.

It Just Knows

Ever wonder how TikTok exploded into popularity? Its recommendation system plays a major role. The short-form video platform's parent company ByteDance developed recommendation algorithms that plug into almost every app the company creates. Its recommender is built based on the activities of tens of millions of users of Toutiao, a news app popular in China years before the Chinese version of TikTok, called Douyin, even became available. The system is also continually updated.

The company's recommender never slows down. TikTok videos range from fifteen to sixty seconds in length, allowing a user to watch 60 to 240 videos in an hour. Compare this to YouTube, where average video length is five to eight minutes, allowing a user to watch about ten videos an hour. Essentially, TikTok's recommender gets more data, faster, so it can serve up more tuned-in videos to further refine its algorithms. The videos, with their watermark, are also designed for easy sharing and to bring people back to the platform when videos are shared on other social media channels like Instagram and Twitter.[23]

Recommender algorithms that "just know" are one of many ways that IDEAS-based technologies are being used to create tuned-in experiences. Chatbots that provide quality conversations are another. Research suggests that making chatbots too smart alienates users, but if they're too dim, people aren't much interested in using them.[24] In other words, users judge chatbots in terms of both warmth and competence (just as they judge people and companies, as we saw in chapter 7). Designers must therefore walk a fine line in determining the just-right setting for a chatbot. The research also suggests that design teams should include people from a wider range of backgrounds to teach chatbots—writers or actors, for example, who are experienced in recognizing subtle tone shifts and how conversational style reveals personality traits. Eventually, users themselves could be able to modify the level of a chatbot's conversation by choosing a preference at the start of an interaction.

Not Your Father's Muzak

A composer of more than sixty soundtracks has teamed up with a co-creator of Siri, Apple's personal assistant, to develop AI software that not only tracks emotions, as emotional AI does, but enhances them with music. In the famed Abbey Road studios in London, composer Phil Sheppard works with top-flight musicians to compose and record musical building blocks—not computer-generated sounds, but music played by real performers on real instruments. These snippets of musical phrases are then processed by an AI platform that generates a personal soundtrack that adapts to the listener's environment and inputs—a soundtrack that is unique each time you engage it.

Says the former Apple executive Tom Gruber, "It's early days to say exactly how this thing works, but we're opening up the possibility to have music adapt to any human signals. We're just beginning to learn from the human data, from the data of how humans respond. It's kind of like the early days of biofeedback."[25]

Called LifeScore, the system's software and bank of musical building blocks are managed in the cloud. That allows the company to deploy the service within any physical space or on any desktop, mobile device, or hardware. The aim is to license it to industries that could enhance their offerings with adaptive music—video game companies, automakers, wellness apps, and streaming services. For instance, video games often feature various musical sequences that recur throughout the game, eventually becoming repetitive. LifeScore, by contrast, is capable of thousands of hours of emotionally appropriate music that doesn't repeat itself.

LifeScore decidedly isn't Muzak (now called Mood Media), the venerable service that produces saccharine, lowest common denominator versions of vaguely familiar music and pipes it into elevators, stores, and other businesses. But where Muzak operates in the background, lulling the listener with a canned playlist, LifeScore means to engage listeners with foregrounded music that they, in effect, create themselves through their emotions and environment.

One of its first public applications came recently on *Artificial*, an Emmy award-winning, live audience-interactive sci-fi series on Twitch, the live video streaming service operated by a subsidiary of Amazon. The show follows the adventures of an AI-being on a quest to become human. The audience interacts directly with the characters in the show to transform the story, actively participate in it through live

Q&A and story-driven polls, and even create new characters in special episodes.

In the third season, which premiered in May 2020, the audience gained the ability to collectively shift the emotion and intensity of the music through LifeScore. But viewers don't directly focus on influencing the music. Instead, they simply engage in live chat as they normally would. LifeScore looks at the chat for keywords that indicate how the audience feels and then adapts the music to that collective sentiment. As the story unfolds, and sentiments change, the music continues to adapt.

For personal as opposed to collective soundtracks, the company sees LifeScore adapting to information about the physical environment and getting the user into a desired state of focus, relaxation, or mindfulness. It might also create immersive musical experiences in any physical or digital space for any product that adapts to measurable inputs like color, flavor, smell, or touch. Or on one of those long car trips, where the highway mile markers pass in numbing succession, it might provide a nonrepetitive musical experience that keeps the driver continually energized.

Education at Scale

One of Stanford's most popular online classes is called Code in Place that, in a recent semester, enrolled more than 12,000 students from 148 countries. In an experiment, researchers at the university unleashed a well-trained AI to critique student coding work. So far, student evaluations have been exceedingly positive. "We've deployed this in the real world, and it works better than we expected," Chelsea Finn, a Stanford professor and AI researcher who helped build the new system, told the *New York Times*.[26]

Part of the system's success hinges on its immense data records specific to the course. For more than a decade, the class has been populated by thousands of students who take a midterm test that includes numerous and various programming challenges. Stanford's digital records of those results, which include student code as well as human expertise in the form of instructor critiques, were used to train the AI, while additional coding problems and critiques were added for the most recent semester. In spring of 2021, the system provided 16,000 critiques. Students agreed with the feedback 97.9 percent of the time, slightly higher than the rate of student agreement with human critiques at 96.7 percent.

The class is a case of intelligent systems and data coming together to create a new experience for students and instructors alike. Students get more pointed feedback than they normally would in such a large class, and instructors aren't burdened with the task of grading mountains of code. It's unlikely that the automated critiques will completely replace instructors, but it points to a future where, with enough structured data, systems can be built to give excellent and useful support to students on increasingly large scales, while helping to minimize teacher burnout.[27]

While Stanford's online course offerings are breaking new ground with automated feedback, the online education provider Coursera is using its massive stores of data and AI to help broaden educational opportunities. The education software company taps expertise with its human-in-the-loop design and data and intelligence for individualized learning pathways for its students. The company has also expanded its auto-captioning capabilities and translation, both of which are improving accessibility for a variety of people globally.[28]

In the depths of the pandemic, education all over the world went remote. The sudden shift created opportunities for instructors, educational institutions, and technology providers to consider the most important, human-forward features they want designed into their platforms. Those who recognized the potential of their own data, instructor expertise, and platform flexibility are zooming ahead of the competition and are better positioned to lead the way to more hybrid models of education in the future.

Responsible Experiences

The food scientists at Impossible Burger have accomplished something that few thought achievable just five years ago: a plant-based burger that is virtually indistinguishable from meat. The key is the heme-containing protein at the root of soy plants. Scientists produce the protein by inserting its DNA into genetically engineered yeast, in effect brewing the burger. But to achieve a texture and flavor that truly mimics meat, scientists turned to AI to churn through innumerable ingredient combinations for the most viable solutions.[29] One food scientist likened the approach of composing the right flavors with the help of AI to "playing a piano with 5,000 keys."[30]

One major impact of designing more palatable and widely available plant-based "meats" is the reduction of global carbon emissions. A 2019 study found that an Impossible Burger has an 89 percent smaller carbon footprint than a traditional beef burger. It also uses 87 percent less water than beef, 96 percent less land, and reduces water contamination by 92 percent.[31]

The sustainability ethos at Impossible Burger demonstrates what can happen when intelligence, data, expertise, and strategy are harnessed not only for the good of the individual, but also for a larger cause like our shared and interconnected ecosystems. Responsible experiences are defined by far-reaching benefits that have the potential to tip industries in directions that strengthen the bottom line as well as communities and the environment—experiences that many people now demand of brands today, with eight in ten consumers saying purpose is at least as important to them as traditional customer experience.[32]

Nudges for a Better World

For years, brands have experimented with slight changes to the designs of their digital portals in order to provide nudges for user behavior.

So-called A/B testing tries out various font updates, for example, to increase engagement and customer satisfaction, among other metrics. More recently, some brands are making use of design nudges for potential social good as well. The Google Maps app will draw on its extensive stores of geodata (road type, incline, traffic congestion), to let users choose the most environmentally friendly route. Users in New York and London will also start to see mass transit and bicycling routes more prominently displayed.

"This benefits the planet and also helps drivers save money, as routes that require higher fuel consumption also lead to higher gas bills," says Russel Dicker, director of transportation product at Google Maps.[33]

Twitter has tested a new feature called "humanization prompts," aimed to improve "conversational health" on the platform. During the test, about 10 percent of English-speaking Android phone users saw shared interests and mutual followers of the accounts they were replying to. The idea is that the more you realize you have in common with someone, the more respectfully you will treat them.[34]

In a move toward better privacy and data transparency, researchers at Carnegie Mellon are pushing a tech-labeling scheme that's similar to nutrition labels on food packaging. But these labels would apply to smart refrigerators and other devices that make up the internet-of-things. Vetted by researchers and privacy experts, the labels would tell consumers how their data will be used and by whom.

The labels would be provided free of charge to IoT device makers, standards organizations, and others and appear on products' packaging and the websites where products are sold. If the idea takes off, consumers could have a much better understanding of how their use of these products produces data and where the data flows, allowing more informed purchasing decisions.[35]

But even if you have all the information you think you need about a purchase, sometimes the item simply doesn't work out. Large online retailers like Amazon, Walmart, and others know the pain of processing

returns and are always looking for ways to make it easier for customers and more economic for themselves. Both companies have
tested a system that uses AI to determine whether it makes sense to
process a return at all. Very large and very small items simply
might not be worth it. Letting customers keep the product saves
the retailer's money and the customer's time. It also reduces the
carbon footprint by reducing shipping and further packaging. And
customers are encouraged to donate unwanted items that can't be
put to use.[36]

Easing Loneliness

Long before the pandemic hit, social isolation was a reality for many
around the globe. From the *hikikomori* in Japan to those with chronic
illness to elderly people in care facilities or in their own homes, loneliness is and has been prevalent in the modern world. Recent studies
have shown that social isolation rivals smoking, obesity, and physical
activity for increasing a person's risk of premature death. Indeed, it
is associated with a roughly 50 percent increased risk of dementia
and a four-fold increased risk of death among patients with heart
failure.[37]

A small but growing international industry now offers technology
solutions for loneliness. It's a tricky challenge. Some argue that com-
panion robots like the interactive stuffed seal named Paro relieve the
duties of family members and of the community to support ageing or
isolated populations. Others argue that even if most technology solutions don't completely vanquish the loneliness problem, they have been
shown to have positive effects on their users, providing a kind of comfort where there was none before.[38]

One project that aims to quell loneliness uses a technology solution
in combination with a goal of connecting an older population with
younger generations as well as those far in the future. Memory Lane

is the brainchild of Sweden's largest energy supplier, Stockholm Exergi, and Accenture Interactive. Using Google Voice Assistant, the team has created a conversational AI that invites a person to share their stories, which the system then turns into a physical book and a podcast to share with others and future generations. Meanwhile, a person who might have few visitors can find some solace in conversations with the surprisingly intuitive AI.

Memory Lane's AI was developed over the course of two years for a small pilot study in Stockholm, where more than 250,000 residents suffer from acute loneliness.[39] The AI asks personal questions and understands the correlation between different answers, triggering relevant follow-up questions. Every day, the system analyzes the previous conversation to get at the heart of the topic and to create a memory graph—a structured virtual version of a person's memory.

This is a technology solution that aims to not only improve health and quality of life of its users but to go beyond the individual and connect future generations to stories that would have otherwise been lost.[40]

The Human Journey

The Memory Lane project spans all four of the experiential categories we've outlined in this chapter. The project *empowers* its users to share their stories, which is *rewarding* to them and to those who listen or read. The conversational AI is expressly *tuned in* to draw out personal stories and details and to offer a sense of interest and companionship. And finally, the system has been *responsibly* conceived of and implemented as a way to help maintain the health of individuals and build community.

Such more expansively human experiences point the way to the future. The radically human revolution in technology we've been discussing throughout this book makes it possible to get there.

This will require a simple but profound shift in mindset. Leading companies will think not merely in terms of the customer journey but of the journeys of people, including employees, through their lives. In the course of that journey, people are seeking experiences that are empowering, rewarding, tuned-in, responsible, and more. Companies that provide the best, most relevant experiences in that larger context will become an indispensable part of their customers' and employees' lives, setting themselves up for meaningful differentiation and sustained growth—and outdistancing their less imaginative peers.

That human journey is itself situated in a larger context—sustainability, to which we turn in the next chapter. Because sustainability is so all-encompassing, affecting everyone on the planet, it is perhaps the most consequential of the differentiators being considered here and—the good news—it is an area where the application of IDEAS holds out great hope.

SUSTAINABILITY

Planet IDEAS

The radically human turns represented by IDEAS come together in the most radically human turn of all: sustainability, the existential struggle to save our planet and those who inhabit it. Machine learning and related digital technologies hold immense promise for helping us overcome our biggest challenges. At the same time, digital technologies have a dark side in terms of the environment. For example, training a single AI model can emit as much carbon as five ordinary cars do over their lifetimes.[1] Companies will need to address this reality directly in order to keep the damage from outpacing the gain. They must adopt a dual focus: using technology as a powerful tool to create new solutions that promote sustainability, while also improving the sustainability of technology itself.

Living Systems for Our Living Planet

The vast computing power of the cloud and the wide net cast by edge technologies are being put to work monitoring and analyzing a whole host of environmental and climate phenomena: ocean temperatures, rainfall patterns, the effect of soot and sulfate from cargo ships on clouds, and much more.[2] AWS, for example, is seeing more organizations using its machine-learning services on dozens of climate-related projects, ranging from soil-data analysis and ocean-conservation efforts to forest preservation.[3] And its Sage Maker tool is enabling domain experts, with no training in AI, to bring the power of machine teaching to highly specific sustainability projects. Remote sensors and other edge technology make it possible to track water pollution, deforestation, and "dark fleets" of vessels whose fishing practices breach environmental regulations.[4] These technologies are being woven together into dynamic living systems—the boundaryless, adaptable, and ultimately radically human approach to technology architecture we detailed in chapter 4. These systems, with humans very much in the loop, are being used to take on a host of environmental challenges that threaten habitats, humans, and virtually every business in every sector.

The Porsche, Audi, and Volkswagen brands are using an AI-powered early warning system to identify sustainability risks such as environmental pollution, human rights abuses, and corruption among direct business partners and at the lower levels of the supply chain.[5] An algorithm created by Austrian start-up Prewave identifies and analyzes publicly available media and social networks in more than fifty languages and over 150 countries. The brands are notified if the system finds indications of a sustainability risk in their supply chains. They then look more closely at the situation and decide what measures should be taken. Since the pilot project began in October 2020, the three VW brands have analyzed more than 5,000 keywords and are keeping an eye on over 4,000 suppliers. It's hard to understate the potential of such systems since the typical multinational's supply chain generates 5.5 times more emissions than its direct operations.[6]

The World Mosquito Program (WMP), a not-for-profit initiative, uses the cloud and AI to protect communities around the world from mosquito-borne diseases like dengue, Zika, chikungunya, and yellow fever. Pioneered by Australian researchers at Monash University, the technique involves introducing into the mosquito population in disease-prone areas a natural bacteria called Wolbachia, which stops the spread of disease.[7]

But deciding where to release mosquitos carrying Wolbachia is a resource-intensive process. Without proper models, researchers run the risk of missing human settlement areas and also releasing mosquitos into protected areas. So WMP uses Azure and machine learning in a key part of the process.[8] The goal is to pinpoint multiple high-impact release points within blocks of as little as 100 square meters. WMP gathers high-resolution satellite imagery and then sends it through a pipeline built on Microsoft Azure to train models, build footprints, and create grids. The grids and maps are processed, and the pipeline provides maps that allow WMP experts to identify human settlement, view building areas, and determine spatial relationships. A process that used to take two to three weeks to complete is performed by the model in just one day and allows Wolbachia to be introduced to populations more effectively, and at lower cost.

Dendra Systems helps companies like Glencore and RioTinto restore ecosystems.[9] Dendra drones, using swarm technology, map every square inch of the area to be restored and gather data, including erosion trends, that the company's ecologists and AI use to determine what seeding plan to pursue. Seeding drones, capable of spreading at least 420 million seeds every day, containing up to fifty-three different species, then seed the area to be restored. It's far faster and more accurate than manual seeding and doesn't risk ecosystem damage from boots-on-the-ground and wheeled vehicle seeding methods.

Consider, also, the concerted effort by a number of stakeholders to combat deforestation in the major cocoa-producing regions of the world. The clearing of primary forest cover causes significant increases in greenhouse gasses. One way to prevent it is to help farmers optimize yields on existing land. FarmGrow, established by the Rainforest Alliance and Grameen Foundation, supports cocoa farmers through an Android-based decision-making platform that helps them improve the productivity and long-term sustainability of their farms.

Mars and global cocoa trader Touton were among the first companies to embrace FarmGrow. Mars, maker of M&M's, Snickers, Mars bars, and many other global brands, has declared a commitment to achieving a deforestation-free cocoa supply chain by 2025.[10] The company aims to map 100 percent of its supply chain down to the farmer level and to create risk assessment and action plans for all of the countries where they source cocoa, including Côte d'Ivoire, Ghana, Indonesia, Brazil, Cameroon, and Ecuador.

Using FarmGrow, suppliers' field teams—the humans in the loop—can provide customized coaching on farming practices, help farmers prioritize investments, share information about crop management, and monitor adoption methods to improve farmers' yields. By the end of 2019, Mars had mapped almost 100 percent of the farms in Ghana and 62 percent in Côte d'Ivoire and had made significant progress in tracing the cocoa it sourced. Meanwhile, Touton had reached more than 4,500 farmers in Ghana, of which 1,650 farmers effectively adopted a FarmGrow plan.

The FarmGrow platform uses information supplied by Satelligence, a Netherlands-based company whose technology combines remote sensors, satellite imagery, and cloud-based AI. Satelligence was founded in 2016 with the mission of achieving sustainable agricultural production and moving toward zero deforestation, zero extinction, and zero emissions. How do their satellites "see" deforestation? Rens Masselink, the company's head of operations, explains it this way:[11] satellites can create images of the earth's surface through clouds and transform them into radar signals. The signals that come back from forests are higher in altitude than signals from deforested areas. Then an algorithm, developed in collaboration with Wageningen University, calculates the probability that an area is deforested and "stacks" probabilities in an iterative way to attain a higher degree of certainty about the deforestation event.

The area that the company monitors for soft commodity-related deforestation covers about 3 million square kilometers. Each pixel from the satellite represents 100 square meters. That means more than 3 billion pixels need to be processed in near real time, so it is done at one of the major cloud providers with a processing engine developed by Satelligence. The engine efficiently processes these huge amounts of data and distills actionable information that enables customers to know what is happening in their supply chains immediately, anywhere on the planet.

The processing engine is also highly flexible, one of the hallmarks of living systems. When a customer wants to add new monitoring areas, Satelligence can add them instantly. In addition, the company's data science and engineering teams are continuously developing new algorithms and implementing them in the processing engine, leading to new services like tree age, carbon stock, burned area, and crop performance indicators.

These systems will unlock troves of sustainability information and put more pressure on companies to use them for more accurate and granular disclosure of sustainability performance. In the United Kingdom, the "Spatial Finance Initiative" was established in 2019 to find ways to analyze geospatial data and translate it into financial decision making for impact investors. Tiny satellites, augmented by drones, will be used to take high-resolution images of every point on the globe daily, and the resulting data will be scanned and interpreted by AI.[12] Investors will be able to use the technology to see with an unprecedented level of detail how businesses are affecting the environment, including those with big, complex geographical operations and supply chains. As the threat of ecological catastrophe becomes increasingly clear, even investors with little emotional attachment to environmental issues are likely to pay careful attention to sustainability metrics—and companies will need to have in place living systems to provide them at an unprecedented level of specificity and transparency.

Sustainability in Silico

As we write, less than ten years remain to achieve the 2030 Agenda for Sustainable Development. The 2030 Agenda, adopted by all United Nations member states in 2015, sets out seventeen sustainable development goals (SDGs) and an urgent call for action by all countries, developed and developing, to tackle poverty, improve health and education, reduce inequality, and spur economic growth—all while tackling climate change and working to preserve the world's oceans and forests.[13] Meanwhile, the landmark COP26 Climate Summit in Glasgow in 2021 added fresh urgency to meeting the still unfulfilled climate goals of the Paris Accord.

The transformation needed to achieve the world's ambitious targets will require new ways to create circular economies, to manage products and services over their entire lifecycle, to make cities ecologically smarter, and to repair and protect complex interdependent ecosystems. One way to accelerate this transformation is through digital twins.

Digital twins are used to model complex systems—from cars to cities to human hearts—and simulate their functioning with an accuracy that allows the user to go directly from the virtual model to creating a solution to the problem at hand without spending the years it normally takes to prototype and incrementally improve designs and systems.

Digital twins can help companies reduce their costs, resource use, and carbon footprint, and they can support disruptive innovation and agile, customer-centric, circular business models. Digital twins can help city planners coordinate complex urban systems—from traffic control to waste disposal to public parks—for greater efficiency and sustainability. Climatologists can use digital twins to understand how myriad factors are interacting to produce climate change and to identify urgently needed interventions.

Singapore has created Virtual Singapore, a high-fidelity, real-time-data digital twin of the city.[14] Powered by sophisticated analysis of images and data collected from public agencies and sensors, Virtual Singapore aims to virtually match all moving parts of the city in real time. It will enable city planners to test various possible responses to everything from population growth and resource management to public events and building patterns and then implement those that create the safest, most positive experiences, including sustainability initiatives.[15]

Meanwhile, the European Union is creating a digital twin of the Earth. Called Destination Earth (DestinE), the project will enable the modelling of Earth's physical resources.[16] DestinE's federated cloud-based modeling and simulation platform—providing access to data, advanced computing infrastructure, software, AI applications, and analytics—will integrate digital twins of planetary subsystems, such as weather and climate, food and water security, global ocean circulation, and the biogeochemistry of the oceans. Users will have access to thematic information, services, models, scenarios, simulations, forecasts, and visualizations that can be used to test interventions that would enable more sustainable development.

In the commercial world, digital twins can deliver not only richer design options and rapid prototyping, but also greater production process efficiency; improved quality; better operational performance, life extension, and decommissioning of assets; and more robust supply chain scenario planning and resiliency—all of which can contribute to a more circular economy. A full 100 percent of the world's top electric vehicle (EV) manufacturers, and 90 percent of the top drug and healthcare laboratories, use digital twin solutions. But the vast majority of private and public organizations globally have yet to pilot and scale such solutions. That's unfortunate given the great promise digital twins hold for improved business and sustainability performance.

To find out precisely how much promise exists, Accenture teamed up with Dassault Systèmes, one of the largest providers of collaborative twins of the real world, to explore the potential of digital twins to design and deliver the new products and systems we need for zero-carbon, circular economies. Together, we quantitatively assessed five industry-specific use cases for their sustainability impact up until 2030, with a focus on reducing environmental sustainability and greenhouse gas (GHG) emissions.[17]

The assessment examined use cases within the construction, consumer packaged goods, transportation, life sciences, and electrical and electronics industries. The analysis found that these five cases alone could deliver combined incremental benefits of $1.3 trillion of economic value and the equivalent of 7.5 gigatons of CO_2 emissions reductions by 2030. For example, commercial and residential buildings currently account for about 40 percent of global energy demand (60 percent of the world's electricity) and 25 percent of our global water usage. They are also responsible for approximately a third of global GHG emissions.[18] Energy consumption in buildings can be reduced by 30 to 80 percent using proven and commercially available digital twin technologies, often as part of a broader smart cities plan. The assessment found that the potential of implementing digital twins in new construction globally between 2020 and 2030 amounts to $288 billion of reduced building operating costs and the equivalent of a reduction of 6.9 gigatons of CO_2 emissions.

When combined with AI, digital twins can enable an entirely new, intelligent, and resilient level of product design. Product development can be pushed closer to the supply chain and to the customer. Design and manufacturing cycles shrink from years to weeks, as newfound creativity unleashes greater efficiency. For example, Volkswagen used Autodesk's AI-driven generative design capabilities to develop a lighter and greener concept version of its iconic VW bus—and completed the process in a matter of months, compared to a previous cycle of one and a half years.[19] Such experiments help explain why 44 percent of global CEOs Accenture surveyed said that digital twin technology will make a significant impact on sustainability in their industry over the next five years, even as 53 percent of CEOs said that they struggle to understand which technologies can enhance their sustainability performance.

But beyond these benefits and challenges, it is humans who will ultimately determine the fate of sustainability. Another Autodesk project, this one undertaken in partnership with the Smithsonian Institution, underlines the point.[20] The two organizations recently teamed up on an exhibit at the Smithsonian's historic Arts and Industries Building (AIB), America's original National Museum, to demonstrate how a digital twin can be used to help communities design a more sustainable city, much like the objectives of Virtual Singapore.

Visitors to the "Future Communities" interactive exhibit can work with each other to design a city block from scratch—with help from sophisticated AI. Participants, working in teams, manually place virtual models of buildings, parks, and other urban features directly onto the design space. The changes individual users make at small computer screens are reflected in real time on a shared big screen with a virtual twin of the group's growing city. The AI considers what the group does and suggests other, more efficient or more sustainable possibilities.

But there is an intensely human wrinkle in the experience that also mirrors the real world. Team members role-play various interested parties, who may have conflicting priorities. One member may be focused on environmental impact, another member on accessibility, another on public transit, and so on. While the suggestions of the AI help bridge the differences, the team must ultimately agree on mutually acceptable solutions. That requires that they collaborate successfully with each other. Says Brad MacDonald, AIB's director of creative media, "We're looking for ways in which tech can give us the space to be better."[21]

The End of the ICE Age?

Ambient air pollution accounts for an estimated 4.2 million deaths per year due to stroke, heart disease, lung cancer, and chronic respiratory diseases.[22] Around 91 percent of the world's population lives in places where air quality levels exceed World Health Organization limits. One of the biggest sources of air pollution is the internal combustion engine (ICE). Phasing it out could be one of the most radically human turns, in terms of lives saved, that the auto industry could undertake.

Automakers have dabbled in EVs for decades, and Tesla, which deals exclusively in EVs, has been around since 2003. But in early 2021, an extraordinary series of announcements by the likes of GM and Ford held out the hope that the ICE age was waning. In January, General Motors said that it would phase out gasoline-powered cars and trucks and sell only vehicles that have zero tailpipe emissions by 2035, as part of a larger plan to become carbon neutral by 2040. The following month, Ford announced that all of its passenger cars would be all electric by 2030. In May, the company unveiled the F-150 Lightning pickup truck, an all-electric version of the gas-powered F-150, the number-one-selling vehicle in the United States. Volkswagen had previously promised electric versions of all of its models by 2030. And Volvo plans to build only electric vehicles by the end of the decade.

Although EVs are the fastest growing segment in the auto industry, they commanded only about 3 percent of the market globally as of 2021. A major obstacle to widespread adoption of EVs has been battery performance: from charging speed to driving range to vehicle lifetime to cost of materials. Only by overcoming these obstacles will EVs reach price parity with gas-powered vehicles.

AI is being widely employed to speed up development of batteries across a wide variety of areas, including capacitor development, battery materials, anodes, cathodes, and electrolytes.[23] Significantly, AI is dramatically speeding up analyses of battery performance. For example, IBM researchers have been using AI to develop a battery that is fast-charging and free of heavy metals like nickel and cobalt, which are expensive, hard to recycle, and come with concerns about human rights where they are mined. One set of materials under consideration included 20,000 potential compounds. Screening them using traditional methods could have taken five years. Machine learning did the job in nine days.[24] The battery under development uses three new materials never before combined in a battery and uses no heavy metals or other substances with sourcing concerns. The materials can be extracted from seawater, laying the groundwork for less damaging sourcing techniques than current material mining methods.[25] Such speed and innovation are critical as the world struggles to prevent catastrophic climate change.

In the quest for a better battery, IBM Research has adopted a key characteristic of IDEA-powered strategy: seeding the developer and industry ecosystems that potentially lead to exponential improvements in technology. IBM researchers have collaborated on exploring this space with Mercedes-Benz Research and Development North America; Central Glass, one of the top battery electrolyte suppliers in the world; and Sidus, a battery manufacturer. IBM says that its aspiration is "to build an ecosystem to bring the batteries into commercial reality."[26]

A team of researchers from Stanford, MIT, and the Toyota Research Institute has developed a machine-learning approach that cuts the time required to evaluate batteries by 98 percent.[27] "In battery testing, you have to try a massive number of things, because the performance you get will vary drastically," says Stefano Ermon, an assistant professor of computer science who helped lead the team. "With AI, we're able to quickly identify the most promising approaches and cut out a lot of unnecessary experiments."

Their goal was to be able to charge an EV battery in ten minutes while maximizing the battery's life. In the traditional trial-and-error method, researchers must wait months and even years to gather data on how changes to a battery affect its life. But the Stanford team's AI is able to predict lifetime performance based on only a few charging cycles. The team then predicts the cycling life and sends it to a data-efficient Bayesian optimization algorithm to test the next charging protocol. Learning from previous experiences, the AI was able to predict which charging methods found the sweet spot between rapid charging and long battery life. The traditional approach would have required 500 days of charging and discharging, but the Stanford team's algorithm identified the best charging protocols among 224 candidates in sixteen days.[28]

To help stimulate the wider ecosystem of battery research, the team made all of its data publicly available so that other researchers could use it to train their machine-learning algorithms. The Argonne National Laboratory, a US Department of Energy multidisciplinary science and engineering research center, hopes to stimulate the ecosystem even further.[29] A team at the Argonne is mobilizing research institutions and companies to share their data via a platform developed at the University of Chicago called Data Stations. The platform, using a unique privacy-preserving machine learning (PPML) architecture, offers what its developers call a "neutral zone" where data is shared but sealed.[30] Users cannot see, access, or download the original datasets, viewing only a broad catalog of available data. Users query the collected data—for example, asking about the effectiveness of particular compounds in prolonging battery life. The Data Station automatically finds the right data, combines it or uses it to train AI models, and provides the user with the answer without disclosing the underlying raw data. As we saw in chapter 4, the MELLODY project uses AI and federated learning to speed up drug discovery among normally competitive pharmaceutical companies. Similar efforts in sustainability could go a long way toward achieving a decarbonized future.

Freeing Humans to Do What They Do Best

A San Francisco Bay Area biotechnology startup looks for innovative solutions to some of the world's biggest environmental challenges—protecting crops from drought, defending against insect-borne diseases, and reducing plastic waste. Using software, AI, robotics, and advanced genetic engineering techniques, it makes industrial microbes to optimize the production of chemicals or create brand new compounds. While many existing approaches to genetically engineered microbes involve petroleum-based products that harm the environment, the company seeks less damaging biology-based solutions.

With proprietary simulation software, it can digitally predict a molecule's properties. From there, it rapidly prototypes candidate molecules, evaluates their performance, and chooses the ones ultimately best suited to address a problem. Once the winning biomolecule has been identified, company scientists design microorganisms that can produce it.

Typically in microbe optimization, scientists draw on the existing scientific literature, their experience, and intuition to develop hypotheses, design experiments, and conduct manual tests. While that approach is not exactly hit-or-miss, it leans heavily on the scientist's "genius"—as well as a bit of luck—and yields a limited number of experiments. Manually conducting the experiments also engages highly educated, high-value employees in often low-value tasks.

Rather than propose specific tests, company scientists design strategies for finding effective changes that are generally applicable. For a given project, they draw on their expert knowledge to choose a strategy from among the available strategies and then auto-generate a large volume of changes to try. As we saw in chapter 3, the radically human turn in expertise is not about greater and greater degrees of specialization, but instead is about working with AI in a way that yields maximum leverage from one's knowledge and experience. Instead of laboriously generating a necessarily limited number of experiment designs, the company's scientists bring their expertise to bear at a higher strategic level, while letting AI generate a much greater number of promising experiments. As a result, the experiments are simultaneously more targeted and more comprehensive than experiments conducted using either the age-old hypothesis approach or brute-force AI.

So far, the company has announced three products, two of which directly address the protection of crops against pests. All three products are reported to be completely novel, never-used-before molecules. That is in line with the company's aim to create new biology-based products rather than green alternatives to existing products. And for the planet, the payoff could be a new generation of biology-based products that not only reduce environmental harm, but also directly address sustainability issues.

Consider, also, machine teaching at Japanese steelmaker JFE. JFE was among the top ten makers of heavy goods like steel, cement, and glass that led the *Wall Street Journal*'s 2020 list for best practices in addressing environmental risk.[31] In addition to using AI to monitor production and avoid downtime and defective products,[32] the company has harnessed AI systems and applications to more broadly save energy and reduce CO_2 emissions. The company has set a 2030 goal of reducing emissions from its steel operations by more than 20 percent from 2013 levels. By 2050, JFE wants to be carbon neutral—the same target set by the Japanese government.[33]

To accelerate the adoption of AI and machine learning across the enterprise, JFE uses DotData, an AI and machine-learning platform that seeks to automate the entire data science life-cycle.[34] Using Dot-Data, the company can complete machine-learning projects in days instead of months. Most important, DotData democratizes data science. Business analysts, with no coding skills, can execute AI and machine-learning projects based on their intimate knowledge of the business, turning machine learning into machine teaching. Moreover, DotData makes AI transparent and explainable, automatically producing a "human-readable" explanation of each feature as well as a blueprint that visually outlines the logic used to generate features.

Clothes with a Conscience

According to H&M, the second largest clothing retailer in the world, the fashion industry is one of the most polluting and water intensive industries in the world. Producing one T-shirt consumes 2,700 liters of water.[35] Dyeing and finishing products in textile production is estimated to be responsible for about 20 percent of global clean water pollution. The washing of synthetic fabrics accounts for 35 percent of the microplastics released into the environment. Clothing and footwear production accounts for 10 percent of global gas emissions. Fast fashion—the constant provision of new styles at low prices—has greatly increased the quantity of clothes produced and thrown away. The average consumer now buys 60 percent more clothing than fifteen years ago, and more than 80 percent of garments wind up in landfills or incinerators.[36] Production often takes place in countries with spotty environmental regulations, low wages, and human rights abuses like child labor.

Many organizations and companies, including some of the most recognizable brand names as well as innovative upstarts, are working to change those numbers through supply chain traceability, more eco-friendly fibers, recycling programs, wiser land use, and better water management.

The Stella McCartney fashion brand has collaborated with Google Cloud to develop a tool that uses data analytics and machine learning to give brands a more comprehensive view into their supply chain, particularly at the level of raw material production.[37] Initially, they are looking at cotton, which accounts for 25 percent of all fibers used in making clothes and involves significant amounts of water and pesticides. They are also looking at viscose, a semi-synthetic material derived from wood pulp that has links to deforestation. Working with fashion brands, experts, nongovernmental organizations, and industry bodies, they hope to create an open industrywide tool that will let companies better measure the impact of their raw materials in key areas such as air pollution, greenhouse gas emissions, land use, and water scarcity.

Inditex, the parent company of Zara, the world's largest clothing retailer, has developed a proprietary technology platform to run all of the company's integrated digital operations. The platform is flexible and scalable, with a microservices architecture that enables customized projects in response to specific business needs. It uses machine learning to determine optimal stock levels and an analytical engine developed with MIT to estimate the distribution of new products, all of which helps avoid overproduction that damages the environment. With far more accurate demand forecasting, 85 percent of Zara's production is now done during the current season.[38]

Finesse, an online startup launched in January 2021, is upending the traditional fast-fashion operating model and fighting wasteful overproduction in the process. Traditionally, fast-fashion brands rely on design teams to determine what to make and on buyers to determine how much to produce. Finesse begins the creative process with social media. Using proprietary algorithms and combining time series analysis, natural language processing, and computer vision, the company's machine learning system scours the internet for creative cues about fashion trends among Gen Zers (the generation born after 1997). "Fashion's birthplace has moved from the catwalks of New York [and] Paris to social media," says the company's founder, Ramin Ahmari.[39]

Guided by the trends detected on social media, the company then creates three potential outfits that it posts on the Finesse website, where shoppers vote for the one they prefer. The winner is put into production. But instead of iterating on physical samples back and forth between the company and the factory, Finesse uses 3D virtual prototyping to arrive at a final design. The company then uses its data to determine how many units to manufacture. The result is even faster fashion—the process cuts lead times from five months to just twenty-five days[40]—but with less waste.

Amplified Intelligence at H&M

For its part, H&M appears to be pursuing a thoroughgoing sustainability-first appeal to customers. Its app not only owns up to the industry's shortcomings, it also foregrounds sustainability at every turn, showcasing products made from ecofriendly materials like organic cotton, pineapple-leaf fiber, recycled polyester, and polylactic fiber. When online shoppers click on an H&M product, they can find out the materials used to make the product, the countries involved in its production, the suppliers and factories (right down to street addresses) that H&M partnered with to make it, and information about how to recycle clothes. In H&M stores, shoppers can open the app and scan a product's tag, and the app will take them to available sustainability information online. Shoppers can also bring unwanted clothes or home textiles—any brand and in any condition—and they will be rewoven, reused, or recycled.

But perhaps the strongest signal of commitment to sustainability came in 2020, when the company appointed Helena Helmersson as its new CEO. Helmersson had served as the company's head of sustainability from 2010 to 2014. Since her appointment, the company announced that by 2025 it aims to use 30 percent recycled materials and reduce emissions from its operations by 20 percent. The company also piloted blockchain technology for greater traceability in its supply chain of more than 1,600 primary factories and nearly 300 secondary suppliers. Now more than 65 percent of its materials are from recycled or more sustainable sources, and 100 percent of its cotton is organic, recycled, or sourced in a more sustainable way. The company also expanded its use of 3D tools to design garments in a way that minimizes waste.

Although H&M came relatively late to AI and machine learning—conducting its first proof-of-concept project in 2016—the technology quickly became critical to its sustainability efforts. In 2018, the company created an AI department with the express purpose of making more sustainable business decisions. Arti Zeighami, global head of advanced analytics and AI at H&M, sees AI as the road to using fewer resources, creating fewer emissions, and reducing waste. Only he doesn't call it artificial intelligence; he calls it "amplified intelligence" to stress

AI's dependence on humans to be fully effective. "When we do the combination of AI and human, the gut feeling and the data, the art and science—that's when we get the most out of it."[41] That's why instead of developing use cases without the involvement of business users, he brought business users into the process of refining the business application. He found that the algorithm alone performed a few percentage points better than humans, but when combined with humans, the results were twice as good as the algorithm by itself.[42]

The company has adopted other aspects of the radically human turn in technology. It is democratizing AI and machine learning by creating component libraries in areas like fashion forecasting and logistics that can be deployed across the organization. It is also building a new data platform named Yggdrasil, after the sacred tree in Norse mythology, that will allow teams throughout H&M to help themselves to central data assets.[43] To create more flexible predictive modeling capabilities, the company digitally decoupled from a cumbersome legacy architecture and moved to the Microsoft Azure cloud. It is stimulating the industry ecosystem through a platform called Treadler, which will give other companies access to H&M's global supply chain and even help them with product development. The aim, says Gustaf Asp, Treadler's managing director, is to take advantage of "the full potential of H&M Group's extensive investments and progressive sustainability work by catering to clients' needs and contributing to driving long-term growth for H&M Group, while driving change in our industry."[44]

Turning AI from Red to Green

Without a doubt, AI will be one of—if not the—driving technological force behind the world's collective response to climate change. But advanced AI software, in some cases, worsens many of the environmental problems it aims to solve.

That's because the way in which AI software is developed can be extremely energy intensive. Consider an experiment conducted by Accenture researchers. They trained an AI model on a small, publicly available dataset of iris flowers. Using only 964 joules of energy, the AI model achieved accuracy of 96.17 percent in classifying the flowers' different species. Achieving an additional 1.74 percent-point increase in accuracy required 2,815 joules of energy. That means the last 0.08 percent increase in accuracy took nearly 400 percent more energy than was required to reach 96.17 percent accuracy.

In another experiment, using a medium-size publicly available image dataset, the researchers showed that a 70 percent smaller subset of the training data could achieve nearly the same level of accuracy with a significantly lower energy cost. The model consumed 47 percent more energy when trained on the entire dataset compared to the smaller subset, but achieved less than 1 percent more accuracy. Further, the bigger and more unwieldy AI software became, the more energy required of the machines that ran it, further increasing its carbon footprint.

In a highly influential study, a group of researchers led by Oren Etzioni, chief executive of the Allen Institute, proposed a shift toward what they call "Green AI," which they define as AI research that is more environmentally friendly, as well as more inclusive.[45]

To help promote more sustainable software development, Accenture, GitHub, Microsoft, and ThoughtWorks launched the nonprofit Green Software Foundation (GSF) in early 2021 with the Linux Foundation and the Joint Development Foundation. Born out of a mutual desire and need to collaborate across the software industry, GSF wants to build a trusted ecosystem of people, standards, tooling, and leading practices for creating green software. The foundation aims to help the software industry contribute to the information and communications technology sector's broader targets for reducing greenhouse gas emissions by 45 percent by 2030, in line with the Paris Climate Agreement. After all, the data centers and communications networks that power smartphones and other devices will produce an estimated 14 percent of the world's greenhouse gas emissions by 2040, according to researchers at McMaster University in Canada.[46]

Green AI, Etzioni and his colleagues say, could actually move us in a more "cognitively plausible direction." Why? Because the brain is highly efficient. A number of companies and researchers are now exploring the development of "neuromorphic chips"—computer chips designed to resemble the circuitry and electrical behavior of the neurons that make up biological brains. Most computers today are based on what is known as the von Neumann architecture, where data travels back and forth between a central processor and memory chips, in a linear fashion.

Neuromorphic chips move data back and forth the way the brain does, in a series of electrical bursts. Synapses in biological brains react to stimuli and alter their connections based on learned experience. Neuromorphic chips aim to mimic this by etching the brain's neural networks into silicon. These chips are highly energy-efficient, just like the brain, because their neurons aren't constantly firing, as occurs with traditional silicon technology, but activated only when they receive a spiking signal.[47]

Neuromorphic technologies will help solve business challenges that require AI at the edge, such as responsive voice control for vehicles, full-body gesture recognition for touchless interfaces, and on-board intelligence for assistive robotics. In a recent collaboration with an automotive client, our firm demonstrated that spiking neural networks running on a neuromorphic processor can recognize simple voice commands up to 0.2 seconds faster than a commonly used embedded GPU accelerator, while using up to a thousand times less power. This brings truly intelligent, low-latency interactions into play, at the edge, even within the power-limited constraints of a parked vehicle.

While neuromorphic chips advance, there is also hope in replacing older CPUs (central processing units) with newer energy-efficient chip architectures, such as graphics processing units (GPUs) and field-programmable gate arrays (FPGAs).[48] GPUs have numerous advantages over CPUs. The latter process fewer high-volume streams of data simultaneously. GPUs, meanwhile, are more energy-efficient because they specialize their memory architecture to support high-speed data streaming for intensive applications. GPUs are built specifically for rendering and other graphic applications that support extensive parallel processing.

FPGAs are based on a matrix of configurable, interconnected logic blocks that make them more energy efficient. FPGA technology is seeing a notable uptake across industries, including aerospace and defense, automotive, and consumer electronics, with the global market expected to see a compound-annual growth rate of 8.6 percent from 2019 to 2024.[49]

Graphcore, a UK startup, has produced an Intelligence Processing Unit (IPU) that is even more energy-efficient than GPUs. The company has said that its IPU processes data ten to fifty times faster than GPUs, saving large amounts of energy.[50]

How does the IPU work? To process data faster, it deploys built-in memory processing, which reduces the amount of data sent between chips. IPUs also increase throughput (the amount of data delivered during any given period) by about 300 percent while decreasing latency (the time it takes data to be delivered) by 20 percent compared with GPUs.[51]

Further, IPUs are designed to make computer brains more human-like. To do this, IPUs forgo the slower, heavier, number-crunching typical of GPUs in favor of a speedier process that relies on less precise math. The upshot: IPUs were able to train Google's natural language processing model, BERT-large, in 36.3 hours, which is 25 percent faster than the standard GPU time for the task.[52]

Carbon emissions can also be reduced by migration to the public cloud—as much as 59 million tons per year, according to our analysis.[53] This represents a 5.9 percent reduction in total IT emissions and equates to taking 22 million cars off the road. This magnitude of reduction can go a long way in meeting climate change commitments, particularly for data-intensive businesses.

The first step toward a sustainable cloud-first journey begins with selecting a carbon-thoughtful provider. Cloud providers set different corporate commitments towards sustainability, which in turn determine how they plan, build, power, operate, and retire their data centers. AWS's expansive infrastructure is 3.6 times more energy efficient compared to median US enterprise data centers, largely due to efficient servers and high-capacity utilization rates.[54] The company's water-cooled facilities actively measure water efficiency and select conservation options in the context of regional climate patterns and local resources.[55] Google currently utilizes a carbon-intelligent computing platform that shifts timing of non-urgent data center workloads to times when low-carbon sources of energy are most plentiful. The company has made a bold commitment to operate its data centers carbon-free 24/7 by 2030. Microsoft, carbon neutral since 2012, has committed to shifting its data centers to 100 percent renewable energy by 2025 through power purchase agreements (PPAs). Microsoft Azure's customers can even access a carbon calculator that tracks emissions associated with their own workload on the cloud.[56]

Our analysis of the largest public cloud service providers shows average enterprise-owned-to-cloud migrations can lead to an impressive 65 percent energy reduction and 84 percent carbon reduction.[57] Companies drive even greater carbon reductions through cloud-native architectures and deployments. Our analysis shows that customizing applications to be cloud-native can stretch carbon emission reduction to 98 percent, another example of Green AI's enormous environmental promise.

The Most Important Differentiator of All

The world will need that kind of human cooperation and collaboration at scale if we are to forestall the worst effects of climate change. In August 2021, the United Nations issued a devastating new report on our climate future.[58] Approved by 195 governments and based on more than 14,000 studies, the report concluded that global warming will continue to intensify over the coming twenty years, even if nations begin reducing carbon emissions immediately. Deadly heat waves, severe droughts, violent weather and flooding, plant and animal extinctions, and the dying off of coral reefs that support fisheries around the globe will grow in intensity and frequency. These are not speculative scenarios. Many of the technologies we've been discussing in this book—especially cloud/edge monitoring systems and AI-driven modeling—have given these climate predictions unprecedented precision.

As the effects of climate change become more immediate, sustainability will increasingly be top of mind for billions of people. For companies, that means sustainability will become one of the most compelling differentiators of all. While governments, politicians, and other officials continue to set often toothless aspirational goals, companies can take concrete, consequential actions now, as automakers did by shifting production to electric vehicles. Talent, customers, and investors—all acutely aware of the stakes in a way they never have been before—will gravitate in ever larger numbers to companies that excel in terms of sustainability.

And that advantage will drop straight to the bottom line. Our research shows that sustainability strongly correlates with superior financial performance. Between 2013 and 2019, companies with consistently high ratings for environmental, social, and governance (ESG) performance enjoyed 4.7 times higher operating margins than low ESG performers over the same period. High performers generated 2.3 times higher annual total returns to shareholders than their peers. Even as global markets faced tremendous pressures and volatility, companies with high ESG scores continued to outperform, experiencing less volatility and generating a cumulative relative return 6.3 percent higher than bottom performers.[59]

Over the next two decades, as climate change becomes impossible for even the most casual observer to ignore, we are likely to see this performance gap widen for sustainability-first companies. But to maintain their lead, companies must begin to immediately embrace the twin imperatives we outlined at the beginning of this chapter, using technology as a sustainability catalyst while also making technology more sustainable. Of all the differentiators a company might pursue, sustainability is the one that could generate the biggest boost to radically human performance—while offering the most radically human path to protecting the planet.

CONCLUSION

Three Truths and a New Opportunity

Over the past five years, three truths have emerged with undeniable clarity.

First, all companies are now technology companies. The first stirrings of this development, when AI began to remake one business process after another, were what moved us to write *Human + Machine.* Amid widespread fears of job displacement by AI, employee unease with smart machines, and the ethical and technical complexities of machine learning and its implementation, we laid out a road map organizations could use to responsibly bring humans and machines together to form new kinds of jobs and work experiences and achieve significant performance improvements.

In the intervening years, intelligent technologies have become the animating force throughout many leading organizations. These now-ubiquitous technologies are not only remaking processes, they are also opening up new sources of value, underpinning new business and operating models, addressing some of the most intractable business and social challenges, and moving leaders to see technology and strategy

229

as inseparable. That exponential expansion—from processes to products, algorithms to architecture, systems to platforms, strategy to sustainability—is the new reality for all organizations, no matter the business they are in.

Second, companies have proved that they can wield technology to innovate and change with unprecedented speed. Before the pandemic, many companies, faced with a widening gap in digital performance, had already begun to fast forward their transformation agendas. The Covid crisis greatly accelerated those plans. Leaders focused intensely on building a digital core to simultaneously transform multiple parts of their enterprises and rapidly reorient their talent to the demands of intelligent technologies. Major shifts that were predicted to materialize in years happened in months: industry convergence, localized supply chains, and mass virtualization—all against a backdrop of fast and continuously changing customer expectations. Enterprises everywhere pivoted quicker than they believed they could and demonstrated the adaptability, innovation, and agility that many mistakenly thought they'd already achieved. The pandemic also awakened some sleeping giants, as former laggards leapfrogged their peers, turning around mediocre performance virtually overnight.

That the pace of change is picking up is of course a cliché of business literature in every era. But this time there's a big difference. It's not just that potentially game-changing technology will keep appearing at what seems like a faster rate, but that a great many companies now know that they can change far faster than they, or anyone, believed possible. Until Roger Bannister ran the first sub-four-minute mile in 1954, it was a speed widely believed to be unattainable.[1] But within forty-six days of Bannister's breaking the barrier, another runner did it. A year later, three runners in a single race did it. Since then, more than a thousand runners have accomplished the feat, including eleven high schoolers. Something like that has occurred in business over the past two years. The many companies that accomplished lightning-like transformations have set a new standard for speed that more and more enterprises will now see that they, too, can attain. The old cliché carries new weight: the pace of change is picking up, doubly so.

Third, in the human-technology nexus, the human is in the ascendant. The IDEAS framework offers new approaches to the building blocks of comprehensive digital transformation. The major differentiator of these approaches is not only do they push technical boundaries, but they do so while taking on a distinctly human character. Artificial intelligence that more closely resembles the way humans reason and feel promises greater explainability, transparency, and comfort in our interactions with machines. The new utility of small data, including the ability to create data where none exists, is democratizing AI, bringing it within reach of enterprises and researchers previously locked out of it by the cost and scale of computing power. The cloud is similarly leveling the playing field with big data. Putting the professional, social, and personal expertise of people in the driver's seat through machine teaching will mean even more human-centered and accessible technology. Radically human technology is transforming differentiators like talent, trust, experiences, and sustainability, challenging companies to take them to a new level of distinctiveness.

Of these three truths, this third one is perhaps the least well understood, and the reason we wrote this book. Its full implications are still unfolding. As people's skills, experiences, and, in some senses, humanity evolve in tune with new technologies, the technologies and their design will, of course, need to further adapt. And as they adapt, individual and collective capabilities and perspectives will further evolve. In reality, this has always been the nature of the human-tool symbiosis. What's different now is that it's happening much faster and with much broader reach.

Taken together, these three truths and recent history have brought us to a new inflection point. We're facing a set of global circumstances we've never seen before. Radically human technology and the ability to transform at astonishing speed have given us the power to break through many of the traditional constraints of business and create almost anything we can dream up. On the other hand, the journey of reinvention has only just begun. Virtually every industry remains a blank slate waiting to be defined. It's a once-in-a-generation opportunity to actively shape our future from the ground up. To finally, definitively operationalize values. To move fast and *fix* things. At this moment of truth for technology and for people, companies that fully embrace their newfound power to reimagine everything from their talent to data, architecture, and strategy will lead the way in business performance and to a future that works better for everyone.

The stakes couldn't be higher; the opportunity couldn't be greater. All of the phenomena we examine throughout this book—more natural artificial intelligence, manageable small data, machine teaching, living systems, trustworthy AI, the unleashing of talent—make technologies more recognizably human. As these new terms of our relationship with technology unfold, we will find ourselves moving deeper and deeper into reflections about what makes us truly human. In the final analysis, that may offer the most radically human hope for the future.

Our Commitment to Making the Skills for a Radically Human Future Available to All

In our book *Human + Machine*, we made a commitment to donate the proceeds to organizations that help people develop the skills they'll need to be successful in the Age of AI. And through the support of so many readers around the world who made the book a success, we were able to have a significant impact on a number of organizations, such as LaunchCode, a US nonprofit that creates pathways through job-ready training and apprenticeships for people seeking careers in technology; East London Business Alliance (ELBA), a British charity that brings positive change to East London and beyond by connecting the public, private, and volunteer sectors in order to tackle issues of social mobility and community well-being; La Cruz Roja, Spain's humanitarian arm of the International Red Cross, which focuses on aid, social inclusion, health, education, and employment for vulnerable people; and New Profit, a US venture philanthropy organization created by and for social entrepreneurs that is behind the XPRIZE Rapid Reskilling prize and the MIT Solve Reimagining Pathways to Employment in the US Challenge.

Postscript

Now, with the publication of *Radically Human*, we are pleased to extend this commitment. We are donating our net royalties from the sale of this book to help fund education and training programs focused on individuals in the middle of their careers who need extra support as they develop new skills that will enable them to succeed in the radically human future ahead of us.

NOTES

Introduction

1. Bhaskar Ghosh, Adam Burden, and James Wilson, "Full Value. Full Stop. How to Scale Innovation and Achieve Full Value with Future Systems," Accenture, 2019, https://www.accenture.com/us-en/insights/future-systems/future-ready-enterprise-systems.

2. Paul Daugherty, Bhaskar Ghosh, Annette Rippert, Ramnath Venkataraman, and H. James Wilson, "Make the Leap, Take the Lead," Accenture, April 28, 2021, https://www.accenture.com/us-en/insights/technology/scaling-enterprise-digital-transformation.

3. Here, we are, of course, paraphrasing Marshall McLuhan's observation, https://mcluhangalaxy.wordpress.com/2013/04/01/we-shape-our-tools-and-thereafter-our-tools-shape-us/.

Chapter 1

1. Alan Turing, "Computing Machinery and Intelligence," *Mind*, LIX (236): 433–460, October 1950, https://doi.org/10.1093/mind/LIX.236.433.

2. Alison Gopnik, "The Ultimate Learning Machines," *Wall Street Journal*, October 11, 2019, https://www.wsj.com/articles/the-ultimate-learning-machines-11570806023.

3. Brenden M. Lake, Tomer D. Ullman, Joshua B. Tenenbaum, and Samuel J. Gershman, "Building Machines That Learn and Think Like People," *Behavioral and Brain Sciences*, 40, 2017, https://www.cambridge.org/core/journals/behavioral-and-brain-sciences/article/building-machines-that-learn-and-think-like-people/A9535B1D745A0377E16C590E14B94993.

4. Paul R. Daugherty and H. James Wilson, *Human + Machine: Reimagining Work in the Age of AI* (Boston: Harvard Business Review Press, 2018).

5. Alison DeNisco Rayome, "Why Companies Plan to Double AI Projects in the Next Year," TechRepublic, July 15, 2019, https://tek.io/2Y3heCK.

6. Bhaskar Ghosh, Adam Burden, and James Wilson, "Full Value. Full Stop. How to Scale Innovation and Achieve Full Value with Future Systems," Accenture, 2019, https://www.accenture.com/us-en/insights/future-systems/future-ready-enterprise-systems.

7. Karen Hao, "We Analyzed 16,625 Papers to Figure Out Where AI Is Headed Next," *MIT Technology Review*, January 25, 2019, https://www.technologyreview.com/2019/01/25/1436/we-analyzed-16625-papers-to-figure-out-where-ai-is-headed-next/.

8. Tristan Greene, "AI Fails to Recognize These Nature Images 98% of the Time," TNW, July 18, 2019, https://thenextweb.com/artificial-intelligence/2019/07/18/ai-fails-to-recognize-these-nature-images-98-of-the-time/.

235

9. Carlos Zednick, "Solving the Black Box Problem: A Normative Framework for Explainable Artificial Intelligence," arXiv, 2020, https://arxiv.org/ftp/arxiv/papers/1903/1903.04361.pdf.

10. Gary Marcus and Ernest Davis, *Rebooting AI: Building Artificial Intelligence We Can Trust* (New York: Pantheon Books, 2019), 69.

11. Marcus and Davis, *Rebooting AI*, 162.

12. Brian Bergstein, "What AI Still Can't Do," *MIT Technology Review*, February 19, 2020, https://www.technologyreview.com/s/615189/what-ai-still-cant-do/.

13. Brenden M. Lake, Tomer D. Ullman, Joshua B. Tenenbaum, and Samuel J. Gershman, "Building Machines That Learn and Think Like People," arXiv, April 1, 2016, https://arxiv.org/abs/1604.00289.

14. "Covariant Launches from Stealth to Bring Universal AI to Robots," Covariant, January 29, 2020, https://www.prnewswire.com/news-releases/covariant-launches-from-stealth-to-bring-universal-ai-to-robots-300995185.html.

15. Karen Hao, "AI-Powered Robot Warehouse Pickers Are Now Ready to Go to Work," *MIT Technology Review*, January 29, 2020, https://www.technologyreview.com/s/615109/ai-powered-robot-warehouse-pickers-are-now-ready-to-go-to-work/.

16. Evan Ackerman, "Covariant Uses Simple Robot and Gigantic Neural Net to Automate Warehouse Picking," *IEEE Spectrum*, January 29, 2020, https://spectrum.ieee.org/automaton/robotics/industrial-robots/covariant-ai-gigantic-neural-network-to-automate-warehouse-picking.

17. Daniela Hernandez and Parmy Olson, "Smarter Delivery Hinges on Smarter Robots," *Wall Street Journal*, January 29, 2020, https://www.wsj.com/articles/smarter-delivery-hinges-on-smarter-robots-11580288408.

18. Hernandez and Olson, "Smarter Delivery Hinges on Smarter Robots."

19. Jared Council, "At Zappos, Algorithms Teach Themselves," *Wall Street Journal*, July 8, 2019, https://www.wsj.com/articles/at-zappos-algorithms-teach-themselves-11562578200.

20. Hilary Milnes, "How Zappos Used AI to Rebuild its Search Engine," *Modern Retail*, August 2, 2019, https://www.modernretail.co/retailers/how-zappos-used-ai-to-rebuild-its-search-engine/.

21. Cade Metz, "Machine Learning Invades the Real World on Internet Balloons," *Wired*, February 17, 2017, https://www.wired.com/2017/02/machine-learning-drifting-real-world-internet-balloons/.

22. Tony Quested, "Great Decision as Secondmind Blooms from PROWLER.io," *BusinessWeekly*, September 29, 2020, https://www.businessweekly.co.uk/news/hi-tech/great-decision-secondmind-blooms-prowlerio.

23. Cade Metz, "AI Is about to Learn More Like Humans—with a Little Uncertainty," *Wired*, February 3, 2017, https://www.wired.com/2017/02/ai-learn-like-humans-little-uncertainty/.

24. Rahul K. Das et al., "Bayesian Machine Learning on CALGB/SWOG 80405 (Alliance) and PEAK Data Identifies Heterogeneous Landscape of Clinical Predictors of Overall Survival (OS) in Different Populations of Metastatic Colorectal Cancer (mCRC)," GNS Healthcare, July 4, 2019, https://info.gnshealthcare.com/hubfs/Publications_2019/ESMO_GI_Final_Poster_Printed_PD_20.pdf.

25. "GNS Healthcare Chosen to Present Discovery of New Clinical Predictors of Overall Survival in Metastatic Colorectal Cancer at ESMO 2019 in Collaboration with the Alliance for Clinical Trials in Oncology," GNS Healthcare, July 2, 2019, https://www.gnshealthcare.com/discovery-of-new-clinical-predictors-of-overall-survival/.

26. Maryam Mohsin, "10 YouTube Stats Every Marketer Should Know in 2021," Oberlo, January 25, 2021, https://www.oberlo.com/blog/youtube-statistics.

27. Ji Lin, Chuang Gan, and Song Han, "TSM: Temporal Shift Module for Efficient Video Understanding," arXiv, August 22, 2019, https://arxiv.org/pdf/1811.08383.pdf.

28. Karen Hao, "Powerful Computer Vision Algorithms Are Now Small Enough to Run on Your Phone," *MIT Technology Review*, October 11, 2019, https://www.technology review.com/f/614551/ai-computer-vision-algorithms-on-your-phone-mit-ibm/.

29. Chelsea Gohd, "It's Really Hard to Give AI 'Common Sense,'" Futurism, March 11, 2018, https://futurism.com/teaching-ai-common-sense.

30. H. James Wilson, Paul R. Daugherty, and Chase Davenport, "The Future of AI Will Be about Less Data, Not More," *Harvard Business Review*, January 14, 2019, https:// hbr.org/2019/01/the-future-of-ai-will-be-about-less-data-not-more. https://hbr.org/2019/01 /the-future-of-ai-will-be-about-less-data-not-more.

31. Gary Marcus, "AI's Hardest Problem? Developing Common Sense," LinkedIn, October 4, 2019, https://www.linkedin.com/pulse/ais-hardest-problem-developing -common-sense-gary-marcus/.

32. "Distracted Driving," National Highway Traffic Safety Administration, n.d., https://www.nhtsa.gov/risky-driving/distracted-driving.

33. "Drowsy Driving: Asleep at the Wheel," Centers for Disease Control and Prevention, November 7, 2019, https://www.cdc.gov/features/dsdrowsydriving/index.html.

34. "Road Rage Statistics Filled with Surprising Facts," https://drivingschool.net/road -rage-statistics-filled-surprising-facts/.

35. Elizabeth Bramson-Boudreaum, "When Our Devices Can Read Our Emotions: Affectiva's Gabi Zijderveld," *MIT Technology Review*, Feb 28, 2019, https://www.technologyreview .com/2019/02/28/136839/when-our-devices-can-read-our-emotions-affectivas-gabi-zijderveld/.

36. Bramson-Boudreaum, "When Our Devices Can Read Our Emotions."

37. Rana el Kaliouby, "Emotionally Aware Technology Could Help Us Beat Zoom Fatigue," *Fast Company*, June 15, 2020, https://www.fastcompany.com/90515714/emotionally -aware-technology-could-help-us-beat-zoom-fatigue.

38. el Kaliouby, "Emotionally Aware Technology Could Help Us Beat Zoom Fatigue."

39. Neil C. Rabinowitz, Frank Perbet, H. Francis Song, Chiyuan Zhang, S. M. Ali Eslami, and Matthew Botvinick, "Machine Theory of Mind," arXiv, March 12, 2018, https://arxiv.org/abs/1802.07740.

40. Matthew Hutson, "Artificial Intelligence Has Learned to Probe the Minds of Other Computers," *Science*, July 27, 2018, https://www.sciencemag.org/news/2018/07 /computer-programs-can-learn-what-other-programs-are-thinking.

41. Christian Blum, Alan F. T. Winfield, and Verena V. Hafner, "Simulation-Based Internal Models for Safer Robots," *Computational Intelligence in Robotics*, January 11, 2018, https://www.frontiersin.org/articles/10.3389/frobt.2017.00074/full.

42. Shelly Fan, "Thinking Like a Human: What It Means to Give AI a Theory of Mind," SingularityHub, September 19, 2018, https://singularityhub.com/2018/09/19 /thinking-like-a-human-what-it-means-to-give-ai-a-theory-of-mind/.

Chapter 2

1. "IoT Growth Demands Rethink of Long-Term Storage Strategies, Says IDC," IDC, July 27, 2020, https://www.idc.com/getdoc.jsp?containerId=prAP46737220.

2. Stefan Seltz-Axmacher, "The End of Starsky Robotics," Medium, March 19, 2020, https://medium.com/starsky-robotics-blog/the-end-of-starsky-robotics-acb8a6a8a5f5.

Notes

3. Gary Marcus and Ernest Davis, *Rebooting AI: Building Artificial Intelligence We Can Trust* (New York: Pantheon Books, 2019), 56.

4. "How Big Data Analysis Helped Increase Walmart's Sales Turnover?" ProjectPro, July 4, 2021, https://www.dezyre.com/article/how-big-data-analysis-helped-increase -walmarts-sales-turnover/109.

5. Jacquelyn Bulao, "How Much Data Is Created Every Day in 2021?" Techjury, May 18, 2021, https://techjury.net/blog/how-much-data-is-created-every-day/#gref.

6. Alex Woodie, "Deep Learning Has Hit a Wall, Intel's Rao Says," Datanami, November 13, 2019, https://www.datanami.com/2019/11/13/deep-learning-has-hit-a-wall -intels-rao-says/.

7. Dhruv Mahajan, Ross Girshick, Vignesh Ramanathan, Manohar Paluri, and Laurens Van Der Maaten, "Advancing State-of-the-Art Image Recognition with Deep Learning on Hashtags," Facebook, May 2, 2018, https://ai.facebook.com/blog/advancing -state-of-the-art-image-recognition-with-deep-learning-on-hashtags/.

8. Roy Schwartz, Jesse Dodge, Noah A. Smith, and Oren Etzioni, "Green AI," arXiv, August 13, 2019, https://arxiv.org/abs/1907.10597.

9. Emma Strubell, Ananya Ganesh, and Andrew McCallum, "Energy and Policy Considerations for Deep Learning in NLP," arXiv, June 5, 2019, https://www .technologyreview.com/s/613630/training-a-single-ai-model-can-emit-as-much-carbon-as -five-cars-in-their-lifetimes/.

10. "COVID-19 Consumer Data Protection Act of 2020," Congress.gov, https://www .congress.gov/bill/116th-congress/senate-bill/3663.

11. Bradley Arsenault, "Why Small Data Is the Future of AI," Towards Data Science, August 7, 2018, https://towardsdatascience.com/why-small-data-is-the-future-of-ai -cb7d705b7f0a.

12. Christopher Mims, "How AI Is Taking Over Our Gadgets," *Wall Street Journal*, June 26, 2021, https://www.wsj.com/articles/how-ai-is-taking-over-our-gadgets -11624680004?page=1.

13. David J. Harris and Tom Croonenborghs, "Bayesian Product Ranking at Wayfair," Wayfair, January 20, 2020, https://tech.wayfair.com/data-science/2020/01/bayesian -product-ranking-at-wayfair/.

14. Swami Sivasubramanian, VP of AI and Machine Learning at AWS, AWS Machine Learning Summit, Opening Keynote, June 2, 2021, https://www.youtube.com/watch?v =dRcA_2Xw2FU.

15. "Amazon Rekognition Custom Labels," AWS, https://aws.amazon.com/rekognition /custom-labels-features/; "Building Your Own Brand Detection and Visibility Using Amazon SageMaker Ground Truth and Amazon Rekognition Custom Labels—Part 1: End-to-End Solution," AWS Machine Learning Blog, January 25, 2021, https://aws.amazon.com/blogs /machine-learning/part-1-end-to-end-solution-building-your-own-brand-detection-and -visibility-using-amazon-sagemaker-ground-truth-and-amazon-rekognition-custom -labels/.

16. Tom Simonite, "These Industrial Robots Get More Adept with Every Task," *Wired*, March 10, 2020, https://www.wired.com/story/these-industrial-robots-adept-every-task/.

17. "How Case Mason Deployed Vicarious Robots to Pack over 500,000 Sephora PLAY! Kits," Vicarious x Case Mason case study, n.d., https://f.hubspotusercontent30.net /hubfs/8180830/Case%20Studies/Vicarious%20x%20Case%20Mason%20Case%20Study.pdf.

18. "Replace Pick-to-Light Systems with Smart Robots Powered by Neuroscience-Inspired AI," Vicarious blog, March 2021, https://www.vicarious.com/posts/replace-pick -to-light-systems-with-smart-robots-powered-by-neuroscience-inspired-ai/.

19. "Attacking Machine Learning with Adversarial Examples," OpenAI, February 24, 2017, https://openai.com/blog/adversarial-example-research/.

20. Tony Peng, "Vicarious.ai Is Teaching Robots to See the World Like Humans," Synced Review, November 10, 2017, https://medium.com/syncedreview/rvicarious-ai-is-teaching-robots-to-see-the-world-like-humans-8f0464202e5.

21. Simonite, "These Industrial Robots Get More Adept with Every Task."

22. Daniel P. Sawyer, Miguel Lazaro-Gredilla, and Dileep George, "A Model of Fast Concept Inference with Object-Factorized Cognitive Programs," arXiv: 2002.04021, https://arxiv.org/pdf/2002.04021.pdf.

23. D. George, W. Lehrach, K. Kansky, M. Lázaro-Gredilla, C. Laan, B. Marthi, X. Lou, Z. Meng, Y. Liu, H. Wang, et al., "A Generative Vision Model That Trains with High Data Efficiency and Breaks Text-Based CAPTCHAs," Science, October 27, 2017, https://media.theobjective.com/2017/10/science.aag-CAPCHA.pdf; Ivan Y. Tyukin, Alexander N. Gorban, Muhammad H. Alkhudaydi, and Qinghua Zhou, "Demystification of Few-Shot and One-Shot Learning," arXiv, May 29, 2021 https://arxiv.org/pdf/2104.12174.pdf; Jun Shu, Zongben Xu, and Deyu Meng, "Small Sample Learning in Big Data Era," arXiv, August 22, 2018, https://arxiv.org/pdf/1808.04572.pdf.

24. Oriol Vinyals, Charles Blundell, Timothy Lillicrap, Koray Kavukcuoglu, and Daan Wierstra, "Matching Networks for One Shot Learning," arXiv, December 29, 2017, https://arxiv.org/pdf/1606.04080.pdf.

25. Egor Zakharov, Aliaksandra Shysheya, Egor Burkov, and Victor Lempitsky, "Few-Shot Adversarial Learning of Realistic Neural Talking Head Models," arXiv, September 25, 2019, arXiv:1905.08233v2.

26. Zakharov et al., "Few-Shot Adversarial Learning of Realistic Neural Talking Head Models."

27. Egor Zakharov, Aliaksandra Shysheya, Egor Burkov, and Victor Lempitsky, "Personal Statement," https://www.youtube.com/watch?v=p1b5aiTrGzY.

28. Elizabeth Payne, "Ottawa Hospital Team Pioneers Virtual Reality to Treat Parkinson's Patients," Kingston Whig-Standard, March 19, 2019, https://www.thewhig.com/news/local-news/ottawa-hospital-team-pioneers-virtual-reality-to-treat-parkinsons-patients/wcm/24914de3-697f-4964-b106-db0877dc0730?fb_comment_id=2004219489677092_2174866382612401.

29. Mandy Erickson, "Virtual Reality System Helps Surgeons, Reassures Patients," (Stanford University Medical Center), Medical X Press, July 12, 2017, https://med.stanford.edu/news/all-news/2017/07/virtual-reality-system-helps-surgeons-reassures-patients.html.

30. Paul Daugherty, Bhaskar Ghosh, Annette Rippert, Ramnath Venkataraman, and H. James Wilson, "Make the Leap, Take the Lead: Tech Strategies for Innovation and Growth," Accenture, April 2021, https://www.accenture.com/us-en/insights/technology/scaling-enterprise-digital-transformation.

Chapter 3

1. Jon Pareles, Caryn Ganz, and Giovanni Russonello, "The Playlist: Anderson .Paak's Soulful Strut, and 12 More New Songs," New York Times, March 15, 2019, https://www.nytimes.com/2019/03/15/arts/music/playlist-anderson-paak-sean-paul-j-balvin.html.

2. Emily Mackay, "Holly Herndon: Making Music with Her AI Child Spawn," BBC, May 11, 2019, https://www.bbc.com/culture/article/20190511-holly-herndon-making-music-with-her-ai-child-spawn.

Notes

3. Katie Hawthorne, "Holly Herndon: The Musician Who Birthed an AI Baby," *Guardian*, May 2, 2019, https://www.theguardian.com/music/2019/may/02/holly-herndon-on-her-musical-baby-spawn-i-wanted-to-find-a-new-sound.

4. Jared Newman, "'Machine Teaching'" Is a Thing, and Microsoft Wants to Own It," *Fast Company*, April 23, 2019, https://www.fastcompany.com/90338498/machine-teaching-is-a-thing-and-microsoft-wants-to-own-it.

5. Dina Bass, "Microsoft Wants to Teach Drones, Robots and Drills How to Think," *Bloomberg News*, November 4, 2019, https://www.bloomberg.com/news/articles/2019-11-04/microsoft-wants-to-teach-drones-robots-and-drills-how-to-think.

6. Jennifer Langston, "Machine Teaching: How People's Expertise Makes AI Even More Powerful," Microsoft, April 23, 2019, https://blogs.microsoft.com/ai/machine-teaching/.

7. The examples that follow are drawn from Bass, "Microsoft Wants to Teach Drones, Robots and Drills How to Think."

8. Zachary Kew-Denniss, "Google's Latest AI Experiment Wants You to Lip-Sync a Song to Help It Learn How We Speak," Android Police, September 24, 2020, https://www.androidpolice.com/2020/09/24/googles-latest-ai-experiment-wants-you-to-lip-sync-a-song-to-help-it-learn-how-we-speak/.

9. "Volkmar Sterzing and Steffen Udluft Rank among the First Inventors of Data-Efficient AI Applications in the World," Siemens, n.d., https://assets.new.siemens.com/siemens/assets/api/uuid:9e0034a9-229a-4e24-a1cf-e0eae8f23117/inventor-2017-sterzing-udluft-e.pdf.

10. H. James Wilson and Paul R. Daugherty, "Small Data Can Play a Big Role in AI," *Harvard Business Review*, February 17, 2020, https://hbr.org/2020/02/small-data-can-play-a-big-role-in-ai.

11. Fred Morstatter, Aram Galstyan, Gleb Satyukov, Daniel Benjamin, Andres Abeliuk, Mehrnoosh Mirtaheri, KSM Tozammel Hossain, Pedro Szekely, Emilio Ferrara, Akira Matsui, et al., "SAGE: A Hybrid Geopolitical Event Forecasting System," *Proceedings of the Twenty-Eighth International Joint Conference on Artificial Intelligence* (IJCAI-19), 2019, pp. 6557–6559, https://www.ijcai.org/Proceedings/2019/0955.pdf.

12. Philip E. Tetlock, *Expert Political Judgment: How Good Is It? How Can We Know?* (Princeton, NJ: Princeton University Press, 2017).

13. James Surowiecki, *The Wisdom of Crowds: Why the Many Are Smarter Than the Few and How Collective Wisdom Shapes Business, Economies, Societies and Nations* (New York: Doubleday, May 2004).

14. Gregg Willcox, Louis Rosenberg, and Hans Schumann, "Sales Forecasting, Polls vs Swarms," Unanimous AI, 2019, https://11s1ty2quyfy2qbmao3bwxzc-wpengine.netdna-ssl.com/wp-content/uploads/2019/11/Sales-Forecasting-Polls-vs-Swarms-Future-Technology-Conference-2019.pdf.

15. Megan Scudellari, "AI-Human 'Hive Mind' Diagnoses Pneumonia," *IEEE Spectrum*, September 13, 2018, https://spectrum.ieee.org/the-human-os/biomedical/diagnostics/ai-human-hive-mind-diagnoses-pneumonia.

16. Hans Schumann, Louis Rosenberg, Niccolo Pescetelli, and Gregg Willcox, "Human Swarms Amplify Accuracy in Financial Predictions," Ubiquitous Computing, Electronics & Mobile Communication Conference (UEMCON), IEEE Annual, New York, October 2017, https://11s1ty2quyfy2qbmao3bwxzc-wpengine.netdna-ssl.com/wp-content/uploads/2019/09/Forecasting-Financial-Markets-by-Swarm-IEEE-HCC-2019.pdf.

17. Josh Penn-Pierson, "Zendesk," Lilt, n.d., https://support.lilt.com/hc/en-us/articles/360053368573-Zendesk.

18. Hao Jiang, Aakash Sabharwal, Adam Henderson, Diane Hu, and Liangjie Hong, "Understanding the Role of Style in E-commerce Shopping," Association for Computing

Machinery KDD (Knowledge Discovery and Data Mining) Conference, Anchorage, August 2019, https://dl.acm.org/doi/pdf/10.1145/3292500.3330760.

19. Harry McCracken, "How Etsy Taught Style to an Algorithm," *Fast Company*, July 11, 2019, https://www.fastcompany.com/90374429/how-etsy-taught-style-to-an-algorithm. The description of how Etsy taught style to its system draws heavily on this article.

20. McCracken, "How Etsy Taught Style to an Algorithm."

21. Alan Murray and David Meyer, Fortune CEO Daily newsletter, April 20, 2021, https://fortune.com/2021/04/20/etsy-ceo-josh-silverman-pandemic-was-our-dunkirk-moment-ceo-daily/.

22. Murray and Meyer, Fortune CEO Daily newsletter.

23. Jeffrey Dastin, "Gap Rushes in More Robots to Warehouses to Solve Virus Disruption," Reuters, May 21, 2020, https://www.reuters.com/article/us-health-coronavirus-gap-automation-foc/gap-rushes-in-more-robots-to-warehouses-to-solve-virus-disruption-idUSKBN22X14Y.

24. "Hybrid Intelligence Is the Future of Supply Chain Management," April 12, 2019, https://www.borndigital.com/2019/04/12/hybrid-intelligence-is-the-future-of-supply-chain-management.

25. "Surgical Tool Annotation for Workflow Analysis," Quadrant and Siemens case study, n.d., https://cataracts.grand-challenge.org/home/.

Chapter 4

1. "L.L.Bean: Modernizing the IT Architecture at a 105-Year-Old Retailer, Google, n.d., https://cloud.google.com/customers/l-l-bean.

2. Emma Sopadjieva, Utpal M. Dholakia, and Beth Benjamin, "A Study of 46,000 Shoppers Shows That Omnichannel Retailing Works," *Harvard Business Review*, January 3, 2017, https://hbr.org/2017/01/a-study-of-46000-shoppers-shows-that-omnichannel-retailing-works.

3. Andre Israel, Brett Goode, Jason Mark, and Edwin Van der Ouderaa, "Digital Decoupling: A Maturing Concept in Digital Disruption," Accenture, March 27, 2019, https://bankingblog.accenture.com/digital-decoupling-maturing-concept-digital-disruption.

4. Bhaskar Ghosh, Adam Burden, and James Wilson, "Full Value. Full Stop. How to Scale Innovation and Achieve Full Value with Future Systems," Accenture, 2019, https://www.accenture.com/us-en/insights/future-systems/future-ready-enterprise-systems.

5. Adam Burden, Edwin Van der Ouderaa, Ramnath Venkataraman, Tomas Nyström, and Prashant P. Shukla, "Technical Debt Might Be Hindering Your Digital Transformation," *Sloan Management Review*, June 19, 2018, https://sloanreview.mit.edu/article/technical-debt-might-be-hindering-your-digital-transformation/.

6. "Smiths Group Unites Data from Five Global Divisions and Hundreds of Apps with Azure Data Lake Storage," Microsoft, March 10, 2020, https://customers.microsoft.com/en-GB/story/769823-smiths-group-manufacturing-azure.

7. "Smiths Group Unites Data from Five Global Divisions and Hundreds of Apps with Azure Data Lake Storage."

8. Werner Vogels, "Modern Applications at AWS," All Things Distributed Weblog, August 28, 2019, https://www.allthingsdistributed.com/2019/08/modern-applications-at-aws.html.

9. Einas Haddad, "Service-Oriented Architecture: Scaling the Uber Engineering Codebase as We Grow," Uber Engineering, September 8, 2015, https://eng.uber.com/service-oriented-architecture/.

Notes

10. Haddad, "Service-Oriented Architecture: Scaling the Uber Engineering Codebase as We Grow."

11. Haddad, "Service-Oriented Architecture."

12. Adam Gluck, "Introducing Domain-Oriented Microservice Architecture," Uber Engineering, July 23, 2020, https://eng.uber.com/microservice-architecture/.

13. "Ever–ready for Every Opportunity," Accenture, 2021, https://www.accenture.com/_acnmedia/Thought-Leadership-Assets/PDF-5/Accenture-Unleashing-Competitiveness-on-the-Cloud-Continuum-Executive-Summary.pdf.

14. Will Knight, "Meet the Chinese Finance Giant That's Secretly an AI Company," *MIT Technology Review,* June 16, 2017, https://www.technologyreview.com/s/608103/ant-financial-chinas-giant-of-mobile-payments-is-rethinking-finance-with-ai/.

15. Kevin McLaughlin, "After Strategy Reboot JPMorgan Going Deeper in the Cloud," The Information, May 7, 2019, https://www.theinformation.com/articles/after-strategy-reboot-jpmorgan-going-deeper-in-cloud.

16. Jacob Devlin, Ming-Wei Chang, Kenton Lee, and Kristina Toutanova, "BERT: Pre-training of Deep Bidirectional Transformers for Language Understanding," arXiv, May 24, 2018, https://arxiv.org/pdf/1810.04805.pdf.

17. Will Douglas Heaven, "OpenAI's New Language Generator GPT-3 Is Shockingly Good—and Completely Mindless," *MIT Technology Review*, July 20, 2020, https://www.technologyreview.com/2020/07/20/1005454/openai-machine-learning-language-generator-gpt-3-nlp/.

18. Steve Lohr, "The Internet Eats Up Less Energy Than You Might Think," *New York Times*, June 24, 2021, https://www.nytimes.com/2021/06/24/technology/computer-energy-use-study.html.

19. "AI Gives Ukrainian Internet Taxi Start-up Real Competitive Edge," Microsoft, April 19, 2018, https://customers.microsoft.com/en-gb/story/uklon-transportation-powerbi-azure-machine-learning-ukraine.

20. Van Baker, "Technology Insight for Cloud AI Developer Services," October 1, 2019, Gartner, https://www.gartner.com/en/documents/3969932/technology-insight-for-cloud-ai-developer-services.

21. "Edge Artificial Intelligence Chips Market Size, Share & Trends Analysis Report by Processor (CPU, GPU, ASIC), Device Type (Consumer, Enterprise Devices), Function (Training, Inference), by Region, and Segment Forecasts, 2020–2027," Grand View Research, May 2020, https://www.grandviewresearch.com/industry-analysis/edge-artificial-intelligence-chips-market.

22. "Geotechnical Company Generates Environmental Insights Faster and More Reliably with Edge Computing," Microsoft, February 17, 2020, https://customers.microsoft.com/en-gb/story/772599-fugro-professional-services-azure-sql-database-edge.

23. "Geotechnical Company Generates Environmental Insights Faster and More Reliably with Edge Computing."

24. "Geotechnical Company Generates Environmental Insights Faster and More Reliably with Edge Computing."

25. "Oil and Gas Experts Use Machine Learning to Deploy Predictive Analytics at the Edge," Microsoft, September 25, 2017, https://customers.microsoft.com/en-gb/story/schneider-electric-process-mfg-resources-azure-machine-learning.

26. "Oil and Gas Experts Use Machine Learning to Deploy Predictive Analytics at the Edge."

27. Omar Abbosh and Larry Downes, "5G's Potential, and Why Businesses Should Start Preparing for It," *Harvard Business Review*, March 5, 2019, https://hbr.org/2019/03/5gs-potential-and-why-businesses-should-start-preparing-for-it.

28. Catherine Sbeglia, "Verizon to Offer 5G Network Edge Computing with AWS Wavelength," *RCRWirelessNews*, December 4, 2019, https://www.rcrwireless.com/20191204/5g/verizon-5g-network-edge-computing-with-aws-wavelength.

29. Brendan McMahan and Daniel Ramage, "Federated Learning: Collaborative Machine Learning without Centralized Training Data," Google, April 6, 2017, https://ai.googleblog.com/2017/04/federated-learning-collaborative.html.

30. Talha Burki, "Pharma Blockchains AI for Drug Development," *Lancet*, June 15, 2019, https://www.thelancet.com/journals/lancet/article/PIIS0140-6736(19)31401-1/fulltext.

31. Jared Council, "Bayer Looks to Emerging Technique to Overcome AI Data Challenges," *Wall Street Journal*, January 27, 2020, https://www.wsj.com/articles/bayer-looks-to-emerging-technique-to-overcome-ai-data-challenges.

32. Duska Anastasijevic, "Mayo Clinic Launches Its First Platform Initiative," Mayo Clinic, January 14, 2020, https://newsnetwork.mayoclinic.org/discussion/mayo-clinic-launches-its-first-platform-initiative/.

33. Anastasijevic, "Mayo Clinic Launches Its First Platform Initiative."

34. Khari Johnson, "Nvidia Launches Clara Guardian to Power Smart Hospitals with Surveillance, Sensors, and Edge AI," Venture Beat, May 14, 2020, https://venturebeat.com/2020/05/14/nvidia-launches-clara-guardian-to-power-smart-hospitals-with-surveillance-sensors-and-edge-ai/.

35. "Nvidia Clara Guardian," Nvidia, 2021, https://www.nvidia.com/en-us/clara/smart-hospitals/; Arya Goswami, "Ouva's Hospital Intelligence Platform Uses NVIDIA Clara Guardian Framework to Monitor Patients in a Contact Free Environment," MarkTech-Post, September 17, 2020, https://www.marktechpost.com/2020/09/17/ouvas-hospital-intelligence-platform-uses-nvidia-clara-guardian-framework-to-monitor-patients-in-a-contact-free-environment/; "Diycam Brings AI to the Edge of Healthcare with NVIDIA Clara Guardian," *Times of India*, May 27, 2020, https://timesofindia.indiatimes.com/business/india-business/diycam-bringsai-to-the-edge-of-healthcare-with-nvidia-clara-guardian/articleshow/76035783.cms.

36. Johnson, "Nvidia Launches Clara Guardian to Power Smart Hospitals with Surveillance, Sensors, and Edge AI."

37. Ghosh et al., "Full Value. Full Stop."

Chapter 5

1. "How Starbucks Is Using COVID-19 Crisis to Differentiate the Brand," WARC, March 8, 2020, https://www.warc.com/newsandopinion/news/how-starbucks-is-using-covid-19-crisis-to-differentiate-the-brand/43929.

2. Chris Walton, "3 Ways Starbucks Will Emerge from COVID-19 Stronger Than Before," *Forbes*, April 3, 2020, https://www.forbes.com/sites/christopherwalton/2020/04/03/3-ways-starbucks-will-emerge-from-covid-19-stronger-than-before/?sh=60ac5f3d1844.

3. James Vincent, "Welcome to the Automated Warehouse of the Future," The Verge, May 8, 2018, https://www.theverge.com/2018/5/8/17331250/automated-warehouses-jobs-ocado-andover-amazon; "See Inside Ocado's Warehouse Where Robots Pick

Groceries," BT, May 31, 2018, https://home.bt.com/tech-gadgets/tech-news/see-the-ocado -robots-whizz-around-their-automated-supermarket-warehouse-11364269826882.

4. Max Smolaks, "Robots and Software: How Ocado Is Creating New Business Models," DCD, August 29, 2018, https://www.datacenterdynamics.com/en/analysis/robots -and-software-how-ocado-creating-new-business-models/.

5. Michael Moore, "How Ocado and AWS Are Teaming Up to Keep Your Shopping Fresh," ITProPortal, June 29, 2017, https://www.itproportal.com/features/how-ocado-and -aws-are-teaming-up-to-keep-your-shopping-fresh/.

6. "The Art of the Pivot: How Enterprises Do It in the Cloud," Amazon, 2019, https://pages.awscloud.com/rs/112-TZM-766/images/AWS_The_Art_of_the_Pivot_2019.pdf.

7. Moore, "How Ocado and AWS Are Teaming Up to Keep Your Shopping Fresh."

8. "Our Strategy," Ocado Group, https://www.ocadogroup.com/about-us/our -strategy#ip-anchor-4162.

9. Simon Read, "Ocado Says Switch to Online Shopping Is Permanent," BBC.com, July 14, 2020, https://www.bbc.com/news/business-53402767.

10. Vincent, "Welcome to the Automated Warehouse of the Future."

11. Elon Musk, "The Secret Tesla Motors Master Plan (Just between You and Me)," Tesla, August 2, 2006, https://www.tesla.com/es_ES/blog/secret-tesla-motors-master-plan -just-between-you-and-me.

12. Bernard Marr, "The Amazing Ways Tesla Is Using Artificial Intelligence and Big Data," BernardMarr.com, Retrieved October 4, 2020, https://bernardmarr.com/the -amazing-ways-tesla-is-using-artificial-intelligence-and-big-data/.

13. Nathan Furr and Jeff Dyer, "Lessons from Tesla's Approach to Innovation," *Harvard Business Review*, February 12, 2020, https://hbr.org/2020/02/lessons-from-teslas -approach-to-innovation.

14. Ry Crist, "Samsung's Bixby Will Soon ID the Foods in Your Family Hub Fridge," CNET, January 10, 2019, https://www.cnet.com/news/samsungs-bixby-will-soon-id-the -foods-in-your-family-hub-fridge/.

15. "DEWA Power Plants, Dubai," Signify Holding, 2019, https://www.assets.signify .com/is/content/PhilipsLighting/Assets/signify/global/20191211-dewa-case-study.pdf.

16. "Philips Lighting Underlines Leadership in Lighting for the Internet of Things with New IoT Platform," Signify, March 19, 2018, https://www.signify.com/global/our -company/news/press-release-archive/2018/20180319-philips-lighting-underlines -leadership-in-lighting-for-the-internet-of-things-with-new-iot-platform.

17. Shai Wininger, "Lemonade Launch Metrics Exposed," Lemonade, November 22, 2016, https://www.lemonade.com/blog/lemonade-launch-metrics-exposed/.

18. "Lemonade Shareholder Letter, Q2 2020," https://s24.q4cdn.com/139015699/files /doc_downloads/2020/08/Shareholder-Letter-Q2-2020-(1).pdf.

19. Daniel Schreiber, "Lemonade Sets New World Record," Lemonade, January 5, 2017, https://stories.lemonade.com/lemonade-sets-new-world-record-706ef8674110.

20. "Lemonade Shareholder Letter, Q2 2020."

21. Dan Ariely, "Social Impact in 100 Days: Transparency Chronicles Part 4, Insurance as a Social Good," Lemonade, January 31, 2017, https://www.lemonade.com /blog/lemonade-social-impact-100-days/.

22. Daniel Schreiber, "Precision Underwriting," Lemonade, April 3, 2018, https://www .lemonade.com/blog/precision-underwriting/.

23. José María Álvarez-Pallete, "The New Telefónica," Telefónica, November 27, 2019, https://www.telefonica.com/ext/the-new-telefonica/letter-ceo-alvarez-pallete.pdf.

24. Álvarez-Pallete, "The New Telefónica."

25. "ElevenPaths Has Achieved Amazon Web Services (AWS) Security Competency Status," Telefónica, May 26, 2020, https://www.telefonica.com/en/web/press-office/-/elevenpaths-achieves-amazon-web-services-aws-security-competence-status.

26. "Telefónica Tech Reinforces Its Cybersecurity Consulting Capabilities with the Acquisition of Govertis," Telefónica, August 25, 2020, https://www.telefonica.com/en/web/press-office/-/telefonica-tech-reinforces-its-cybersecurity-consulting-capabilities-with-the-acquisition-of-govertis.

27. "Telefónica Tech Fosters the Training of Cybersecurity Professionals with the Acquisition of iHackLabs," Telefónica, September 7, 2020, https://www.telefonica.com/en/web/press-office/-/telefonica-tech-fosters-the-training-of-cybersecurity-professionals-with-the-acquisition-of-ihacklabs.

28. "Telefónica Introduces Telefónica Tech Ventures, Its Investment Vehicle Specialized in Cybersecurity," Telefónica, October 22, 2020, https://www.telefonica.com/en/web/press-office/-/telefonica-introduces-telefonica-tech-ventures-its-investment-vehicle-specialized-in-cybersecurity.

29. Daisuke Tanaka, "Re-Energizing Small Molecule Drug Discovery by Centaur Chemist," presentation at British Embassy, Tokyo, July 25, 2018, https://www.ebi.ac.uk/sites/ebi.ac.uk/files/groups/industry_office/industry-events/japan-2018-event/British%20Embassy%20conference_Japan_Daisuke%20Tanaka.pdf.

30. Joanne Kotz, "In Silico Drug Design," Science-Business eXchange, January 24, 2013, https://link.springer.com/article/10.1038/scibx.2013.50.

31. "Europe's Largest Initiative Launches to Accelerate Therapy Development for COVID-19 and Future Coronavirus Threats," BioSpace, August 18, 2020, https://www.biospace.com/article/releases/europe-s-largest-initiative-launches-to-accelerate-therapy-development-for-covid-19-and-future-coronavirus-threats/.

32. "More than 23 Million People in the WHO European Region Fall Ill from Unsafe Food Every Year," World Health Organization, March 12, 2015, https://www.euro.who.int/en/health-topics/disease-prevention/food-safety/news/news/2015/12/more-than-23-million-people-in-the-who-european-region-fall-ill-from-unsafe-food-every-year#:~:text=New%20report%20on%20the%20burden%20of%20foodborne%20diseases&text=Each%20year%2C%20as%20many%20as,the%20age%20of%205%20years.

33. "LumoVision: Saving Lives and Improving Livelihoods with Revolutionary Data-Driven Maize Sorting Technology," Bühler, n.d., https://digital.buhlergroup.com/lumovision/.

34. "Bühler LumoVision: Saving Lives and Improving Livelihoods with Revolutionary Data-Driven Grain Sorting Technology," Milling and Grain, April 23, 2018, https://millingandgrain.com/entrada/buhler-lumovision--saving-lives-and-improving-livelihoods-with-revolutionary-data-driven-grain-sorting-technology-18263/.

35. "LumoVision: Saving Lives and Improving Livelihoods with Revolutionary Data-Driven Maize Sorting Technology."

36. Sharon LaFraniere, Katie Thomas, Noah Weiland, David Gelles, Sheryl Gay Stolberg, and Denise Grady, "Politics, Science and the Remarkable Race for a Coronavirus Vaccine," New York Times, November 21, 2020, https://www.nytimes.com/2020/11/21/us/politics/coronavirus-vaccine.html?login=smartlock&auth=login-smartlock.

37. LaFraniere et al., "Politics, Science and the Remarkable Race for a Coronavirus Vaccine."

38. Joe Palco, "Moderna's COVID-19 Vaccine Shines in Clinical Trial," NPR Morning Edition, November 16, 2020, https://www.npr.org/sections/health-shots/2020/11/16/935239294/modernas-covid-19-vaccine-shines-in-clinical-trial.

Notes

39. "How Building a Digital Biotech Is Mission-Critical to Moderna," Moderna, n.d., https://www.modernatx.com/sites/default/files/Moderna_Digital_WhitePaper_Final.pdf. The account that follows of Moderna's operations is largely taken from this document.

Part Two

1. Bhaskar Ghosh, Adam Burden, and James Wilson, "Full Value. Full Stop.: How to Scale Innovation and Achieve Full Value with Future Systems," Accenture, 2019, https://www.accenture.com/us-en/insights/future-systems/future-ready-enterprise-systems.

2. Frank Gens, Meredith Whalen, Deepak Mohan, Philip Carnelley, Larry Carvalho, Gary Chen, Ruthbea Yesner, Arnal Dayaratna, Frank Della Rosa, James Wester, et al., "IDC FutureScape: Worldwide IT Industry 2020 Predictions," IDC, October 28, 1919, https://www.idc.com/getdoc.jsp?containerId=US45599219.

3. Aaron Tan, "Getting Threat Intelligence Right," TechTarget, May 30, 2017, https://www.computerweekly.com/feature/Getting-threat-intelligence-right.

Chapter 6

1. Claudia Nemat, "Resilience: A Success Factor for Deutsche Telekom," Deutsche Telekom, July 16, 2020, https://www.telekom.com/en/company/management-unplugged /details/resilience-a-success-factor-for-deutsche-telekom-604006.

2. Julie Sweet and Ellyn Shook, "The Hidden Value of Culture Makers," Accenture, 2020, https://www.accenture.com/ie-en/about/inclusion-diversity/_acnmedia/Thought -Leadership-Assets/PDF-3/Accenture-Getting-To-Equal-2020-Research-Report-IE.pdf.

3. Authors' correspondence with the company, October 2021.

4. "Why LexisNexis Is 'in Awe' of Automation Hub and Task Capture," UiPath, 2020, https://www.uipath.com/resources/automation-case-studies/lexisnexis-risk-solutions -rpa.

5. Roberto Torres, "Low Code Helped Put Out COVID-19 Fires: How Can Leaders Sustain Momentum?" CIO Dive, June 18, 2020, https://www.ciodive.com/news/low-code -implementation-coronavirus-2020/580024/.

6. Jeff Barr, "Introducing Amazon Honeycode—Build Web & Mobile Apps without Writing Code," AWS, June 24, 2020, https://aws.amazon.com/blogs/aws/introducing -amazon-honeycode-build-web-mobile-apps-without-writing-code/.

7. Stephanie Condon, "Salesforce Rolls Out New Low-Code Features for Lightning App Builder," ZDNet, May 7, 2020, https://www.zdnet.com/article/salesforce-rolls-out-new -low-code-features-for-lightning-app-builder/.

8. "Add an App to Microsoft Teams, Microsoft Power Apps," September 15, 2020, https://docs.microsoft.com/en-us/powerapps/user/open-app-embedded-in-teams.

9. John Moore, "RPA Journey: Schneider Electric's Global Plan Taps Blue Prism, UiPath," TechTarget, August 19, 2019, https://searchcio.techtarget.com/feature/RPA -journey-Schneider-Electrics-global-plan-taps-Blue-Prism-UiPath.

10. "DevOps tech: Empowering Teams to Choose Tools," Google Cloud, November 16, 2020, https://cloud.google.com/solutions/devops/devops-tech-teams-empowered-to -choose-tools.

11. "Statistics," National Girls Collaborative Project, 2021, https://ngcproject.org/statistics.

12. Pierre Nanterme and Bruno Sanguinetti, "It's Learning: Just Not as We Know It," Accenture, n.d., https://www.accenture.com/_acnmedia/Thought-Leadership-Assets/PDF /Accenture-Education-and-Technology-Skills-Research.pdf.

13. Paul R. Daugherty, H. James Wilson, and Rumman Chowdhury, "Using Artificial Intelligence to Promote Diversity," *Sloan Management Review*, November 21, 2018, https://sloanreview.mit.edu/article/using-artificial-intelligence-to-promote-diversity/.

14. Kimberly A. Houser, "Can AI Solve the Diversity Problem in the Tech Industry? Mitigating Noise and Bias in Employment Decision-Making," *Stanford Technology Law Review*, Spring 2019, https://law.stanford.edu/wp-content/uploads/2019/08/Houser _20190830_test.pdf.

15. "Future Skills Pilot Report," World Economic Forum, Unilever, Walmart, SkyHive and Accenture, 2021, https://www.accenture.com/_acnmedia/PDF-149/Accenture-Future -Skills-Case-Study.pdf.

16. "The STEM Gap: Women and Girls in Science, Technology, Engineering and Math," AAUW, n.d., https://www.aauw.org/resources/research/the-stem-gap/.

17. Amy Edmondson, "Psychological Safety and Learning Behavior in Work Teams," *Administrative Science Quarterly*, Vol. 44, No. 2, June 1999, https://www.jstor.org/stable /2666999?seq=1#page_scan_tab_contents.

18. Charles Duhigg, "What Google Learned from Its Quest to Build the Perfect Team," *New York Times Magazine*, February 25, 2016, https://www.nytimes.com/2016/02/28 /magazine/what-google-learned-from-its-quest-to-build-the-perfect-team.html?smid=pl -share.

19. "The Missing Element in Nearly Every Learning Strategy," Gartner Research, September 22, 2020, https://www.gartner.com/en/documents/3990788/the-missing -element-in-nearly-every-learning-strategy; Andy Young, Edwin Van der Ouderaa, Monica Juneja, and Diana Barea, "Fearless: How Safety and Trust Can Help Financial Services Thrive Even During Disruption and Transformational Change," Accenture, 2019, https://www.criticaleye.com/inspiring/insights-servfile.cfm?id=5657; Paul J. Zak, "The Neuroscience of Trust," *Harvard Business Review*, January–February 2017, https:// hbr.org/2017/01/the-neuroscience-of-trust.

20. Bhaskar Ghosh, Adam Burden, and James Wilson, "Full Value. Full Stop. How to Scale Innovation and Achieve Full Value with Future Systems," Accenture, 2019, https:// www.accenture.com/us-en/insights/future-systems/future-ready-enterprise-systems.

21. Paul Daugherty, Bhaskar Ghosh, Annette Rippert, Ramnath Venkataraman, and H. James Wilson, "Make the Leap, Take the Lead," Accenture, April 28, 2021, https:// www.accenture.com/us-en/insights/technology/scaling-enterprise-digital-transformation.

22. Yaarit Silverstone, Sarah Bartel, and Philippe Chauffard, "Modern Cloud Champions," Accenture, August 13, 2021, https://www.accenture.com/us-en/insights /consulting/cloud-workforce.

23. "IOOF Gives Developers a New Lease on Life with OutSystems," OutSystems, n.d., https://www.outsystems.com/case-studies/it-modernization-wealth-management/.

24. "AWS Announces the DeepRacer League (DRL)," Amazon Web Services, November 29, 2018, https://press.aboutamazon.com/news-releases/news-release-details /aws-announces-deepracer-league-drl.

25. Sara Castellanos, "Ready, Set, Algorithms! Teams Learn AI by Racing Cars," *Wall Street Journal*, October 1, 2019, https://www.wsj.com/articles/ready-set-algorithms-teams -learn-ai-by-racing-cars-11569922202.

26. "Morningstar Launches Global AWS DeepRacer Corporate Competition to Accelerate Application of Machine Learning," Morningstar, May 30, 2019, https:// newsroom.morningstar.com/newsroom/news-archive/press-release-details/2019 /Morningstar-Launches-Global-AWS-DeepRacer-Corporate-Competition-to-Accelerate -Application-of-Machine-Learning/default.aspx.

27. Peter High, "How Capital One Became a Leading Digital Bank," *Forbes*, December 12, 2016, https://www.forbes.com/sites/peterhigh/2016/12/12/how-capital-one-became-a-leading-digital-bank/#6d99271315ee.

28. "Capital One Financial Corporation," Agreatplacetowork, 2020, https://www.greatplacetowork.com/certified-company/1000049.

29. Santo Milasi, Ignacio González-Vázquez, and Enrique Fernández-Macías, "Telework in the EU before and after the COVID-19: Where We Were, Where We Head To," European Commission, 2020, https://ec.europa.eu/jrc/sites/jrcsh/files/jrc120945_policy_brief_-_covid_and_telework_final.pdf.

30. Nicholas Bloom, "How Working from Home Works Out," Stanford: Institute for Economic Policy Research, June 2020, https://siepr.stanford.edu/research/publications/how-working-home-works-out.

31. Lynda Gratton, "How to Do Hybrid Right," *Harvard Business Review*, May–June 2021, https://hbr.org/2021/05/how-to-do-hybrid-right.

32. Matthew Haag, "Remote Work Is Here to Stay: Manhattan May Never Be the Same," *New York Times*, March 29, 2021, https://www.nytimes.com/2021/03/29/nyregion/remote-work-coronavirus-pandemic.html?action=click&module=Top%20Stories&pgtype=Homepage.

33. "National Landlord Survey," KayoCloud, March 2021, https://kayocloud.com/KayoCloud_LandlordReport_March2021.pdf.

34. Kristin Stoller, "Never Want to Go Back to the Office? Here's Where You Should Work," *Forbes*, January 31, 2021, https://www.forbes.com/sites/kristinstoller/2021/01/31/never-want-to-go-back-to-the-office-heres-where-you-should-work/?sh=8958bdb67127.

35. Victoria Gill, "Robotic Scientists Will 'Speed Up Discovery,'" BBC News, July 6, 2020, https://www.bbc.com/news/science-environment-53029854.

36. "Fujitsu Embarks towards 'New Normal,' Redefining Working Styles for Its Japan Offices," Fujitsu Limited, July 6, 2020, https://www.fujitsu.com/global/about/resources/news/press-releases/2020/0706-01.html.

37. Alan Kohll, "New Study Shows Correlation between Employee Engagement and the Long-Lost Lunch Break," *Forbes*, May 29, 2018, https://www.forbes.com/sites/alankohll/2018/05/29/new-study-shows-correlation-between-employee-engagement-and-the-long-lost-lunch-break/

38. "Humana Uses Microsoft Viva Insights to Help Balance the Workplace Experience," Microsoft, April 30, 2021, https://customers.microsoft.com/en-ca/story/1366153368901617436-humana-healthcare-microsoft-365-viva-insights.

39. Shannon Bond, "Facebook Expects Half Its Employees to Work Remotely Permanently," NPR, May 21, 2020, https://www.npr.org/sections/coronavirus-live-updates/2020/05/21/860382831/facebook-expects-half-its-employees-to-work-remotely-forever.

40. Adam D'Angelo, "Remote First at Quora," The Quora Blog, June 25, 2020, https://www.quora.com/q/quora/Remote-First-at-Quora.

41. Mike Robuck, "Verizon Takes Covid WFH Lessons into Next Stage of Hiring 950 New Employees," Fierce Telecom, September 4, 2020, https://www.fiercetelecom.com/telecom/verizon-takes-covid-wfh-home-lessons-into-next-stage-of-hiring-950-new-employees.

42. Elizabeth Dwoskin, "Americans Might Never Come Back to the Office, and Twitter Is Leading the Charge," *Washington Post*, October 1, 2020, https://www.washingtonpost.com/technology/2020/10/01/twitter-work-from-home/.

43. Christie Smith, Yaarit Silverstone, Nicholas Whittall, David Shaw, and Kent McMillan, "The Future of Work: A Hybrid Work Model," Accenture, April 30, 2021, https://www.accenture.com/us-en/insights/consulting/future-work.

Notes

Chapter 7

1. Jerry M. Evensky, "Adam Smith's Essentials: On Trust, Faith, and Free Markets," *Journal of the History of Economic Thought*, Vol. 33, No. 2, June 2011.

2. Susan T. Fiske, Amy J. C. Cuddy, Peter Glick, and Jun Xu, "A Model of (Often Mixed) Stereotype Content: Competence and Warmth Respectively Follow from Perceived Status and Competition," *Journal of Personality and Social Psychology*, Vol. 82, No. 6, 2002, 878–902, https://cos.gatech.edu/facultyres/Diversity_Studies/Fiske _StereotypeContent.pdf.

3. Chris Malone and Susan T. Fiske, *The Human Brand: How We Relate to People, Products, and Companies*, Jossey-Bass, 2013, 28.

4. Shoshana Zuboff, *The Age of Surveillance Capitalism: The Fight for a Human Future at the New Frontier of Power*, Public Affairs, 2019.

5. Schumpeter, "Getting a Handle on a Scandal," *Economist*, March 18, 2018, https://www.economist.com/business/2018/03/28/getting-a-handle-on-a-scandal.

6. Julie Sweet and Paul Daugherty, "Foreword," Accenture Technology Vision 2021, https://www.accenture.com/us-en/insights/technology/_acnmedia/Thought-Leadership -Assets/PDF-3/Accenture-Tech-Vision-2021-Full-Report.pdf.

7. Allan Dafoe, Yoram Bachrach, Gillian Hadfield, Eric Horvitz, Kate Larson, and Thore Graepel, "Cooperative AI: Machines Must Learn to Find Common Ground," *Nature*, Vol. 593, May 6, 2021, https://www.nature.com/articles/d41586-021-01170-0.

8. Dafoe et al., "Cooperative AI: Machines Must Learn to Find Common Ground."

9. Paul R. Daugherty and H. James Wilson, *Human + Machine: Reimagining Work in the Age of AI* (Boston: Harvard Business Review Press, 2018). The phenomenon of "algorithm aversion" was describe by Berkeley J. Dietvorst, Joseph P. Simmons, and Cade Massey, "Algorithm Aversion: People Erroneously Avoid Algorithms after Seeing Them Err," *Journal of Experimental Psychology: General*, July 16, 2014, https://papers.ssrn.com /sol3/papers.cfm?abstract_id=2466040.

10. J. M. Logg, J. A. Minson, and D. A. Moore, "Algorithm Appreciation: People Prefer Algorithmic to Human Judgment," *Organizational Behavior and Human Decision Processes*, Vol. 151, 2019, 90–103.

11. Jared Council, "Alexa Has a New Skill: Asking When It Doesn't Know," *Wall Street Journal*, December 11, 2020, https://www.wsj.com/articles/alexa-has-a-new-skill-asking -when-it-doesnt-know-11607732175.

12. The Husain Experience, Museum of Art and Photography (MAP), Bangalore, India, https://map-india.org/the-ai-husain-experience/.

13. Will Knight, "A New Artificial Intelligence Makes Mistakes—on Purpose," *Wired*, February 13, 2021, https://www.wired.com/story/new-artificial-intelligence-mistakes -purpose-chess/.

14. R. Rideaux and A. E. Welchman, "Exploring and Explaining Properties of Motion Processing in Biological Brains Using a Neural Network," *Journal of Vision*, Vol. 21, No. 11, February 2021, https://www.biorxiv.org/content/10.1101/2020.09.03.281030v1.full.

15. Bobby Allyn, "'The Computer Got It Wrong': How Facial Recognition Led to False Arrest of Black Man," NPR, June 24, 2020, https://www.npr.org/2020/06/24/882683463 /the-computer-got-it-wrong-how-facial-recognition-led-to-a-false-arrest-in-michig.

16. Joy Buolamwini and Timnit Gebru, "Gender Shades: Intersectional Accuracy Disparities in Commercial Gender Classification," *Proceedings of Machine Learning Research,* Vol. 81, 2018, 1–15, http://proceedings.mlr.press/v81/buolamwini18a/buolam wini18a.pdf.

17. Benjamin Wilson, Judy Hoffman, and Jamie Morgenstern, "Predictive Inequity in Object Detection," arXiv, February 21, 2019, https://arxiv.org/abs/1902.11097.

18. Ben Dickson, "Artificial Intelligence Has a Bias Problem, and It's Our Fault," *PCMag*, June 14, 2018, https://www.pcmag.com/news/artificial-intelligence-has-a-bias-problem-and-its-our-fault.

19. Matthew Hutson, "The Language Machines," *Nature*, Vol. 591, March 4, 2021, https://www.nature.com/articles/d41586-021-00530-0.

20. Jay Greene, "Microsoft Won't Sell Police Its Facial-Recognition Technology, Following Similar Moves by Amazon and IBM," *Washington Post*, June 11, 2020, https://www.washingtonpost.com/technology/2020/06/11/microsoft-facial-recognition/.

21. Sarah Todd, "People Are Terrible Judges of Talent: Can Algorithms Do Better?" *Quartz*, November 19, 2019, https://qz.com/work/1742847/pymetrics-ceo-frida-polli-on-the-ai-solution-to-hiring-bias/.

22. Todd, "People Are Terrible Judges of Talent: Can Algorithms Do Better?"

23. Sara Castellanos, "Tech Giants Launch New AI Tools as Worries Mount about Explainability," *Wall Street Journal*, September 26, 2018, https://www.wsj.com/articles/tech-giants-launch-new-ai-tools-as-worries-mount-about-explainability-1537975652?tesla=y.

24. Neil Vigdor, "Apple Card Investigated after Gender Discrimination Complaints," *New York Times*, November 10, 2019, https://www.nytimes.com/2019/11/10/business/Apple-credit-card-investigation.html.

25. Mariusz Bojarski, Philip Yeres, Anna Choromanaska, Krzysztof Choromanski, Bernhard Firner, Lawrence Jackel, and Urs Muller, "Explaining How a Deep Neural Network Trained with End-to-End Learning Steers a Car," arXiv, April 25, 2017, https://arxiv.org/pdf/1704.07911.pdf.

26. Will Knight, "Nvidia Lets You Peer Inside the Black Box of Its Self-Driving AI," *MIT Technology Review*, May 3, 2017, https://www.technologyreview.com/2017/05/03/105964/nvidia-lets-you-peer-inside-the-black-box-of-its-self-driving-ai/.

27. Danny Shapiro, "Reading an AI Car's Mind: How NVIDIA's Neural Net Makes Decisions," NVIDIA, April 27, 2017, https://blogs.nvidia.com/blog/2017/04/27/how-nvidias-neural-net-makes-decisions/.

28. Castellanos, "Tech Giants Launch New AI Tools as Worries Mount about Explainability."

29. Ben Dickson, "Inside DARPA's Effort to Create Explainable Artificial Intelligence," TechTalks, January 10, 2019, https://bdtechtalks.com/2019/01/10/darpa-xai-explainable-artificial-intelligence/.

30. Dickson, "Inside DARPA's Effort to Create Explainable Artificial Intelligence."

31. "Apple CEO Tim Cook: 'Privacy Is a Fundamental Human Right,'" *All Things Considered*, NPR, October 1, 2015, https://www.npr.org/sections/alltechconsidered/2015/10/01/445026470/apple-ceo-tim-cook-privacy-is-a-fundamental-human-right.

32. Michael Grothaus, "Forget the New iPhones: Apple's Best Product Is Now Privacy," *Fast Company*, September 13, 2018, https://www.fastcompany.com/90236195/forget-the-new-iphones-apples-best-product-is-now-privacy.

33. Michael Grothaus, "Use These 11 Critical iPhone Privacy and Security Settings Right Now," *Fast Company*, February 18, 2020, https://www.fastcompany.com/90254589/use-these-11-critical-iphone-privacy-and-security-settings-right-now.

34. "Differential Privacy," Apple, n.d., https://www.apple.com/privacy/docs/Differential_Privacy_Overview.pdf, accessed December 7, 2020.

35. Gerrit De Vynck, "Sonos Launched a Speaker That Won't Record Your Conversations," *Bloomberg News*, September 5, 2019, https://www.bloomberg.com/news/articles/2019-09-05/anti-alexa-this-sonos-speaker-won-t-record-your-conversations.

Notes

36. Baobao Zhang and Allan Dafoe. "Artificial Intelligence: American Attitudes and Trends," Center for the Governance of AI, Future of Humanity Institute, University of Oxford, 2019, https://governanceai.github.io/US-Public-Opinion-Report-Jan-2019/us _public_opinion_report_jan_2019.pdf.

37. Richard Stengel, "The Untold Story of the Sony Hack: How North Korea's Battle with Seth Rogen and George Clooney Foreshadowed Russian Election Meddling In 2016," *Vanity Fair*, October 6, 2019, https://www.vanityfair.com/news/2019/10/the-untold -story-of-the-sony-hack.

38. David E. Sanger and Nicole Perlroth, "FireEye, a Top Cybersecurity Firm, Says It Was Hacked by a Nation-State," *New York Times*, Dec. 8, 2020, https://www.nytimes.com /2020/12/08/technology/fireeye-hacked-russians.html.

39. Alex Schiffer, "How a Fish Tank Helped Hack a Casino," *Washington Post*, July 21, 2017, https://www.washingtonpost.com/news/innovations/wp/2017/07/21/how-a-fish-tank -helped-hack-a-casino/.

40. "Internet Growth Statistics," Internet World Stats, https://www.internetworldstats .com/emarketing.htm.

41. H. Tankovska, "Internet of Things—Active Connections Worldwide 2015–2025," Statista, September 1, 2020, https://www.statista.com/statistics/1101442/iot-number-of -connected-devices-worldwide/.

42. Andy Greenberg, "The Untold Story of NotPetya, the Most Devastating Cyberat-tack in History," *Wired*, August 22, 2018, https://www.wired.com/story/notpetya -cyberattack-ukraine-russia-code-crashed-the-world/.

43. Danny Palmer, "This Is How Much the WannaCry Ransomware Attack Cost the NHS," ZDNet, October 12, 2018, https://www.zdnet.com/article/this-is-how-much-the -wannacry-ransomware-attack-cost-the-nhs/.

44. Scott Ikeda, "New Security Report Breaks Down Increase in Cyber Attacks Due to Remote Work; Lack of Training, Overwhelmed IT Departments Are the Main Issues," *CPO Magazine*, October 16, 2020, https://www.cpomagazine.com/cyber-security/new -security-report-breaks-down-increase-in-cyber-attacks-due-to-remote-work-lack-of -training-overwhelmed-it-departments-are-the-main-issues/.

45. Aaron Tan, "Getting Threat Intelligence Right," TechTarget, May 30, 2017, https://www.computerweekly.com/feature/Getting-threat-intelligence-right.

46. Aaron Tan, "Why Predictive Threat Intelligence Is Key," TechTarget, September 7, 2020, https://www.computerweekly.com/news/252488666/Why-predictive-threat -intelligence-is-key.

47. "Cyber Security Market Size, Share & Trends Analysis Report by Component, by Security Type, by Solution, by Service, by Deployment, by Organization, by Application, by Region, and Segment Forecasts, 2020–2027," Grand View Research, June 2020, https:// www.grandviewresearch.com/industry-analysis/cyber-security-market.

Chapter 8

1. Liz Stinson, "A Coffee Cup Designed to Let Astronauts Sip Espresso in Space," *Wired*, January 27, 2015, https://www.wired.com/2015/01/coffee-cup-designed-let -astronauts-sip-espresso-space/.

2. Baiju Shah, Lisa De Bonis, Flaviano Faleiro, and Nevine El-Warraky, "Growth: It Comes Down to Experience," Accenture, 2020, https://www.accenture.com/_acnmedia /Thought-Leadership-Assets/PDF-3/Accenture-Interactive-Business-of-Experience-Full -Report.pdf#zoom=50.

3. Shah et al., "Growth: It Comes Down to Experience."

4. Shah et al., "Growth: It Comes Down to Experience."

5. Shiho Takezawa, "Car Crashes in World's Oldest Nation Spur Changes by Automakers," Bloomberg, January 18, 2021, https://www.bloomberg.com/news/articles /2021-01-18/automakers-redesign-cars-for-millions-of-aging-drivers-in-japan.

6. *See*, official trailer, aired September 10, 2019, on Apple TV+, https://www.youtube .com/watch?v=03RAKJipMeM.

7. Katie Deighton, "Evinced, a Web Accessibility Startup, Raises $17 Million," *Wall Street Journal*, February 3, 2021, https://www.wsj.com/articles/evinced-a-web-accessibility -startup-raises-17-million-11612353609.

8. Manuel Matuzovic, "Building the Most Inaccessible Site Possible with a Perfect Lighthouse Score," Matuzo.at, May 31, 2019, https://www.matuzo.at/blog/building-the -most-inaccessible-site-possible-with-a-perfect-lighthouse-score/.

9. Marcy Sutton, "Evinced Is Pushing the Limits of Automated Accessibility Testing," Marcy Sutton.com, February 1, 2021, https://marcysutton.com/evinced-automated -accessibility-testing.

10. Katie Deighton, "Evinced, a Web Accessibility Startup, Raises $17 Million," *Wall Street Journal*, February 3, 2021, https://www.wsj.com/articles/evinced-a-web-accessibility -startup-raises-17-million-11612353609.

11. Shah et al., "Growth: It Comes Down to Experience."

12. Shah et al., "Growth: It Comes Down to Experience."

13. Tom Huddleston Jr., "How 'Animal Crossing' and the Coronavirus Pandemic Made the Nintendo Switch Fly Off Shelves," CNBC, June 2, 2020, https://www.cnbc.com /2020/06/02/nintendo-switch-animal-crossing-and-coronavirus-led-to-record-sales.html.

14. Jordan Valinsky, "Peloton Sales Surge 172% as Pandemic Bolsters Home Fitness Industry," CNN Business, September 11, 2020, https://www.cnn.com/2020/09/11/business /peloton-stock-earnings/index.html.

15. Jono Bacon, "The Five Ways Peloton Weave Community and Content Beautifully," *Forbes*, December 6, 2018, https://www.forbes.com/sites/jonobacon/2018/12/06/the-five -ways-peloton-weave-community-and-content-beautifully/?sh=445203576b59.

16. Ann-Marie Alcántara, "Fitness Platform Obé Rolls Out Workout Parties for Remote Friends," *Wall Street Journal*, December 3, 2020, https://www.wsj.com/articles /fitness-platform-obe-rolls-out-workout-parties-for-remote-friends-11607034060.

17. "Peloton Breaks Out Checkbook for AI, Hardware Acquisitions," PYMNTS.com, March 22, 2021, https://www.pymnts.com/news/partnerships-acquisitions/2021/peloton -artificial-intelligence-hardware-acquisitions/.

18. Paul Daugherty, Marc Carrel-Billiard, and Michael Biltz "We, the Post-Digital People," Accenture, 2020, p. 39, https://www.accenture.com/_acnmedia/Thought-Leadership -Assets/PDF-2/Accenture-Technology-Vision-2020-Full-Report.pdf.

19. Tess Stenzel, "Men's Wearhouse Opens a Newly Designed Modern Retail Experi- ence," *Fashion United*, February 4, 2021, https://fashionunited.com/news/fashion/men-s -wearhouse-opens-a-newly-designed-modern-retail-experience/2021020437897.

20. Daugherty et al., "We, the Post-Digital People."

21. Adrienne Mayor, *Gods and Robots: Myths, Machines, and Ancient Dreams of Technol- ogy* (Princeton University Press, 2018), 151.

22. Katie Deighton, "Volvo Aims to Ease the Queasiness of Riding in Self-Driving Vehicles," *Wall Street Journal*, February 10, 2021, https://www.wsj.com/articles/volvo-aims -to-ease-the-queasiness-of-riding-in-self-driving-vehicles-11612970951.

23. Azeem Azhar, "TikTok's Atmospheric Growth; Kim Stanley Robinson on Climate & China's Area 51 ++ #330," Exponential View, July 11, 2021, https://www.exponentialview .co/ev-330/.

24. Cheryl Winokur Munk, "Consumers Like Chatbots to Be Smart—but Not Too Smart," *Wall Street Journal*, May 21, 2021, https://www.wsj.com/articles/chatbot-consumers -smart-11621535198?mod=djemCXO.

25. Remus Noronha "'Artificial': LifeScore's Tom Gruber Hints at Possibility of Music 'Adapting to Human Signals,'" Media Entertainment Arts WorldWide, May 29, 2020, https://meaww.com/artificial-remote-intelligence-tom-gruber-lifescore-siri-twitch -adaptive-music-exclusive-interview.

26. Cade Metz, "Can A.I. Grade Your Next Test?" *New York Times*, July 20, 2021, https://www.nytimes.com/2021/07/20/technology/ai-education-neural-networks .html.

27. Metz, "Can A.I. Grade Your Next Test?"

28. Shravan Goli, "Announcing New Products, Tools, and Features to Support Learners, Educators, and Institutions with Their Rapidly Evolving Teaching and Learning Needs," Coursera, April 19, 2021, https://blog.coursera.org/announcing-new -products-tools-and-features-to-support-learners-educators-and-institutions-with-their -rapidly-evolving-teaching-and-learning-needs/.

29. Kamal Rawal, "Artificial Intelligence in 'Artificial' Meat Burger—Precision Foods," LinkedIn, June 14, 2014, https://www.linkedin.com/pulse/artificial-intelligence -meat-burger-precision-foods-kamal-rawal.

30. Nathalie Olof-Ors, "AI Beefs Up Veggie Burgers as Market Booms," Phys Org, July 14, 2021, https://phys.org/news/2021-07-ai-beefs-veggie-burgers-booms.html.

31. "Impossible Burger Has 89% Smaller Carbon Footprint than Beef," Vanderbilt University, March 29, 2019, https://www.vanderbilt.edu/sustainability/2019/03/impossible -burger-has-89-smaller-carbon-footprint-than-beef/.

32. Rachel Barton, Jürgen Morath, Kevin Quiring, and Bill Theofilou, "Generation P(urpose): From Fidelity to Future Value," Accenture, 2021, https://www.accenture.com /_acnmedia/PDF-117/Accenture-Generation-P-urpose-PoV.pdf#zoom%3D40.

33. Ann-Marie Alcántara, "Google Maps to Add a Greenest Route to Its Driving Directions," *Wall Street Journal*, April 23, 2021, https://www.wsj.com/articles/google-maps -to-add-a-greenest-route-to-its-driving-directions-11619197255.

34. Jack Morse, "Twitter Tests 'Humanization Prompts' in Effort to Reduce Toxic Replies," Mashable, December 17, 2020, https://mashable.com/article/twitter-humanization -prompts.

35. Cheryl Winokur Munk, "Imagine a Nutrition Label—for Cybersecurity," *Wall Street Journal*, December 8, 2020, https://www.wsj.com/articles/imagine-a-nutrition -labelfor-cybersecurity-11607436000.

36. Suzanne Kapner and Paul Ziobro, "Amazon, Walmart Tell Consumers to Skip Returns of Unwanted Items," *Wall Street Journal*, January 10, 2021, https://www.wsj.com /articles/amazon-walmart-tell-consumers-to-skip-returns-of-unwanted-items-11610274600.

37. "Loneliness and Social Isolation Linked to Serious Health Conditions," Centers for Disease Control and Prevention, April 29, 2021, https://www.cdc.gov/aging/publications /features/lonely-older-adults.html.

38. Mathias Rosenzweig, "Boyfriends for Rent, Robots, Camming: How the Business of Loneliness Is Booming," *Guardian*, November 1, 2020, https://www.theguardian.com /society/2020/nov/01/loneliness-business-booming-pandemic.

39. Larry Dignan, "Accenture Interactive, Stockholm Exergi Aim to Combat Elderly Loneliness with AI," ZDNet, April 30, 2019, https://www.zdnet.com/article/accenture -interactive-stockholm-exergi-aim-to-combat-elderly-loneliness-with-ai/.

40. "Making Stockholm Warm with Compassion and Purpose," Accenture, n.d., https://www.accenture.com/us-en/case-studies/interactive/memory-lane-conversational-ai -solution.

Chapter 9

1. Karen Hao, "Training a Single AI Model Can Emit as Much Carbon as Five Cars in Their Lifetimes," *MIT Technology Review*, June 5, 2019, https://www.technologyreview .com/2019/06/06/239031/training-a-single-ai-model-can-emit-as-much-carbon-as-five-cars -in-their-lifetimes/.

2. Sara Castellanos, "Climate Researchers Enlist Big Cloud Providers for Big Data Challenges," *Wall Street Journal*, November 25, 2020, https://www.wsj.com/articles/climate -researchers-enlist-big-cloud-providers-for-big-data-challenges-11606300202.

3. Castellanos, "Climate Researchers Enlist Big Cloud Providers for Big Data Challenges."

4. Sarah Murray, "Finance Chiefs Face Pressure to Get to Grips with Sustainability," *Financial Times*, December 14, 2020, https://www.ft.com/content/65d1eb06-188a-41cc -ba28-94ff1581c2de.

5. "Porsche, Audi and Volkswagen Use Artificial Intelligence to Minimize Sustainability Risks," Porsche, March 3, 2021, https://newsroom.porsche.com/en/2021 /sustainability/porsche-audi-volkswagen-pilot-project-artificial-intelligence-minimisation -sustainability-risks-supply-chain-23801.html.

6. "Cascading Commitments: Driving Ambitious Action through Supply Chain Engagement," CDP Supply Chain Report 2018/19, https://6fefcbb86e61af1b2fc4-c70d8ead 6ced550b4d987d7c03fcdd1d.ssl.cf3.rackcdn.com/cms/reports/documents/000/004/072 /original/CDP_Supply_Chain_Report_2019.pdf?1550490556.

7. "Protecting Communities from Disease," World Mosquito Program, n.d., https://www.worldmosquitoprogram.org/.

8. "Machine Learning Helps Communities Fight Disease Globally," Microsoft, n.d., https://www.microsoft.com/en-us/ai/ai-for-earth-world-mosquito-program.

9. "Drive Faster Restoration for Environment and Community at Scale," Dendra Systems, n.d., https://www.dendra.io/solutions.

10. "Progress Toward a Deforestation-Free Cocoa Supply Chain," Mars.com, n.d., https://www.mars.com/news-and-stories/articles/achieving-deforestation-free-cocoa -supply-chain.

11. Rens Masselink, "From Millions of Satellite Images to Your Deforestation Alert—3 Most Frequent Questions," Satelligence, n.d., https://satelligence.com/news/2020/1/30 /from-millions-of-satellite-images-to-your-deforestation-alert-answering-the-3-most -frequent-questions.

12. Anna Gross, "High-Tech Tools Shine a Light on Sustainable Farming," *Financial Times*, September 23, 2020, https://www.ft.com/content/2b437c7f-cd38-48af-a263 -bca08e281040.

13. "Transforming Our World: The 2030 Agenda for Sustainable Development," United Nations, September 25, 2015, https://sdgs.un.org/2030agenda.

14. "Virtual Singapore," Government of Singapore, February 20, 2021, https://www .nrf.gov.sg/programmes/virtual-singapore.

Notes

15. Florence Verzelen, Peter Lacy, and Nigel Stacy, "Designing Disruption: The Critical Role of Virtual Twins in Accelerating Sustainability," Accenture, 2021, https://www.3ds.com/sites/default/files/2021-01/dassault-systemes-and-accenture-virtual-twin-and-sustainability.pdf.

16. Verzelen et al., "Designing Disruption."

17. Verzelen et al., "Designing Disruption."

18. UNEP, "Energy Efficiency for Buildings, n.d., https://www.euenergycentre.org/images/unep%20info%20sheet%20-%20ee%20buildings.pdf.

19. Raymond Deplazes, "Autodesk Collaborates with Volkswagen Group on Generative Design in Electric Showcase Vehicle," Autodesk, July 8, 2019, https://adsknews.autodesk.com/news/autodesk-volkswagen-generative-design-electric-showcase-vehicle.

20. Ryan P. Smith, "What If Humans and Artificial Intelligence Teamed Up to Build Better Communities?" *Smithsonian Magazine*, April 21, 2021, https://www.smithsonianmag.com/smithsonian-institution/what-if-humans-and-artificial-intelligence-teamed-build-better-communities-180977541/.

21. Smith, "What If Humans and Artificial Intelligence Teamed Up to Build Better Communities?"

22. "Ambient Air Pollution," World Health Organization, n.d., https://www.who.int/teams/environment-climate-change-and-health/air-quality-and-health/ambient-air-pollution.

23. Ziyi Luo, Xinyi Yang, Yingxue Wang, Weidi Liu, Siliang Liu, Yuankun Zhu, Zihan Huang, Hong Zhang, Shuming Dou, Jie Xu, et al., "A Survey of Artificial Intelligence Techniques Applied in Energy Storage Materials R&D," Frontiers in Energy Research, July 3, 2020, https://www.frontiersin.org/articles/10.3389/fenrg.2020.00116/full.

24. Suzanne Oliver, "Electric-Car Batteries Get a Boost from Artificial Intelligence," *Wall Street Journal*, November 3, 2020, https://www.wsj.com/articles/electric-car-batteries-get-a-boost-from-artificial-intelligence-11604422792#:~:text=Working%20toward%20faster%2Dcharging%2C%20safer,materials%20and%20the%20testing%20process.

25. Young-hye Na, "Free of Heavy Metals, New Battery Design Could Alleviate Environmental Concerns," IBM, December 18, 2019, https://www.ibm.com/blogs/research/2019/12/heavy-metal-free-battery/.

26. Anders Quitzau, "IBM Research Is Reshaping the Scene of Sustainable Batteries," IBM, April 13, 2021, https://www.ibm.com/blogs/nordic-msp/ibm-research-reshaping-scene-of-sustainable-batteries/.

27. Matthew Vollrath, "New Machine Learning Method from Stanford, with Toyota Researchers, Could Supercharge Battery Development for Electric Vehicles," Stanford University, February 19, 2020, https://news.stanford.edu/press-releases/2020/02/19/machine-learninging-electric-car/.

28. Oliver, "Electric-Car Batteries Get a Boost from Artificial Intelligence."

29. Daniel Oberhaus, "AI Is Throwing Battery Development into Overdrive," *Wired*, October 12, 2020, https://www.wired.com/story/ai-is-throwing-battery-development-into-overdrive/.

30. "New Data Stations Project Creates Architecture, Marketplace for Sharing Data," University of Chicago, September 18, 2020, https://www.cs.uchicago.edu/news/article/data-stations/.

31. Dieter Holger, "Best Companies at Managing Environmental Risk," *Wall Street Journal*, October 13, 2020, https://www.wsj.com/articles/best-companies-at-managing-environmental-risk-11602597898.

32. Mikako Yokoyama, "AI Provides Spark of Hope for Japan's Steelmakers," Mainichi Japan, April 4, 2019, https://mainichi.jp/english/articles/20190404/p2a/00m/0bu/016000c.

33. Karl Decena, "Japan's JFE Holdings Eyes 20% Emissions Cut for Steel Unit by FY'30—Reuters," https://www.spglobal.com/marketintelligence/en/news-insights/latest-news-headlines/japan-s-jfe-holdings-eyes-20-emissions-cut-for-steel-unit-by-fy-30-8211-reuters-60364059.

34. Carl Bowen, "dotData Launches dotData Stream—Containerized AI Model for Real-Time Prediction," dotData, July 7, 2020, https://dotdata.com/dotdata-launches-dotdata-stream-containerized-ai-model-for-real-time-prediction/.

35. "The Impact of Textile Production and Waste on the Environment (Infographic)," European Parliament, March 3, 2021, https://www.europarl.europa.eu/news/en/headlines/society/20201208STO93327/the-impact-of-textile-production-and-waste-on-the-environment-infographic. The statistics that follow are drawn from this document.

36. Abigail Beall, "Why Clothes Are So Hard to Recycle," BBC, July 12, 2020, https://www.bbc.com/future/article/20200710-why-clothes-are-so-hard-to-recycle.

37. Nick Martin, "Google's New Pilot Aiming to Measure the Environmental Impact of the Fashion Industry," Google, May 15, 2019, https://cloud.google.com/blog/topics/inside-google-cloud/googles-new-pilot-aiming-to-measure-the-environmental-impact-of-the-fashion-industry.

38. Victor Gosselin, "How Can Zara Maintain Its Leadership in Fast Fashion Thanks to Artificial Intelligence?" Heuritech, December 15, 2020, https://www.heuritech.com/blog/company-analysis/zara-leadership-artificial-intelligence/.

39. Brooke Roberts-Islam, "'Zara Meets Netflix'—The Fashion House Where AI Removes Designers and Overstock," *Forbes*, January 1, 2021, https://www.forbes.com/sites/brookerobertsislam/2021/01/27/zara-meets-netflix-the-fashion-house-where-ai-replaces-designers-eliminating-overstock/?sh=719acb8633ed.

40. Roberts-Islam, "'Zara Meets Netflix.'"

41. "Fashion Forecasting: Arti Zeighami on Implementing AI at H&M Group," Sloan Management Review podcast, November 10, 2020, https://sloanreview.mit.edu/audio/fashion-forecasting-arti-zeighami-on-implementing-ai-at-hm-group/.

42. "Fashion Forecasting: Arti Zeighami on Implementing AI at H&M Group."

43. Roberto Torres, "H&M Wants to Democratize AI with Reusable Components," CIO Dive, October 6, 2020, https://www.ciodive.com/news/HM-data-science-machine-learning/586516/.

44. David Meyer, "H&M Made Its Former Sustainability Chief Its CEO. Now It Wants to Help Other Fashion Houses Become Sustainable—for a Fee," *Fortune*, March 4, 2020, https://fortune.com/2020/03/04/hennes-mauritz-sustainability-treadler-supply-chain/.

45. Roy Schwartz, Jesse Dodge, Noah A. Smith, and Oren Etzioni, "Green AI," arXiv, July 2019, https://arxiv.org/pdf/1907.10597.pdf.

46. Lotfi Belkhir, Ahmed Elmeligi, "Assessing ICT Global Emissions Footprint: Trends to 2040 and Recommendations," *Journal of Cleaner Production*, Vol. 177, March 10, 2018, pp. 448–463, https://www.doi:10.1016/j.jclepro.2017.12.239.

47. Lee Gomes, "Neuromorphic Chips Are Destined for Deep Learning—or Obscurity Researchers," IEEE Spectrum, May 29, 2017, https://spectrum.ieee.org/semiconductors/design/neuromorphic-chips-are-destined-for-deep-learningor-obscurity.

48. In 2019, researchers at Iowa State University and Xilinx Research Labs conducted an experiment to compare the energy efficiency of CPUs, GPUs, and FPGAs for image kernels (i.e., small matrices used to apply Photoshop-like effects, such as blurring, embossing, and sharpening). Their results showed that across a range of kernels—from simple to complex—GPUs and FPGAs were more energy-efficient than CPUs. Murad

Notes

Qasaimeh, Kristof Denolf, Jack Lo, Kees A. Vissers, Joseph Zambreno, and Phillip H. Jones, "Comparing Energy Efficiency of CPU, GPU and FPGA Implementations for Vision Kernels," Iowa State University, 2019, https://lib.dr.iastate.edu/cgi/viewcontent.cgi?article =1219&context=ece_pubs.

49. "Field Programmable Gate Array (FPGA) Market—Growth, Trends, And Forecast (2019–2024)," Industry Research, May 1, 2019, https://www.industryresearch.co/field -programmable-gate-array-fpga-market-14245063.

50. The *Economist*, "The Cost of Training Machines Is Becoming a Problem," June 11, 2020, https://www.economist.com/technology-quarterly/2020/06/11/the-cost-of-training -machines-is-becoming-a-problem.

51. George Leopold, "Microsoft Azure Adds Graphcore's IPU," HPCWire, November 15, 2019, https://www.hpcwire.com/2019/11/15/microsoft-azure-adds-graphcores-ipu/.

52. Graphcore, https://www.graphcore.ai/.

53. Peter Lacy, Paul Daugherty, Kishore Durg, and Pavel Ponomarev, "The Green behind the Cloud," Accenture, September 22, 2020, https://www.accenture.com/us-en /insights/strategy/green-behind-cloud?c=acn_glb_sustainabilitymediarelations _11307639&n=mrl_0920.

54. "Reducing Carbon by Moving to AWS," Amazon, November 26, 2019, https://www .aboutamazon.com/news/sustainability/reducing-carbon-by-moving-to-aws.

55. "Sustainability: Thinking Big," Amazon, September 2019, https://sustainability .aboutamazon.com/pdfBuilderDownload?name=sustainability-thinking-big-december -2019.

56. Noelle Walsh, "Microsoft Sustainability Calculator Helps Enterprises Analyze the Carbon Emissions of Their IT Infrastructure," Microsoft, January 16, 2020, https://azure .microsoft.com/en-us/blog/microsoft-sustainability-calculator-helps-enterprises-analyze -the-carbon-emissions-of-their-it-infrastructure/.

57. Lacy et al., "The Green behind the Cloud."

58. Intergovernmental Panel on Climate Change, "Climate Change 2021: The Physical Science Basis," United Nations, August 7, 2021, https://www.ipcc.ch/report/ar6 /wg1/downloads/report/IPCC_AR6_WGI_Full_Report.pdf.

59. Lacy et al., "The Green behind the Cloud."

Conclusion

1. Bill Taylor, "What Breaking the 4-Minute Mile Taught Us about the Limits of Conventional Thinking," *Harvard Business Review*, March 9, 2018, https://hbr.org/2018/03 /what-breaking-the-4-minute-mile-taught-us-about-the-limits-of-conventional-thinking.

INDEX

Note: Figures are identified by *f* following the page number.

Index

Index

Index

ACKNOWLEDGMENTS

We started discussing the initial set of ideas that eventually became *Radically Human* in late 2018. At the time, we were traveling and speaking extensively to global business and technology audiences about our previous book, *Human + Machine: Reimagining Work in the Age of AI*. That book had a different storyline about AI than the one people had become accustomed to hearing: it emphasized collaboration rather than competition between humans and AI systems. We would like to begin by acknowledging the business executives, entrepreneurs, and other technology experts who embraced and amplified our novel, more positive take on AI and put it into practice. Similarly, we'd like to acknowledge the many economists and researchers who have tested, validated, and added nuance to our thesis that human + machine collaboration is a reality that creates value in today's organizations and in the greater society.

Our sense of urgency for *Radically Human* grew from these roots. *Human + Machine* was validated by real-world evidence. New exponential technology advances held promise but also sparked new questions and concerns. The digitalization of business was creating new winners and losers. The global pandemic rewrote the rules. And human experience and potential was once again at the forefront. The goal of our research and this book is to provide a guide to success in this rapidly changing environment.

We would like to acknowledge the many people (often complemented by smart machines) who contributed in a significant way to this book.

Acknowledgments

Bruce Tucker has been with us from the very start of the project and is one of the best editorial collaborators and creative minds we've encountered in our careers. It's been a pleasure working with a person of such insight and professional grace.

A number of amazing individuals contributed to the global research programs underpinning this book. We would like to acknowledge Bhaskar Ghosh and Francis Hintermann, who steered these research programs and advised the participants at key moments. Ramnath Venkataraman, Adam Burden, Annette Rippert, Karen Bobear, Paul Barbagallo, Justin Herzig, Regina Maruca, and Prashant Shukla deeply influenced our thinking on the evolution of technology. Karthik Narain, Surya Mukherjee, Amy Sagues, Kate Greene, Shalabh Kumar-Singh, Doug Chandler, Gargi Chakrabarty, Dave Light, and Thijs Deblaere deeply informed our sections on cloud computing. Kelly Monahan, Leila Yosef, and Gabriela Burlacu collaborated closely with Christie Smith in advancing our thinking on talent and human potential. Christie has been an amazing collaborator and took our discussions on talent to another level. Thanks also to Ellyn Shook for inspiring many ideas at the intersection of humans and technology.

We would like to call out a few of the visionaries and pioneers who shaped our thinking as we developed this book. While the list is long, we will mention Douglas Hofstadter, Kai-Fu Lee, Albert Borgmann, Hubert Dreyfus, Daniela Rus, Tom Malone, Ken Goldberg, Rodney Brooks, Julie Shah, Fei-Fei Li, Gary Marcus, Geoff Hinton, Erik Brynjolfsson, C.K. Prahalad, Shoshanna Zuboff, Evan Selinger, Douglas Engelbart, Kathy Baxter, Brad Smith, and Andrew Ng.

Thank you to all the technology, strategy, and AI experts who stepped in at critical moments to offer helpful comments and relevant research, especially Shail Jain, Sanjay Podder, Praveen Tanguturi, Ram Ramalingam, Marc Carrel-Billiard, Andy Fano, Michael Biltz, and Edy Liongosari. Mark Goodman and Paul Nunes offered fantastic peer reviews and practical notes on early drafts. We would also like to thank the many research scientists with whom we collaborated at MIT and MIT's Initiative on the Digital Economy (IDE).

We extend a special thanks to Julie Sweet, Accenture's CEO, for supporting us in writing this book. Julie has conceived a corporate purpose centered on technology and human ingenuity, along with a focus on delivering 360-degree value to all stakeholders, that has been inspiring, relevant, and impactful to *Radically Human*.

Several colleagues led case study analyses, made chapter revisions, or facilitated communications with global businesses and within our book's R&D team. Chase Davenport worked with us in developing some of our earliest case studies and stepped in at important moments throughout the project. Mickey Butts brought his discerning eye to key sections of the book and helped us sharpen our graphics. Ed Maney, Michelle Woodward, and Swati Sah led the outreach, vetting, and revision process for the dozens and dozens of company case examples scattered throughout the manuscript. Thanks to Jen Sullivan, who helped us keep up the momentum.

It's been a pleasure to work once again with Jeff Kehoe and the team at Harvard Business Review Press. We look forward to our ongoing collaboration with HBR, Jill Totenberg, and Carolyn Monaco as we bring this book to market.

Our gratitude also extends to the many pioneering clients who entrusted Accenture to guide them on their radically human endeavors. Thanks to these clients, we've had the privilege not only to research the ideas in this book but also to apply the principles in action and observe the results.

Finally, on a personal note, we would like to acknowledge our families and friends for their support.

From Paul: A deep, special thanks to my wife, Beth, for her patience through the countless hours, evenings, and weekends spent on this project, and more importantly, for the many discussions and debates that raised the bar on my radically human ambitions.

Acknowledgments

From Jim: I would like to express a heartfelt thanks to Susan, Benjamin, and Brooke Wilson, who provided so much encouragement and support. I'd also like to thank three friends who added many healthy doses of levity and human connection over the past eighteen months: Bill Coleman, Don Salvucci from Salesforce, and Alan Federman from the robotics company Canvas Construction.

—Paul Daugherty and Jim Wilson

ABOUT THE AUTHORS

PAUL R. DAUGHERTY is a leading authority on how technology innovations are shaping the future of business and society. In his role as Accenture's Group Chief Executive–Technology and CTO, Daugherty leads all aspects of Accenture's Technology business. He sets the firm's technology strategy and directs its technology R&D, ventures, and ecosystem relationships. As the founder of Accenture's businesses in cloud, artificial intelligence (AI), blockchain, and other emerging technologies, Daugherty advises the world's top business and technology leaders on how to apply technology to reimagine and reinvent their organizations' futures.

Daugherty coauthored the bestselling *Human + Machine: Reimagining Work in the Age of AI*, a management playbook on the business of AI. He is a frequent speaker and writer on the future of technology innovation and its implications for business and society and is regularly featured in a variety of media outlets, including Bloomberg Television, Fox Business, and CNBC. He accepted the FASPE Award for Ethical Leadership for his work in applying ethical principles to the development and use of artificial intelligence and other innovative twenty-first-century technologies.

Daugherty is a passionate advocate for gender equality in the workplace and also sponsors STEM-related inclusion and diversity initiatives. He serves on the board of directors of Girls Who Code and was recognized as an "Honorable Guy" by the Institute for Women's Leadership and the "Guys Who Get It Award" for supporting diversity in the workplace and advancement of women, especially in technology and other STEM fields. He also sponsors Accenture's partnership with Code.org, which is focused on bringing computer science education to students around the world. Paul serves on the boards of Avanade, the Computer History Museum, and the Computer Science and Engineering program at the University of Michigan. He lives in Maplewood, New Jersey, with his wife.

H. JAMES (JIM) WILSON is Global Managing Director of IT and Business Research at Accenture, where he leads research programs on the impact of technology on work, innovation, and business performance. He is the coauthor of *Human + Machine* and the author or contributing author of numerous books on the impact of technology on work and society, including, most recently, *HBR's 10 Must Reads on AI, Analytics, and the New Machine Age, How AI Is Transforming the Organization*, and *Artificial Intelligence: The Insights You Need from HBR*.

Wilson's bylined articles appear frequently in *Harvard Business Review* and *MIT Sloan Management Review*; his writing has been shortlisted by *Thinkers50* and has been featured in numerous publications, including the *New Yorker*, the *Economist*, the *Financial Times*, and the *Wall Street Journal*.

Wilson is a frequent keynote speaker and technology conference panelist and has been recognized by Codex as one of the top fifty innovators in the world. He is passionate about education and guest lectures on AI and other emerging technologies at universities such as MIT, NYU, and UCLA. He is an avid mountain biker and triathlete and lives in the San Francisco Bay Area with his family.